PRAISE FOR *THE GLASS LEDGE*

"*The Glass Ledge* provides a simple yet balanced perspective that will help women rewrite their inner dialogue, reject who they have been told to be, and become who they are meant to be."

GRETCHEN CARLSON

acclaimed journalist, cofounder of Lift Our Voices,
bestselling author, empowerment advocate

"Self-sabotage is a slippery slope, and what's the best way to catch your footing? Iman Oubou's brilliant new book, *The Glass Ledge*. If you're a woman and feel that you're getting in your own way, this book can catch you before you fall out of balance."

FRAN HAUSER

former president of Time Inc. Digital, startup investor,
author of *The Myth of the Nice Girl*

"Having questioned myself more than anyone else would ever question me, I know firsthand the negative impact that self-doubt and impostor syndrome can have on your career. Even after making it to the C-suite, these challenges remained a part of my everyday life. For many of us, this is a lifelong struggle, and the struggle is very real. *The Glass Ledge* lays out the ten ways women derail themselves and how they can leverage these holdbacks to propel themselves forward to success. This disruptive guide is a must-buy for every woman looking to reach her potential."

HEATHER MONAHAN

bestselling author of *Overcome Your Villains*

"It's easy to get in your own way, especially when you don't even realize you're doing it. With a world that's constantly trying to reshape us, it's no wonder so many women struggle to silence their voices of self-doubt and self-sabotage. *The Glass Ledge* is about deprogramming yourself from the idea that you are powerless (and deserve to be). It's a brilliant manifesto for navigating a patriarchal world without compromising yourself."

LIZ ELTING

cofounder and former co-CEO of TransPerfect, *Forbes* Richest Self-Made Women list

"*The Glass Ledge* is a much-needed guide to help women cultivate positive self-talk, cut the noise, and become who they truly are."

ASHLEY STAHL

career coach, bestselling author of *You Turn*

"In *The Glass Ledge*, Iman Oubou explores the phenomenon of self-sabotage that women tend to wield on themselves as they're breaking through the glass ceiling. By sharing her own personal and professional experiences, and with the guidance of many iconic women around the world, she lays out the rationale for why we as women allow ourselves to get in our own way and, even more importantly, offers us the very simple steps and homework we should all do to acknowledge and mitigate the glass ledge. This book is funny, thought-provoking, insightful, and a great resource to successfully navigate this wild world as a woman looking to create change."

ALLYSON WITHERSPOON

vice president and chief marketing officer of Nissan U.S.

"This book not only teaches us to re-evaluate ourselves and our circumstances, but it also shows us how to extract insight from our most damaging habits so we can step out of our own way and step into our potential."

EVY POUMPOURAS

former US Secret Service agent, TV personality, author of *Becoming Bulletproof*

"As women, self-sabotage and imposter syndrome can easily creep into our mindset and, at times, even derail our trajectory to success. *The Glass Ledge* offers guidance on how to pave a new path on your own terms while embracing your true, authentic self along the way. A must-read for women in all stages of their careers!"

CINDY ECKERT

founder and CEO of Sprout Pharmaceuticals and The Pink Ceiling

"*The Glass Ledge* is essential reading for making the shift from being your own worst enemy to becoming your own best friend."

MAY BUSCH

former COO for Morgan Stanley Europe, executive coach, speaker, author

"Iman Oubou nails it! *The Glass Ledge* says the quiet parts aloud. This book really allows women to sit in self-reflection, self-acceptance, and self-accountability at the same time. My favorite chapter addresses one of the buzziest business concepts of the moment: authenticity. Iman plainly and boldly identifies authenticity as the current gold standard for leadership, and then she articulates our frustrations. What does authenticity really mean? And how do we lean into our authenticity when we are still figuring out who we REALLY are?

This book answers these questions and more with simple, transformative and empowering guidance. It's organized, easy to process, and an energetic read. *The Glass Ledge* is THE book for all women looking to live their professional dreams while being true to themselves and their personal happiness."

EBONI K. WILLIAMS

attorney, journalist, *Real Housewives of New York* cast member

"How do you prove your value in a fundamentally unequal environment? How do you navigate rooms where you are underrepresented? Author Iman Oubou tackles these common challenges with psychological insights and practical grit. At a time when more corporations are talking up diversity, Oubou confronts how external limits can be internalized—and why deeper progress means not only changing how businesses are run but also changing the way we think. *The Glass Ledge* contributes to an important conversation for everyone who cares about equality—from workplaces to across our society."

ARI MELBER

host of MSNBC's *The Beat with Ari Melber*

THE GLASS LEDGE

IMAN OUBOU

THE
GLASS
LEDGE

HOW TO BREAK THROUGH SELF-SABOTAGE, EMBRACE YOUR POWER, AND CREATE YOUR SUCCESS

sounds true
BOULDER, COLORADO

Sounds True
Boulder, CO 80306

Published 2022

Book design by Linsey Dodaro

The wood used to produce this book is from Forest
Stewardship Council (FSC) certified forests, recycled
materials, or controlled wood.

Printed in Canada

BK06310

Library of Congress Cataloging-in-Publication Data

Names: Oubou, Iman, author.
Title: The glass ledge : how to break through self-sabotage, embrace your
power, and create your success / Iman Oubou.
Description: Boulder, CO : Sounds True, 2022. | Includes bibliographical
references.
Identifiers: LCCN 2021034254 (print) | LCCN 2021034255 (ebook) | ISBN
        9781683648598 (hardcover) | ISBN 9781683648604 (ebook)
Subjects: LCSH: Women in the professions. | Leadership in women. |
        Success--Psychological aspects. | Success in business.
Classification: LCC HD6054 .O93 2022 (print) | LCC HD6054 (ebook) |
DDC
        650.1082--dc23
LC record available at https://lccn.loc.gov/2021034254
LC ebook record available at https://lccn.loc.gov/2021034255

10 9 8 7 6 5 4 3 2 1

To all the women (and men) who feel unsettled
because you know you are meant for more: I
dedicate this book to YOU with the hope that you
may soon experience your own breakthroughs.

◇◇◇◇

"It's only when you have the courage
to step off the [glass] ledge that you'll
realize you've had wings all along."

◇◇◇◇

Contents

Prologue

I t was the first day of summer in 2018, and I will remember it as one of the most gut-wrenching, yet life-altering, days of my life.

I was sitting in a WeWork conference room about to break the bad news to my team. No matter how hard I tried, I couldn't find the right words to communicate that the company might be shutting down and that I needed to let everybody go, effective immediately.

Just a few days before, a potential investor I had been actively pitching since launch had agreed to invest the capital we needed for growth and monetization. However, he'd just informed me that his investment committee no longer wanted to move forward with the deal.

I had been working on overdrive to secure our next round of funding. We were down to our last dollar and could no longer afford to pay the team or the office rent. We had just recruited a new cohort of excited summer interns, and we had to let them go as well.

After I finally made the announcement, I found myself alone in what was left of our office packing my belongings into a large, black trash bag (yep, a trash bag!), which I had to drag into the elevator in front of hundreds of fellow startup warriors.

It was the ultimate walk of shame . . . and I wasn't even in heels.

At home, I rushed into the bathroom. I spent the evening vomiting and at one point lifted up my blouse to reveal a massive rash on the left side of my abdomen. That night I could barely sleep from the discomfort, though my eyes were begging for a break from all the crying.

I suddenly found myself unemployed, unfulfilled, and unwell. Instead of unlocking more of my potential and taking my career and life to the next level, my entrepreneurial journey had hit rock bottom—again! *How do I come back from this? Where do I go from here?*

In the past, when things hadn't worked out or when situations or environments felt too stressful, I would chase the next opportunity. But this time, I couldn't just walk away. It was my business. It was my mission.

I had to rebuild it all, myself included. I had to break the cycle. And that's when it clicked.

All these years, I'd strived to break glass ceilings, but I didn't realize I was also teetering on a glass ledge.

If you haven't heard of the symbolic ledge, it's where physical and emotional exhaustion meet—where we are tempted to damage and distort our self-perspective, blame anyone and everyone for our hard times, internalize rejections, lash out at the ones we love, burn bridges, and ultimately self-sabotage. It leads to a narrow chasm of self-inflicted bitterness, isolation, guilt, and spiraling doubt—where we undermine our own stories and discount our capabilities. The ledge is easy to fall off, and too many of us have stood before it, wondering how to balance or climb down.

I spent years listening to and interviewing some of the most impressive women. These women seem to all have natural talents that change the world. And while I still aspire to reach their levels of success one day, my kind of success has been more modest and accessible. One could say that I am only marginally qualified to be giving advice. My handshake is still not firm enough. My eye-contact game needs work. I still buy a week's worth of fresh vegetables and don't eat any of them. I'm just now learning how to budget my personal expenses properly. And I often ignore emails for weeks because I can be easily overwhelmed, then I write back "somehow this ended up in my spam folder." So yes, I don't have it all figured out. I did, however, fulfill my dream of building and growing my own business and creating financial freedom while living a meaningful and purposeful life.

I write this book now because of my diverse set of pivots and the self-knowledge I acquired along the way. It took me years to recognize that while external barriers do exist, my biggest barrier has been my own flawed self-worth. I wore down, I burned out, I failed, I went broke, my mascara ran and ran out, but ultimately I came out the other side with a different perspective on success, one that aligns me with living my own truth rather than falling victim to expectations set by the outside world.

I stopped allowing a dysfunctional society to turn me into a dysfunctional woman. And my hope is that this book will help you acquire the necessary self-knowledge to stop too.

Introduction

BALANCING ON
THE GLASS LEDGE

I've always felt unclaimed. Like every woman who picks up this book, I am multidimensional. We women carry many complexities that make up who we are, and we intend to embrace them all. Ideally, we're open to evolving and accepting all parts of ourselves, no matter how different they may seem.

Some people may know me as a former beauty queen, and others might know me as "a beauty queen with a PowerPoint and a dream." But there are many facets to me: I'm an immigrant, a scientist, a medical mission-ary, a businesswoman, and a women's advocate. And this is a story of how I created a distinct narrative that shows I am more than just an archipel-ago of identities.

THE AMERICAN DREAM

When I was a teenager, my parents—accomplished executives in Morocco—decided to sacrifice our comfortable lives and their established careers to move across the ocean in pursuit of their children's American Dream.

I find it interesting that most people think of immigrants only as peo-ple who are struggling in their home countries and migrate to better provide for their families. We did the opposite. I had to watch my parents completely level down their lives and start over.

It wasn't long after that move that, at fifteen, I began struggling with depression. I'd been forced to adapt to a new lifestyle. A new culture, a new language, and even a new way of learning. A sense of belonging is crucial for adolescents as it is often associated with being accepted, valued, included, and encouraged—and I no longer had that. I struggled to adapt to a new lifestyle in a different culture. I felt trapped in a new and sudden reality, and the worst part was having no one to talk to about it. I felt misunderstood and lost.

Along with depression, I developed insecurities around my self-image, shame for not speaking perfect English, and guilt for seeing my parents' career downgrades and sacrifices. Isolation was my coping mechanism and journaling my only escape. Journaling helped me realize that my new environment was not the issue. In fact, my reality was mostly positive. It was how I was defining myself in that reality—fueled by my own self-esteem, or lack thereof—that was the problem.

I needed to revise myself from a struggling outsider who didn't belong and was never going to be as good as the other American students. With the help of counselors and the support of my aunt who had gone through the same transition years ago when she, too, moved from Morocco, I learned to normalize my new life, accept responsibility, and harness the restorative power of self-enhancing life choices.

I finished high school and received a college scholarship to study biochemistry and molecular biology. I hoped to fulfill my childhood dream of curing cancer. (Spoiler Alert: I did not end up curing cancer!) After college, I was selected from seven hundred applicants to intern for one of Munich's best emerging biotech startups. This was a stepping-stone to an exciting career as a cancer research scientist.

On the outside it might have looked like I was breaking through obstacle after obstacle. But inside I was riddled with anxiety, as the internalized voice of my new American culture whispered the limits of who I could be. I applied to only two colleges, both in my home state of Colorado, because I didn't think I'd be good enough to get into the Ivy League schools. I followed my friends wherever they were going and did whatever they were doing because I didn't have the confidence to make my own decisions otherwise. I resisted leaving home because I feared I couldn't make it on my own.

TRYING ON THE CROWN FOR SIZE

While I was claiming my place as a research scientist in the male-dominated health-care sector, my mother was encouraging me to "get more in touch with my feminine side."

So she signed me up for a beauty pageant.

Why did I agree to this? I idolized my mother. Growing up, I saw her as the epitome of a woman who truly had it all. She is a confident businesswoman, always dressed to perfection, and she is also a loving wife and a firm yet supportive parent. A fearless risk-taker, my mother has always been the backbone of our family. She left her own family at the age of thirteen to pursue her dreams of becoming an independent and accomplished woman. You could feel her energy just by being in the same room with her. And I am so grateful to have her as a role model.

Although I tended to follow my mother's advice, a beauty pageant was a big ask. I was terrified of being on stage, of public speaking, and frankly, I couldn't handle the thought of putting myself out there for others to deliberately judge. I never thought of myself as a girly girl. I'd avoided joining sororities in college because I was intimidated and insecure around beautiful and accomplished women. And pageants were full of them!

As I'll talk about later, to my surprise, I not only fell in love with pageants but also became obsessed with the preparation process. I think it's because I shifted my focus to the self-development lessons that were there for the taking: poise, communication, confidence, resilience, strength, and courage. To top it off, the unexpectedly supportive pageant community introduced me to a new world in which women encouraged one another to become their best selves.

After several attempts at the Miss Colorado USA pageant, making it as far as a first runner-up, I moved to New York and won the title of Miss New York United States in 2015 on my first attempt. I then went on to place second runner-up at Miss United States 2015 and to serve on the first all-women panel of judges at the 2018 Miss Universe competition in Thailand. I have since judged multiple other state and national pageants, including Miss Teen USA in 2020 and Miss Earth USA in 2022.

WHEN FEMINISM MEETS HUSTLE

While experiencing pageant success and establishing myself as the fresh voice of a generation of millennial women through my emerging media brand SWAAY, I found myself subtly becoming part of a "resistance" culture in which feminism rebranded itself as what we now call Girlboss Capitalism. Amplified by the downfall of the first potential female president and the rise of a misogynist in national office, 2016 became the start of the golden age for women who dared to step out and speak up. And I was ready to rally.

Mass-media feminism took on a new sense of urgency. Women-only clubs popped up across the nation. Grassroots activism reached its peak. And in 2017, the #metoo movement showed men that the old ways of abusing power are no longer acceptable. At the forefront of all these movements were charismatic female founders and leaders who were brave enough to change the narrative by sharing their stories and gracing magazine covers as the new celebrated icons.

I felt so grateful and excited to have had a front-row seat to this historic shift, interviewing and taking in the raw accounts of these icons regarding their experiences as disruptive leaders, while trying to become one of them and navigating my own startup struggles as a female founder myself. The concept of Girlbossery became a representation for the pursuit of female ambition and success, and the women's movement fueled a storm of rebellion against the injustices that made every woman's life taxing. I felt proud to play even a small part in the change that was taking place. But fighting the patriarchy while sustaining a female-forward media startup that further exposed me to unexpected indignities was a double-edged sword. On one hand, I was part of an emerging generation of change agents who were collectively raising their voices and bringing vital issues to light. On the other hand, it felt like I was stuck in an echo chamber where feminism became obsessed with victimhood and where the rhetoric focused more on what we women can't do instead of what we can. Subconsciously, I began to define myself by the wounds of gender-related adversities, which was ultimately disempowering.

The haunting belief that I might be less than others—especially counterparts who were men—hijacked my confidence and triggered my ego. At the time, I saw this dynamic as the foundation of my ambition. It fueled the already-big chip on my shoulder and gave me the motivation to hustle for change, and without it I wouldn't have been able to achieve so many of my goals and transcend the odds.

But during the first years of building my business and navigating repeated rejections, I became defensive and reactive, anticipating rejections and failures before they even happened. And when they did happen, I easily blamed the unfair structural systems in place. Every time a man in power looked at me smugly and then closed the door in my face, I wanted desperately to show him that I was in fact good enough. As I repeated the same validation dance over and over, it became clear to me that my inner dialogue was more condescending than the venture capitalists in the conference rooms. At this point in my journey, I began to pay attention to these voices within me. The voices I'd internalized that trumpeted patriarchy, xenophobia, and women's inferiority. The voices that led me to see myself in ways detrimental to my self-actualization.

These voices were to be expected. After all, the feminist movement is all about exposing a system that isn't designed for our advancement—and we have the research to prove it.

- In 2015, 17 percent of women were in C-suite positions (the highest-ranking individuals in an organization); in 2021, at 21 percent, it's barely grown.
- Women in the US are paid 82 cents for every dollar paid to men, an annual gender wage gap of $10,194. The wage gap is even larger for most women of color.
- Women are starting high-growth businesses more than ever before but are receiving only 2.8 percent of venture capital investments.
- Across all media platforms, men received 63 percent of bylines and credits while women received 37 percent.

These statistics paint a grim picture, one that leaves every woman feeling frustrated and disadvantaged but also motivated for change. I am still as passionate as ever about gender parity and women's rights; let it be known that I am and always will be a proud feminist. But to me feminism is also about encouraging and empowering women (and men) to feel a sense of autonomy and control in their lives while cultivating a sense of accountability. So as I continued to push through the different barriers in my entrepreneurial journey, my perspective began to shift from "things should be different" to "what can I do differently for myself and to pay it forward?"

Galvanized by my personal experience and more research, I set out to create a safe space for women to own their stories and speak their truths, an outlet that would equip them with the guidance and tools to amplify their voices and elevate their credibility. With this hope of shaping a new societal narrative, I pivoted my company, SWAAY Media, from an aspirational feminist media brand to a self-publishing platform where underrepresented voices can build their authority and influence as thought leaders.

Despite the constant struggles in fundraising and growing a sustainable business, in five years SWAAY has become a leading platform and community for female thought leadership and storytelling. The company currently reaches more than two million women and is uplifting thousands of voices. And most importantly, it has become a network of powerful women from all walks of life who mentor and champion one another by sharing stories of resilience, vulnerability, and autonomy.

In the same way that my background and experience aren't easily summarized or labeled, today's women are also a diverse multi-hyphenated, and rich group of individuals. But many face a common obstacle: internalized oppression.

Women face judgment issues in career progression, communication, and appearance, and as a result, we often adopt strategies that hold us further back.

This book explores self-inflicted barriers (internalized oppression) often shaped by preconceived societal expectations and outdated gender stereotypes (external oppression) in a way that doesn't blame women or society. It focuses instead on our individual actions and provides tools to change ourselves faster than the outside world will change for us. I will prompt you to ask yourself tough questions and uncover uncomfortable answers. And rather than asking what society needs to do differently or blaming it for what it hasn't done for us, we will help each other hold sway over our circumstances by asking ourselves,

What can I do differently?

We want to change the narrative for ourselves and pay it forward.

Everyone has heard of "the glass ceiling." Decades ago, this term came into being to describe the invisible barriers to women's workplace advancement. It has since become a rallying cry of corporate feminism that everyone #LovesToHate. And while we've come a long way in breaking through many barriers, many successful women face the same formidable obstacle I have faced: unconscious self-sabotage fueled by internalized oppression. When women affirm negative self-stereotypes and give in to external expectations, I call it "tumbling off the glass ledge."

The **glass ceiling** has become a mainstream idea to describe invisible external oppression and has been at the forefront of conversations around women's empowerment. But it's time we explore the **glass ledge**, a metaphor that represents women adapting thinking and behavior that does not serve them. **Tumbling off the glass ledge** is when we have lost control over our owns paths and fallen prey to fear, panic, and hopelessness because of our self-sabotaging thoughts and behavior (often driven by external pressures and standards), which ultimately hinders our growth potential.

Balancing on the glass ledge or stepping gently off the glass ledge happens when we understand the nuances of why we feel the way we do and act from a place of self-awareness and self-assurance. It involves breaking free from our self-deprecating ways, shattering the poor self-image we've been carrying, and rising above internal and external biases to achieve our rightfully earned success.

This book will explore the ten themes that are most likely to derail us when we least expect it. These themes aren't good or bad in and of themselves. What we will learn are productive strategies for working through potential issues on our own terms. The ten themes are organized as stand-alone chapters:

- Power
- Likability
- Presentation
- Authenticity
- Conflict

- Confidence
- Balance
- Competition
- Expertise
- Belonging

Each chapter begins with examples of sabotaging inner dialogue that will help you identify those voices within yourself. Then I offer stories from my journey to help you unpack how that theme might be showing up in your life. Each chapter also includes advice from accomplished women in my network, credible third-party research, lessons and tips to prevent slipping off the ledge and/or for getting back on the right track, as well as exercises that will help you put the content to work right away. I highly recommend you keep a journal to reflect on the stories shared, to track your answers to the exercises, and to make the most of the information you find throughout the book. You are welcome to share your reflections with me and other women at SWAAY.com or through social media by tagging me (@imanoubou) or using the hashtag #theglassledge.

Although I've written this book from the point of view of a cis-gender, heterosexual woman—which might make my perspective and ideas more familiar to others in this same camp—I hope that no matter how you identify and what ideals you aspire to, you will find some inspiration that resonates and works for you.

It has never been a perfect world. While many social norms may have shifted when it comes to the gender dynamic, both workplace and societal gender polarities remain ingrained. Though we may not have the power as individuals to change this at scale, we women do have the power to control the decisions and behaviors that lead to a story we don't want. We can change our own stories and pay it forward at the same time. We don't have to settle for being labeled, and we don't have to adhere to expectations that are driven by other people's validation.

I hope this book will help women at all stages of life learn to "sway" the narrative, as they approach the glass ledge with balance and clarity. May you grow through your own definition of what it means to be a womxn. But more importantly, may you gain the advantage that will catapult you to the next level personally and professionally.

"I don't want others to think I am power hungry."

"I will never have the power I deserve."

"I don't trust power. It makes people evil."

"Society has to change to provide women with power."

"I am not powerful because I don't have money or resources."

"If I don't work twice as hard, my power will be undermined."

"Having rights and having power are not the same thing."

"I don't have the power to achieve my dreams."

"People won't ever see me as powerful because of my failures."

"I can't create my own reality because of oppressive external barriers."

Chapter One

POWER

Raise your hand if you have experienced powerlessness despite being intelligent, educated, competent, accomplished, confident, etc. Yep! That's why we need to start this book off by understanding nuances around power, because our relationship with power defines everything we do. It affects everything, from how we present ourselves to how we resolve conflict. Every woman needs to define her personal, individual relationship with her own power and with the power of others, but far too often we fall off the ledge by allowing other people or society at large to define power for us. And once that happens, it's very easy for our power to slip away.

In its simplest form, power is the ability to act. Through my own experiences and conversations with mentors, I've learned that power is about charting my life's course on my terms and helping others do the same. It's about having the strength and capacity to champion my values and valuing my accomplishments regardless of what society says. It's so much more than feeling like the Girlboss in a perfectly tailored pantsuit.

Like many people, I have held some negative associations with the idea of power. It is often equated with corruption and forcing your will on others, personified by mobsters, dictators, and incompetent politicians. But I have come to see that power is destructive only when we seek it for its own sake, when we view it as an end instead of a means, a tool. The truth is, the more power you have and the more skillfully you use it, the greater the impact you can have.

Recall Christine Blasey Ford, the American professor of psychology who testified against Supreme Court justice nominee Brett Kavanaugh, citing his sexual assault when they were teenagers growing up outside Washington, DC. Blasey Ford didn't present herself as fierce or loud, but that didn't mean she wasn't powerful. Her voice wavered, and she appeared emotionally vulnerable—but Blasey Ford was still on that stand. And even if she wasn't entirely comfortable with it, she exuded power through her bravery.

Speaking of the Supreme Court, while writing this chapter, one of my longtime heroines, Ruth Bader Ginsburg, passed away. She was the epitome of a woman in pursuit of power. Without her dedication and commitment to women's rights, I might not have had the opportunity to write this book. Ginsburg made it her mission to fight for women's futures. And she did it with grace, poise, and confidence. She was aware of her internal power, and she knew exactly how to use it. Her passing brought a deep and poignant moment of reflection. For me, it signaled the end of an era in which women fought to bring down external barriers and the beginning of a deliberate path to expand our perception of ourselves and what we can accomplish when we embrace our potential.

Since we are looking at power, we should also look at the concept of *empowerment*. When we talk about or advocate for women's empowerment, what's often implied is that we are *asking* (and in certain instances, begging) for power to be given to us—which underscores the preconceived narrative that women do not already have power. We have power. Instead, we should define empowerment as "the process of becoming stronger and more confident, especially in directing one's life and claiming one's rights." My startling confrontation with this concept began in September 2015, when I decided to officially trade my unfulfilling but stable corporate career for an uncertain but exhilarating entrepreneurial adventure.

At the time, it seemed to make sense to turn my podcasting hobby into a media brand. So I spent hours researching and perfecting my first investor pitch for making a difference in a world where women's stories are underrepresented. I fashioned myself as a kind of Wonder Woman fighting for women's voices, and the mission excited me. The only issue? I had no money, no network, and no previous experience in media or running a business.

Nearly immediately after quitting my job, self-doubt dominated my thoughts, and I began to regret my decision. I had already lost most of my savings in my first attempt at a business. That was when I was twenty-three, fresh out of graduate school, and had partnered with the wrong guy. He promised to make my dream of launching a Moroccan-inspired skin-care line a reality but never delivered, and my investment was gone. After this debacle, I'd made it my mission to build a career striving for stability and security. Now, here I was again, risking that career for another entrepreneurial dream. I felt like I was self-sabotaging.

I didn't have the resources to build the business I wanted and could barely pay my bills. Yet I was still fulfilling my duty as Miss New York US, attending fancy events and making red carpet appearances alongside some of New York's most successful people. It felt like a double life. I used my PR skills to land amazing media features about my new company, but deep down I felt like an impostor and a failure.

I was powerless—or so I thought.

Until that first pitch, I'd never considered what power really means to me. As a child of the "girl power" era and fan of the Spice Girls' feminist call, when I was young, the idea that women could not be powerful leaders never crossed my mind. In school, I never questioned my ability to win or to lead. I was motivated by competition, without taking gender into account. But as the years went by and I stepped into my career heels, the rules for women became more numerous. For example, to avoid coming across as weak, I was told to be approachable but not too friendly. I was told not to wear dresses or tight pencil skirts to job interviews to avoid being sexualized by male interviewers (because it was my responsibility not to tempt them). I was told that if I cared about my career, I would put plans of having a family aside. I was even told to squelch my ambition because it intimidated men who might want to date me.

One particular memory stands out. I was pursuing a prominent venture capitalist for a few months before he finally agreed to meet me for coffee. I had learned about the many great investments he'd made in businesses founded by women and knew of his public support for our community of female founders, so I was psyched for our conversation. At first, our conversation was going smoothly. He asked the right questions and was optimistic about my mission to champion women's voices through storytelling. But then he addressed my history with beauty pageants, which he found interesting. Shortly after ordering our second cup of coffee, he said:

"I don't know if you realize that starting a business is hard. Really hard. You would probably make more money quicker if you got involved with beauty brands to inspire women. You know, use your pretty face. It would be such a shame to waste that."

After that meeting, I was never in touch with the man again. The experience had been truly shocking. How could I slip into such preconceived societal expectations as easily as I could a tailored pantsuit? How much of myself must I change or censor to be taken seriously?

While these societal narratives are deplorable, they don't compare to the economic burden placed on women: the persistent and widening pay gap, the lack of gender-neutral policies to normalize diverse caregiving roles, the limited access to funding and resources, the fact that choosing to have a family can be of value to men but detrimental to women, and the fact that existing power dynamics normalize sexual harassment and abuse. To be clear, being paid a lower salary isn't the same as feeling insecure in an outdated pantsuit, but both experiences stem from a power structure that is driven by gender stereotypes that keep men on top.

This power structure has a long history, punctuated by an event in 1995: the United Nations' Fourth World Conference on Women, which took place in Beijing. "The meeting was notable for many reasons, not least because it was, at the time, the largest gathering of women's rights activists around the world," write Rachel Vogelstein and Jennifer Klein in their article for ForeignPolicy.com, "Let's Make Women's Power Culturally Acceptable." "At the conclusion of the meeting, governments meeting in Beijing agreed to the most ambitious Platform for Action on women's rights in history, one that called for the full and equal participation of women in political, civil, economic, social, and cultural life."

In the ensuing years, that Platform for Action has met with varying degrees of success. When it comes to legal rights, health, and education, women have come a long way. But in terms of economic power? Not so much. "Women's participation in the labor force actually dropped from 51 to 47 percent, even before COVID-19 decimated jobs disproportionately held by women and the women who were employed remained saddled with a double burden of caregiving and household work," write Vogelstein and Klein.

They contend that although some legal barriers remain, cultural norms are also responsible for holding women back. "If the twenty-five years since Beijing have been about women naming their rights, the next twenty-five must be about amassing sufficient power to claim them. Societies need to shift the expectations and attitudes that undergird the resistance to women's power," they write. These include stereotypes about women's motives when seeking power, preconceived ideas pegging women as caregivers, and the tolerance of sexual harassment—both a cause and a result of a power imbalance.

Vogelstein and Klein say that the solution is a concerted strategy to push back on outdated norms and divisions of labor. "Campaigns to make women's power culturally acceptable will help ensure that women have the leverage to claim their rights not just in theory but also in practice—and demonstrate that power may come in the form of a woman wearing a mask, rather than a man behind a desk or wielding an army."

Former first lady, secretary of state, and presidential candidate Hillary Rodham Clinton is on the same page. In a 2020 op-ed for *The Atlantic*, she writes that inequality isn't just about rights, but about power—who has it, who doesn't, and how to close the gaps. She cites a book by Mary Beard, *Women & Power: A Manifesto*, which urges readers to reject the notion of power as a zero-sum game.

"If power is seen as a tool only a few people can wield at a time, within systems designed by and for men, an entire gender will forever be excluded from it. Instead, why not look at power more comprehensively? We should think of it as the ability to be effective, to make a difference in the world, and to be taken seriously," Beard writes.

If anyone knows how to do this, it's Hillary Clinton. "In addition to voting for women seeking positions of power, each of us can speak out, support organizations promoting women's rights and power, and engage in peaceful protest movements. We can support mentoring and role modeling, and work to change messages in media. We can call out sexism and racism, and challenge insidious norms in our culture, workplaces, and households," she recommends in *The Atlantic*.

While these leaders make excellent points on the systemic transformative changes needed for women to access real power in practice, they unfortunately fail to address the internal barriers that are holding us back from claiming the power we have and reaching the equality we deserve.

One of my favorite philosophers, Michel Foucault, once said, "Power is everywhere" and "comes from everywhere." But if this is true, what has stopped me and countless other women from getting it and exercising it to sway our own narratives? And what is it about power that causes women to fall off the glass ledge?

In her book *No Excuses: 9 Ways Women Can Change How We Think about Power*, Gloria Feldt writes that "women in general have been so invisible in society's halls of power for so long that we can hardly think of our own ambition as having intrinsic value. We are all called to power. And how we use it is the ultimate question."

She adds: "Women can be at the forefront of changing the power paradigm. After all, women have been at the forefront of almost every major movement for social justice in our nation's history from the Women's March and Black Lives Matter to #metoo and Time's Up."

Remind yourself that fear of power is not real; it is just a self-inflicted barrier that is standing between you and the life you truly want. Of course, answering the call to power is easier said than done. This rest of this chapter will tackle the challenge, addressing what power means to you, how to take responsibility for current barriers to progress, how to develop your internal locus of control, and how to internalize gratitude for the power (and everything else) you already have.

CHOICE AND ACCOUNTABILITY

When I originally told the story of my run-ins with the patriarchy to the media, I did so from a place of external blame. It was clear to me that I should have been treated differently and that it was wrong and unfair for my prospective investors to see me as less than. But I also failed to take accountability for underestimating the power of my own worth. If I didn't see what I was bringing to the table, why should they? Accountability is the obligation to explain, justify, and take responsibility for our beliefs and actions, and if we don't do this, no one else can take up the mantle for us. It was up to me to speak my truth and press for my value, but every time I was presented with a chance to do so, I fell off the ledge.

LEDGE PROTECTOR #1: UNDERSTAND WHAT POWER MEANS TO YOU

I met my dear friend Eboni K. Williams, an attorney, author, and TV personality, at the launch party for her book *Pretty Powerful: Appearance, Substance, and Success*. At the time, I was working on our first SWAAY media campaign, #swaaythenarrative, and when I heard Eboni speak, I knew she'd be an amazing ambassador for challenging women stereotypes.

As a previous host on the Fox News Channel and current co-host of the late-night talk show *State of the Culture* on Revolt TV, Eboni is no stranger to participating in and commentating on social movements or the pursuit of power. "As early as age six, I knew I wanted to be a lawyer because that was a profession unabashedly about having the power in the courtroom and in legislative forums to bring about real change," she told me. "For me, power is synonymous with impact. I'm on an aggressive journey that openly and vocally pursues power because I want to use my gifts to impact communities of color, women, children, and other marginalized groups."

The need to foster your power as an individual is a crucial piece. After all, many of us women still don't know how to feel about our own power. We want to be equal to men. But when we are granted a bigger challenge, a high-level position, or a prestigious accolade, thanks to pesky norms it sits on us like a tight, itchy shirt, and we may unconsciously take steps to sabotage ourselves.

Although women's oppression is nothing new, we are our own worst enemy when we insist on our own powerlessness.

"The truth is that a lot of women are still uncomfortable with power," Eboni said. "Despite movement and progress, and despite that it's now cool to say we have power, when I have quiet conversations with other women, when I pull back the layers, there is conflict around notions of femininity and power. Power is equated with masculinity. Work is being done to eradicate the correlation, but it's still there."

Eboni concurred that while it's self-protective to become part of an outraged culture that blames our individual situations on societal injustices, this move will also result in a fall off the ledge. As she once told me: "One of my favorite sayings is, 'In the meantime, while we wait for systems to change, how are we going to show up?' We women need to hold ourselves accountable to succeed despite systemic oppression. We have to stop waiting for permission and for other people to be comfortable."

I couldn't agree more.

Cindy Eckert, whom I've interviewed on my podcast and for a SWAAY feature, is a fearless entrepreneur known for founding Sprout Pharmaceuticals. She also launched The Pink Ceiling, which invests in companies founded by or delivering products for women. In the last ten years, she has started and sold two pharmaceutical companies for more than $1.5 billion. First, Slate Pharmaceuticals redefined long-acting testosterone treatment for men, and then Sprout Pharmaceuticals broke through with the first FDA-approved drug for low sexual desire in women—dubbed "female Viagra" by the media. One of my favorite power moves by Cindy? After she sold Sprout, she successfully fought to get the female Viagra drug back and launch it on her own terms.

When I asked Cindy about power, she said: "In humans, power is courage times relentlessness. Power isn't about external influence; it is about internal resolve. All of the moments I have been tested throughout my life and career have made one thing clear: the power you have boils down to the amount of courage you have to exercise it. It's what led me to fight the government for women's sexual pleasure, and it is what fuels my mission today."

In the mid-twentieth century, social psychologists John French and Bertram Raven studied the types of power and labeled the following:

- **Legitimate:** A powerful person has a formal right to make demands and expect others to comply with those demands.
- **Reward:** A powerful person ensures compliance by compensating others.
- **Expert:** A powerful person gets that way based on their high level of skill and knowledge.
- **Referent:** A powerful person gets that way because they are perceived as attractive and worthy of others' respect.
- **Coercive:** A powerful person ensures compliance by punishing others.
- **Informational:** A powerful person gets that way by controlling the information others need to accomplish something.

You can probably recognize yourself or leaders you know in each of these categories. Some types of power are more positive (and I'd even go so far as to say more effective) than others. The good news is that you don't have to be wealthy or hold a high position in an organization to cultivate power.

Our early experiences do quite a bit to wire our beliefs and shape our lives, so when considering which type of power speaks to you most clearly, it might be worthwhile to consider your household of origin. What type of power was used most frequently? For example, was there legitimate power between your parents? What about coercive power between you and any siblings? How might these dynamics impact how you now wield or fear power as an adult?

Note too that these types of power all have one thing in common: they pertain to one's ability to influence others. But power can be collective too. We often think of power over or power under, but let's not forget about power that's shared. Just because one person has power doesn't have to mean another person automatically lacks it.

Heifer International, a nonprofit organization striving to end hunger by supporting local farmers and their communities, recently published a variety of perspectives on women's empowerment around the world.

"Women's empowerment is freedom. Freedom is expression, freedom to make decisions, freedom to be happy."
ANAHIT GHAZANCHYAN, ARMENIA

"Women's power is a feeling that has no borders and no limits. You can make things happen. You can challenge yourself and achieve it."
IVANIA LOVO, NICARAGUA

"Women are empowered when their voices are heard."
NIMISHA BHAGAWATY, INDIA

"Women's power is a space of equality, working in a job under equal conditions."
BEATRIZ POZO, HONDURAS

"Women's empowerment means that women are not afraid."
ANGIE AHUYON, US

Of all these answers, Nimisha's resonates with me the most. Through my work with SWAAY and my thought-leadership coaching, I've learned that women's voices are underrepresented because we often hesitate to embrace our power and speak our truths. We can't be heard if we aren't insisting on raising our voices, even when it feels uncomfortable.

When the COVID pandemic hit and all travel was paused, I filled my time by getting to know SWAAY's community of rising thought leaders. I offered free one-on-one coaching sessions to women who feared putting themselves out there. After more than one hundred sessions, I'm still surprised by how many accomplished, smart, and driven women are taking their own power away by convincing themselves that what they have to contribute lacks value.

Nimisha is right about voice, but inside my own notion of power, there are a few additional nuances. First, having the right to be heard is one thing, but choosing to be heard is another. Most women aren't intentionally choosing to use their voices or choosing to accept their value and the positive influence their stories can have on others. These choices, or lack thereof, are often fueled by the voices in our heads that say something like *my story doesn't matter* or *no one cares what I have to say* or *there are so many people out there speaking/writing about X, why would anyone listen to me*, etc.

Regardless of our personal definition of power, we must have the courage to speak it out loud.

Before we move on, I also want to suggest that true power can be held in balance with vulnerability (or leaving yourself exposed to the possibility of being judged or attacked). Most women we admire and respect today—like Malala Yousafzai, Roxane Gay, Simone Biles, and Jacinda Ardern, to name a few—demonstrated power by embracing vulnerability. We will talk more about vulnerability throughout the book, but as we talk about power, I hope you'll keep in mind that vulnerability can be powerful too!

◆ Ledge Work: Visualize Your Own Power

The first step to solidifying your definition of power is to imagine yourself at your most powerful. For this exercise, think back to a time when you, as the saying goes, "Nailed it!" Perhaps you delivered a presentation to enthusiastic applause or conquered internal obstacles to get a controversial but important program off the ground. Maybe you're a swimmer and just shaved seconds off your personal best time, or maybe you finally finished a complex work of art.

Now, recall the details in the self-reflection journal you've set aside specifically for this book. Ask yourself:

What was the situation?

Why did you feel powerful? For instance, did you think you were at the top of your game, were in control, had clarity, or made a difference?

What did the power feel like in your body? For instance, was your heart beating quickly? Were you smiling from ear to ear? Were you calm and still?

What emotions were top of mind? For instance, did you feel competence, excitement, or confidence?

Next, consider a subtler, less obvious demonstration of power in your life. Explore a moment when you felt powerful alone, perhaps while you were meditating or exercising. Answer the same questions about your experience.

Reread your answers every day for a week, so you can train your brain to recall the experience of power and the conditions that brought it about. By readily visualizing this version of yourself, you can recreate it more often in everyday life, where showing up powerfully will become routine.

◆

LEDGE PROTECTOR #2: TAKE RESPONSIBILITY FOR BARRIERS TO PROGRESS

The journey to embracing your power also includes understanding what power is NOT. "Sometimes we find ourselves fighting for our power, holding steady, and standing strong, when the reality of the issue isn't about power at all," says Deirdre Maloney, an author, speaker, and the CEO of Momentum, Inc. "Sometimes what we think is about power is really about getting our way just to get our way. It's really about knowing we are right, to show that others are wrong. It's really about proving we can last longer and play harder at all costs. Sometimes we insist on being powerful not to get things done, not to make our lives better, but simply to feel powerful. That's when power is about pride."

My friend Abby is a veterinarian. Her office director usually gives the complicated cases to the male vets on staff, even if they have less experience. Over the last year, Abby has gotten more and more frustrated about this situation. Instead of confronting the director head on, Abby has talked to numerous people inside and outside the office—including myself and other clients—about her displeasure. And the more she ranted about the biased director, the more power and mental energy she devoted to him.

Abby didn't want to give the office director the satisfaction of addressing the problem diplomatically; instead, she undermined her own success, as well as that of her colleagues. The office environment became so toxic that Abby and several of her women colleagues considered quitting a practice they truly loved.

When she recruited others over to her cause, Abby may have felt powerful temporarily, but she ended up falling off the glass ledge here. Getting even or stirring things up so you can "win" may not result in the best outcome. In fact, it may involve giving away even more of your power.

Perhaps that's why Deirdre Maloney says that the true definition of power is the ability to make our own choices: "Sometimes power means taking something on, but sometimes it means choosing to let something go. Sometimes power means standing strong, but sometimes it means choosing to step aside. Sometimes power means having our say, but sometimes it means choosing to let others have theirs."

In July of 2015, when she was thirty-seven years old, Jen Welter became the first woman coach in NFL history. The Arizona Cardinals, under the direction of head coach Bruce Arians at the time, made the historic decision to hire a woman for a coaching role. While she was training inside linebackers, Jen learned to leverage the different types of powerful actions Maloney described.

I first met Jen at a female founders' pitch competition I judged for Visa during New York Fashion Week in 2019. I missed her uplifting speech because of my judging duties, but luckily I connected with her after the event to get a few signed copies of her book *Play Big: Lessons in Being Limitless from the First Woman to Coach in the NFL*. After reading her book, I reached out again because as the lone but outspoken woman in a male-dominated environment, Jen represented the type of power I was still seeking. "If you are looking for a fight, you can always find one," Jen told me. "But the evolution of gender equality involves women and men learning to be allies for each other, so in some cases it was more powerful to use a conflict to build bridges."

Although most male team leaders and players were supportive, Jen did hear insensitive and ignorant comments. "I'd use humor to diffuse things. I'd say something like, 'You do realize you said that out loud, right?' In this way, I acknowledged an inappropriate remark, but we all laughed and built trust that encouraged them to really listen to me in the future."

In a tough situation, sometimes the more powerful course is a subtle action.

"So many women get mad about remarks that aren't meant to be offensive. They take their own backstories into the interaction, and they feel wronged. I was (and still am at times) one of them. But to be powerful, you have to look at intent and also the larger picture of what you need to accomplish," Jen told me.

This brings us back to my earlier point about responsibility. The word literally means the state of being accountable within one's power, control, or management. Again, when it comes to issues of women's power and empowerment, it's easy to point the finger at others or at "the way things are." It *is* unfair that our gender has been oppressed for millennia. It *is* unfair that women comprise but a small fraction of top public- and private-sector leaders. It *is* unfair that both visible and invisible cultural norms push against us as we pursue positions of power, personally and professionally.

There's a lot about life we can't control, but focusing on those barriers won't help our progress. Instead, consider how you can create change for yourself. If something unfortunate happens, you can acknowledge that, but you can also own your role in helping things go better the next time.

Instead of thinking obsessively about the negative circumstance and feeling helpless, you can change your attitude toward the situation as well as your response moving forward. In doing so, you become an agent rather than a victim in your own life.

"Stop railing, start doing," advises Cindy Eckert. "Do you have a level playing field? Nope. But that doesn't mean you shouldn't get the hell on the field and start scoring anyway. Plenty of male investors laughed at me when I asked them to invest in the little pink pill for women. If their dismissiveness had consumed me, I wouldn't have had the energy left to bring it to market and sell it for a billion dollars. Instead of being frustrated, I was fueled. And you know what? Today, those same people invest in deals alongside me."

Cindy's words struck a nerve. My experience pitching investors who were dismissive had consumed me too—and I let it. I had the power to sway those investors and others who would follow, but instead I chose not to exercise my power because of my own limited self-perception. For months afterward, I felt angry and frustrated, and I operated from a place of fear and unworthiness instead of conviction. I realized my pursuit of power had shifted from being about impact to being about pride.

Cindy's fuel, on the other hand, has been her internal regulation, which is independent of any external event. And that is where true power lies. It took me a few years of trial and error to master this myself, so let's shift our focus now to how you can achieve this too.

LEDGE PROTECTOR #3: HONE YOUR INTERNAL LOCUS OF CONTROL

Locus of control is an idea developed by Julian Rotter, a pioneering American psychologist of the twentieth century. If you believe you control your own destiny, you have an internal locus of control. Alternatively, if you think your destiny is controlled by other forces, like God or fate, your family or your boss, that is an external locus of control.

Research shows that men tend to be more internally focused than women, older people are more internally focused than younger people, and people at higher levels in an organization are more internally focused than those lower on the chain.

You can imagine why it's better to have an internal locus of control. These individuals work harder to get what they want, and their health is better because they don't spend so much time railing against factors they can't do anything about.

Your personal locus of control is probably based on a combination of genetic and environmental circumstances at play when you were a child. That said,

just because an external locus of control is your default doesn't mean you have to stick with it.

You can strive to be more internally focused by doing the following:

Create a checklist

Get into the habit of writing a to-do list at the start of every day. The things on your list should be simple and achievable, such as making a single networking Zoom call or attending a workout class. Every time you check something off the list, you will increase your sense of effecting positive change with your actions. Each time you accomplish a small goal, you will build momentum and energy. It's all about taking manageable steps daily toward creating a sustainable shift and cultivating a sense of control.

Stand on your own

People with an external locus of control often believe others know better than they do. Get in the habit of making decisions on your own, doing your own research, and using a list of pros and cons, so you can build trust in your own judgment and ability to make sound choices. Don't rely on other people's opinions and validation to drive your life decisions.

Silence the helpless voice

Throughout this book, I'll be talking a lot about inner voices that aren't helpful. One of the voices you may hear says, "There's nothing I can do." Dispute these thoughts as quickly as you can by eliminating the word *nothing* from your vocabulary and reflecting on what you *can* do. In most cases, there is always something you *can* do when you're looking for solutions instead of focusing on the problem. For example, while it's true that you can't always control whether you get sick, you can find ways to make the illness bearable today and take steps toward building a healthier you with habits that contribute to a stronger immune system.

Catch yourself catastrophizing

It's hard to feel powerful when the annoyances of everyday life send you into a tailspin. If you tend to allow something as simple as a late or incompetent colleague to ruin your day, practice controlling your negative response by looking at the big picture and how things could be worse or even further outside your control. Do your best to react to a situation that is causing you a lot of anxiety in a productive and actionable way. For example, schedule a mediated meeting between you and that colleague to discuss the consequences of their actions and address the core issues.

LEDGE PROTECTOR #4: INTERNALIZE GRATITUDE

Gratitude is a powerful wellness strategy that aids with a variety of glass ledge–related concerns, which we will have occasion to talk about again. Here, in the context of personal power, gratitude can be an immensely useful tool.

I have come to realize that I feel powerful when I am decisive and have found that gratitude allows me to see a situation more objectively, evaluating the pros and cons more clearly and avoiding snap judgments that could undermine my power. Gratitude enables me to be more focused on the things that matter, so I make choices that align with my values. And what could be more powerful than that?

Although embracing power through gratitude is helpful for all of us, it turns out that not all people are equally adept at being grateful, even when they make a conscious effort. For instance, did you know there's a genetic basis for gratitude? In a study published by the American Psychological Association, researcher Michael Steger and others found that identical twins (who share 100 percent of their DNA) had more similar self-reported levels of gratitude than fraternal twins (who share just 50 percent of their DNA). Researchers at the University of California at Berkeley have identified a specific gene, CD38, involved in the secretion of the neuropeptide oxytocin. Apparently, differences in this gene were significantly associated with the quality and frequency of expressions of gratitude toward romantic partners. In the study, participants were asked to show appreciation to their partners on a daily basis. Subjects with one variant of the CD38 gene reported thanking their partners about 45 percent of the days they were studied, while partners with another gene variant thanked their partners more than 70 percent of the days they were studied. Another contender is the gene COMT, which is involved in recycling the neurotransmitter dopamine in the brain. Another UC Berkeley study, by Jinting Liu, showed that people with one version of this gene were more grateful than those with an alternate version.

Brain structure may play a role too. One research study found that more grateful individuals have more gray matter in their right inferior temporal cortex, an area that UC Berkeley's Greater Good blog author Summer Allen says is linked to interpreting people's intentions. More grateful individuals also have greater activity in brain regions associated with moral cognition, perspective taking, and reward.

Having a gene or a brain that naturally discounts gratitude can make it more difficult to feel powerful. Fortunately, it isn't a lost cause. Allen's blog article included an analysis of thirty-eight gratitude studies, which concluded that "gratitude interventions like gratitude journaling can have positive benefits for people in terms of their well-being, happiness, life satisfaction, grateful mood, grateful disposition, and positive affect."

Hunt for ways to internalize gratitude that resonate with you. Noting and reinforcing the areas in which you are already powerful can help you appreciate how far you've come. For instance, when I did not receive the Forbes 30 Under 30 recognition I was coveting, I shifted my thinking to how highly I must be regarded to have made the short list. Similarly, when I placed second runner-up for Miss United States, I was naturally disappointed in that moment, but eventually I learned to see it as an incredible accomplishment, a celebration of how far I'd come since my shy and insecure teenage years. We often don't stop to appreciate our small wins because we're anticipating a bigger win or living up to others' expectations. Soul Pancake, a group that researches the basis of happiness, did a study in which participants wrote letters to a person they were grateful for. This simple exercise increased their happiness ratings by two percentage points, and when participants took their gratitude to the phone, their happiness levels jumped 15 percent!

The best self-work strategies benefit our relationships with others as well as our own growth,

which is the case with gratitude. By incorporating grateful behaviors into your daily life, you will cultivate both internal and external power.

Voices from the SWAAY Community

What Women's Empowerment Really Means

Dr. Claudia Consolati

Women in the Western world have been sold a faulty dream. Raised in families that encouraged us to be strong and independent, we've strived to become successful—to reach the top—in a world that wasn't designed for us.

The imperative to become empowered has been a driving force in my life for the best part of two decades. My family taught me to work hard, get an education, and become financially independent. I had enough means to pursue my interests with a degree in literature without ever working any odd jobs or worrying about survival.

Still, I was ambitious. At twenty-three, I packed my bags and moved from Italy to the United States. I wanted to get away, to become my own person. I wanted to show the world what a petite woman with a lot of curiosity and drive could achieve. As a rite of passage, I chopped all my hair off.

I made a life for myself. I enrolled in an Ivy League doctorate program, and I reached the top.

Or so I thought.

The Lone Woman on Top

I was proud I accomplished it all by myself. I knew how to get by through efficiency, intellect, determination, creativity, and outstanding organizational skills. As a true high achiever, I didn't like group projects because I knew I could do everything faster (and better) by myself.

I was proud of my grit. I was proud that I didn't need anybody.

When I finished my PhD, I had to face the harsh reality that academia was not the prestigious ivory tower that I had once coveted and that the ideal I had pursued of becoming an empowered "career woman" was not only unsustainable but also unfulfilling after all.

I realized that, like most institutions in this country, higher ed was a patriarchal stronghold (yes, even in the humanities, a field with a higher percentage of women than men). And I realized that the model I was following, a model based on relentless work at any hour of the day and night, continuous criticism marked as "feedback," competition, individualism, and a logic of "always work harder," was not a model in which I could thrive.

I also realized that independence at all costs goes against our basic human need for connection and that the pride I felt in doing it all alone and never ever asking for help was not a strength but a survival mechanism against a world that often leaves women to fend for ourselves. With that came the reckoning that because of my self-proclaimed "strength," I had stayed in toxic situations for too long.

Who Really Is the Empowered, Independent Woman?

Over the past few years, I've thought a lot about this ideal that had become my holy grail—the strong, empowered, independent woman. *Who is she? Where does she come from? And most importantly, who has she become?*

She is who I wanted to be. The alternative? Getting married and finding fulfillment within the home, *à la* 1950s housewife. I *knew* I didn't want that. So I sought out the opposite.

Where first-wave feminism's agenda in the US focused on reaching gender equality in the public sphere, which resulted in white women gaining the right to vote in 1920, second-wave feminism focused, along with legislative change on key issues such as abortion and divorce, on equality in the private sphere. It brought women out of the house and into the streets, and from the streets into the workforce. Its mantra was "the personal is political"; its goal was equality inside and outside the home.

But the problem with equality in a capitalist society is that it gets co-opted by the dominant system, which as I noted earlier is a problematic endeavor in a society based on stark inequalities. As someone who studies and observes gender dynamics for a living, I argue that today the myth of the empowered woman has become a fantasy, something to be consumed. The empowered woman has been made to work within existing institutions instead of questioning them. And at huge costs.

How the Empowered Woman Becomes an Object of Fetishization

Co-opted by capitalism, the stereotype of the strong, independent woman functions culturally as an object of both dread and desire akin to Freud's notion of the fetish. According to Freud, fetishism is the displacement of desire onto alternative objects or body parts in order to avoid facing the fear of castration. In this logic and economy of desire, the fetish becomes a "penis substitute" easing male anxiety around castration (intended metaphorically as loss of manhood).

If you're a cis, hetero woman, living, dating, and relating in the twenty-first century, you've probably wondered at one point or another whether your independence intimidates men. I'll get to that in a second, but first I want to speak about the men who proclaim to actually like strong women.

Is it true? And what do they like about them?

While I cannot speak for all men, I've heard far too many times that men like strong women because they like the "challenge" and they like that they are their "equals." These statements are problematic for a number of reasons. First, being "equals" in a patriarchal society means that women become like men, which is a worthy first step when equal rights are the exception, but it's not enough. Second, this proclamation of equality rests on a cis-male economy of desire—one where the woman becomes a projection of his own ego and a "penis substitute" to ease his own anxieties around masculine power and changing gender dynamics.

He desires her precisely because she reminds him of himself; she becomes a testing ground of cis-male prowess and achievement. As Freud says in his essay on fetishism, the fetish is both "a token of triumph over the threat of castration and a safeguard against it."

In the process, the so-called strong woman is dehumanized. She's treated at best as a capitalist shell of ritualistic efficiency and intellectual stimulation. Something—not someone—to be consumed and exploited. At worst, she's viewed as an object of cis-male desire for his own masturbatory pleasure. She is a "challenge" to be won over and then discarded the moment she becomes human.

Internalizing Our Own Objectification and the Trauma That Follows

And what about women, especially women who have followed and aspired to this model themselves? It's crucial to understand the roles that capitalist and patriarchal narratives have played in transforming the notion of "female empowerment" from something nurtured and cultivated in the women's circles of the 1960s and 1970s to the individualistic nightmare of late capitalism. We're stuck trying to "make it" in a world that wasn't designed for us, while we don't know how to ask for help, we think we have to do everything alone, and therefore we tolerate abusive behavior.

Trying to fit into and succeed in the "world of the father," as Maureen Murdock calls it in *The Heroine's Journey*, we become disconnected from our own inner source of power. We objectify ourselves—sexually, relationally, and professionally. We internalize the notion that we exist only as a function of cis-male desire or to *please* the system (or both).

This state of being cut off from our own voice—which is the deepest, truest, kindest, and most loving part of ourselves—is similar to the trauma response known as "freeze." In buying into ideals that are not our own, we become frozen in body and soul. We become stuck in a survival mechanism that's the result of centuries of oppression and silencing. In the meantime, we think that we have to play by the oppressor's rules—a process of self-betrayal that causes the trauma cycle to perpetuate itself.

And if you're wondering if you're intimidating to men, the answer is yes, you probably are, at least to many (and these are not the right men for you!). But there's a deeper level too. You might think that you're strong and independent, but what if you're actually frozen? What if there's actually a different you behind the shell of strength and empowerment? A you that has even more power, more drive, and more grace than you even believe is possible?

Freeing Your Inner Self from the Fetishization Freeze

Of course, I want all women to be strong, empowered, and independent. But what I'm saying is to reach that state on your own terms, without letting dominant narratives appropriate your identity.

When I realized that my pursuit of strength and independence had actually left me frozen and that I was trying to fit into a box that wasn't built for me in order to gain the approval I was so desperately seeking from within, I took my Ivy League PhD and made the decision to blow my life up in order to put the pieces back together in a way that made sense to me.

In some respects, I have not changed at all. I'm still very driven, ambitious, and goal-oriented—probably more so than before. I'm also 100 percent more resilient because I realized that I couldn't rely on patriarchal institutions to keep me alive and had to find those resources from within.

And what strength looks like for me now is very different from the misguided millennial #girlboss dreams we've been sold—dreams that only reinforce the current power dynamics and risk framing women as projections of patriarchal ego fantasies about masculine prowess.

If you value your professional ambitions and your drive, and if you know that you're here to have a big impact and make waves, I encourage you to look inside and ask yourself: What does empowerment look like for *me*?

For me, it's not about fitting into preexisting institutions of power and losing my heart, health, and soul in the process. It's about creating my own reality and bringing everyone up with it. And yes, I am in a position of privilege to do so, and that's why I feel even more responsibility to make a difference for other women to be able to do so as well.

I'm not someone else's object of desire. I'm not functional to someone else's fantasy. I'm not functional to any fantasy at all. My dreams, ambitions, and goals are mine. My body, my pleasure, and my inner world are mine.

And that is my wish for all women.

"The Empowered Women Fetish You May Not Even Know You Are Fulfilling" by Dr. Claudia Consolati was published on SWAYY.com. Dr. Consolati is assistant professor of film, gender, and sexuality and the founder of the Women Speak Up Project, a platform to help visionary women entrepreneurs.

LEADERSHIP SPOTLIGHT

Do you remember when sexual assault survivor Maria Gallagher confronted Senator Jeff Flake amidst the controversy of the Kavanaugh Supreme Court hearings? She had pinned him into the corner of an elevator, and as he averted his eyes, she said: "You have power when so many women are powerless! Look at me when I'm talking to you!"

When reporting on this in 2018, *The Cut* speculated that Gallagher's fury dominated the space and that she would be remembered as a hero and ultimately the one with the power. But Gallagher could not see that, because the entire notion of her own power was so unfamiliar to her. In that political moment—and in others since—women have been using their collective power to insist on their own powerlessness.

Women leaders are chronically ambivalent. Even when we find ourselves in power and have the spotlight, the authority, the control, and most importantly the microphone, we still allow our power to be undermined. At the beginning of launching SWAAY, I landed a meeting with a successful investor and media industry veteran. This man in his sixties was quick to give his unsolicited strong opinions and observations about everything I said and did—except for my actual business pitch.

"Honey, let me give you one piece of advice. Never mention your beauty pageant past. You're a businesswoman now, and if you want to be taken seriously, you shouldn't bring up your pageant history." Instead of owning the power of my story and leveraging this moment as an opportunity to educate him on why pageantry is a big part of who I am, I simply smiled and nodded as I sat across from him, feeling worthless.

My pageant history has taught me more about myself and my role in society than any other experience I've had. Thanks to pageantry, I discovered my purpose: changing the narrative for women and challenging the status quo. Without it, I wouldn't be the aspiring businesswoman sitting across from this potential investor. And yet, I let an entitled stranger take that away from me in a matter of seconds. I let a man in power usurp the only thing that gives me complete power: speaking my truth.

This wasn't an isolated incident either. There have been times when instead of seizing power moments and using them to push myself forward and reinforce my own authority, I've said and done things that have made me feel smaller. For example, when an investor was being inappropriate and asked to meet in his hotel room, I spent every power-moment opportunity talking about how powerless I felt in that situation. Another time, when a reporter asked me about my accomplishments, I used interview airtime to talk about my powerlessness in the company of other powerful men. And although I'm doing it again in this chapter, this time it's to prove a point.

We women have to be cognizant of our propensity to do this, especially if we are in leadership positions in which we're serving as role models for other women. We can own our power even when it's intimidating to do so.

There will be times when you feel stuck and times when you find yourself slipping off the ledge despite your best efforts.

Above all, encourage other women—and yourself—to be patient and persistent.

Hillary Clinton was at that historic world conference on women in Beijing and gave a speech that would reverberate for decades. "When I spoke in Beijing as First Lady, I thought I'd reached the peak of power and influence that would ever be available to me," she said in 2020. "Yet it turned out my journey was far from over, and I would get the chance to carry those concerns into the highest levels of government and politics. What we think are peaks can turn out to be way stations on a higher climb." Rising to power might be considered an empowering feminist victory, but leading with your inner power is the ultimate triumph.

CUE THE REAL WORLD

Now that you've explored the ledge protectors around power, let's explore how you might employ some or all of the protectors to step into your power. Write your ideas in your journal.

- Explore your own definition of power. What does power mean to you, and how does it manifest in your life?

- Describe a time in your life when you could have done a better job of owning responsibility for personal or professional progress.

- What do you currently feel gratitude for, and how do these things feed your personal definition of power?

POWER LEDGE REVIEW

- In its simplest form, power is the ability to act, but it means something slightly different depending on who you ask. To me, power is about **charting my life's course on my terms** and helping others do the same. It is about having strength and capacity to value my accomplishments regardless of what society says.
- Although some legal barriers remain, cultural norms are also responsible for holding women back. We women must make a concerted effort to push back on **outdated norms and divisions of labor.**
- If you believe that you control your own destiny, you have an **internal locus of control**; if you think your destiny is controlled by other forces, you have an **external locus of control**. Individuals with an internal locus of control work harder to get what they want. Also, their health is better because they don't spend so much time railing against factors they can't do anything about.
- Hunt for ways to internalize **gratitude** that resonate with you. Noting and reinforcing the areas in which you are already powerful can help you appreciate how far you've come.
- Women leaders are chronically ambivalent. Even when we find ourselves in power and have the spotlight, the authority, the control, and most importantly the microphone, we still allow our power to be undermined. Make sure you **own your power in high-stakes situations**, even if it's intimidating to do so.

"Why do I feel the desperate need to be liked?"

◇◇◇◇◇

*"I need to prioritize my relationships with
others over my career ambitions."*

◇◇◇◇◇◇

"I have to say yes to everyone. Otherwise, I'll offend them."

◇◇◇◇◇

"I should do as expected (or as told) if I want to get ahead."

◇◇◇◇◇◇

"I can easily be liked if I follow the rules."

◇◇◇◇◇◇

"If I set this boundary, they'll be mad at me."

◇◇◇◇◇

"I'm the 'nice one,' and if I'm honest, I prefer it that way."

◇◇◇◇◇◇

"I live in fear of giving feedback that will cause people not to like me."

◇◇◇◇◇◇

"To achieve likability, I should refrain from challenging things."

◇◇◇◇◇

"I need to fit into [insert outdated stereotype] in order to be liked."

◇◇◇◇◇◇

Chapter Two

LIKABILITY

The likability conundrum is all too familiar to the many women pursuing power, success, and greatness.

Early on in my career, I was reluctant to embrace power because I was too busy trying to be liked. I struggled with assessing my own worth and based my self-esteem on how others perceived me. As long as this was the status quo, I put others' approval over my own needs and authenticity.

When I made my first few key hires five years ago, I was a first-time founder with the tendency to avoid the confrontation needed for change. I focused on being pleasant and likable rather than asserting my authority and defining clear boundaries. I brought on talented people with more experience in the media industry and felt I had to earn their approval at all times. So I acted like their friend and ultimately put their comfort above my responsibilities as a leader and, most importantly, above our company's needs.

Because of the amount of freedom I granted the team, they didn't think twice before overstepping when it was convenient for them. Some eventually became too comfortable around me, and at times too entitled, which was concerning every time I'd voice my opinions or assign new tasks. I failed to set the proper boundaries early on, and in my pursuit to be a likable boss, I lost my ability to be an effective leader.

It was a disempowering experience that detracted from my company's growth potential. But it taught me an important lesson about overestimating the importance of likability while compromising effective leadership.

I don't want to imply that too much likability is inherently bad. If you cultivate a lot of positive traits in yourself and people want to be around you, likability is a natural result. For example, it's not unusual for a wise, honest, kind, and ethical leader to be universally liked by her staff. Rather, here's the line to keep in mind: when you make decisions for the express purpose of being liked, then you risk losing respect. That's when likability could get in your way.

For the female candidates in the 2020 US presidential election, the likability trait was a persistent and disruptive factor. It was interesting and disappointing to see these candidates disappear from the stage one by one. According to their haters, Amy Klobuchar was too demanding, Kamala Harris used a romantic relationship to advance her career, and Elizabeth Warren was too aggressive and unwilling to compromise. It's important to note that female voters were motivated and mobilized more than ever, the patriarchy was toppling, and it was supposedly "the year of the woman." Yet not one of the immensely qualified female candidates remained on that stage. This statement from one of Marianne Cooper's *Harvard Business Review* op-eds explains it perfectly:

> What is really going on, as peer-reviewed studies continually find, is that high-achieving women experience social backlash because their very success—and specifically, the behaviors that created their success—violates our expectations about how women are supposed to behave. Women are expected to be nice, warm, friendly, and nurturing. Thus, if a woman acts assertively or competitively, if she pushes her team to perform, if she exhibits decisive and forceful leadership, she is deviating from the social script that dictates how she "should" behave. By violating beliefs about what women are like, successful women elicit pushback from others for being insufficiently feminine and too masculine. As descriptions like "Ice Queen," and "Ballbuster" can attest, we are deeply uncomfortable with powerful women. In fact, we often don't really like them.

Likability among high-profile women isn't a new issue. Livia Drusilla, the wife of Augustus, Rome's first emperor, lived more than two thousand years ago. At the time, women were governed by their fathers and husbands and were supposed to be modest and virtuous and fade into the background as much as possible. Through Livia's natural shrewdness, however, she became a prominent adviser in her husband's administration.

Because Roman society was unwilling to accept that a gifted female politician could exist, Livia was strongly disliked. In the fictionalized account of the Julio-Claudian dynasty, *I, Claudius*, Livia is portrayed as evil, as someone who will stop at nothing to cement her family's status. What people today might call independent, outspoken, and savvy in a woman, Robert Graves, the author of *I, Claudius* (as well as most Roman Empire historians), presents as greedy, unethical, and disloyal. Some even went so far as to call Livia a murderer, who routinely poisoned political rivals and possibly her own husband!

Fast forward hundreds of years, and take a look at one of my ultimate idols growing up: Madonna. She's arguably the most accomplished female pop star of all time, yet she has contended with likability since the beginning of her career in the early 1980s. As Matthew Jacobs of *The Huffington Post* puts it: "Today the singer provokes ire and indifference, but Madonna fatigue can be traced to at least 1991." At that time, Madonna was a vocal supporter for LGBTQ and AIDS-patient rights. She produced audio and visual material that was "mature, unconventional, and naked in more ways than one."

Despite her runaway success, Madonna's career nearly screeched to a halt when she refused to lay off the sexual progressivism. Jacobs reminds us of Madonna's comment on VH1's *Behind the Music*. "After the *Sex* book came out, I could not open up a newspaper or magazine and not read something incredibly scathing about myself," Madonna had said. The worst critique came from journalist Ilene Rozenzweig, who in 1994 published *The I Hate Madonna Handbook*, dismissing the artist as a talentless bloodsucker who should start a perfume line and call it a day. Madonna never behaved the way female entertainers were expected to behave, and her likability with both men and women suffered for it.

Then, in the first decade of the new millennium, actress Angelina Jolie replaced Madonna as one of the most disliked female entertainers in America. After the tabloids reported that she'd cozied up to Brad Pitt while he was still married to Jennifer Aniston, Angelina was unceremoniously branded an opportunistic whore. As a man, Brad was given a pass by the public, and the story friends told cast doubt on any infidelity. But Angelina's reputation as a she-devil continued for years. It didn't matter that she directed thought-provoking and important films, served as a Goodwill Ambassador to the United Nations, set up her own charitable foundation, and campaigned to end sexual violence against girls.

On a site appropriately called Villainesse, writer Abigail Johnson felt compelled to stand up for the actress after reading articles titled "Ange's Evil New Plan" and "Kids Flee Evil Ange." "I might have muttered an audible, 'Jesus,'" Johnson said. "I think the world-at-large is afraid of individualistic women who know their own minds. Women who don't kowtow to societal pressures. Women who don't pretend to be something they're not."

Likability is a combination of personality traits that engage another person into an emotional relationship with you. Steven Goldstein, a former producer for the *Oprah Winfrey Show* and a former lawyer for the House Judiciary Committee, has spent his career trying to figure out what makes people likable. In his book, *The Turn-On: How the Powerful Make Us Like Them—From Washington to Wall Street to Hollywood*, Goldstein identified the following four pairs of traits that he believes are key to genuine likability.

- **Captivation and Hope:** You are interesting and memorable in a positive way.
- **Authenticity and Relatability:** You are real, and others can identify with your experiences.
- **Protectiveness and Reliability:** You are there for others, and they can depend on you.
- **Compassion and Perceptiveness:** You empathize with others who are different from you, and you try to understand and meet their needs.

In an interview with the *Washington Post*, Goldstein was careful to distinguish between likability and niceness. "Nice people might have 80, 90, or 100 percent support, but nobody would go to bat and die for them. Likability does involve some degree of polarization. Having a strong enough personality where some people are going to be instantly attracted to it, and others not," he said. And for better or worse, likability matters. "Likability is leverage, a democratizing tool to achieving a better world."

I'm quite familiar with the peril of niceness. Everyone in my family looked to me to be the nice girl, the girl who did what was expected. I was a daughter of immigrants who sacrificed everything for their children's future, so I had no choice but to be the straight-A student with a perfect track record and no attempt at rebellion. And that's exactly who I was for most of my life.

But I bore a darker truth: I had absolutely no clue who I was or where I belonged. In my childhood years, I desperately wanted to be liked by my classmates. Even though I hated wearing skirts and dresses, I begged my parents to buy me girly clothes so I could get the popular girls' approval. My only goal was to fit in, though I knew I was different and felt it in my core.

I may not have realized it at the time, but being well-liked was the only way to make up for my identity crisis and my lack of belonging. But in my early twenties, my mentality began to shift when I embarked on a series of unpredictable experiences that opened up the path to self-discovery. Living overseas by myself, traversing the pageant world, and traveling to third-world countries as a medical missionary, I finally started to accept myself as a multidimensional woman who shouldn't be pigeonholed into one identity. By the time I moved from Colorado to New York, I was ready to try the previously unimaginable. Learning to let go of the "nice girl" label has resulted in an infinitely more authentic life.

The political world epitomizes the tension-filled relationship powerful women have with likability and niceness. Unlike Goldstein, voters put their fingers on exactly what makes candidates likable— or unlikable. Because this "I know it when I see it" mentality has caused confusion for decades (and in the case of Livia Drusilla, a few millennia), the nonpartisan Barbara Lee Family Foundation (BLFF) set out to answer these questions: What makes a woman candidate or officeholder likable to voters? And how can one establish likability and qualifications at the same time?

The BLFF found that 84 percent of men and 90 percent of women feel it's important to like a candidate they support, but male candidates are more likely to be elected without being liked, while female candidates are substantially less likely to be elected. According to the research, the key components of women's likability are presentation and track record. Appearing confident is essential, as voters assess this in a woman in less than thirty seconds. People also want to see that female candidates

- engage with their communities and strive for social impact
- are doing their jobs among constituents
- address their passions and constituent values when promoting accomplishments
- take credit for achievements while also sharing that credit with their teams
- manage everyday issues like sewers and snowstorms
- have a sense of humor and don't take themselves too seriously

Another likability study, recently published in the *Economic Journal* by researchers at the University of Hamburg, found that likability matters for women in every one of their interactions but matters for men only if they interact with the opposite sex. "The observed gender difference in social interactions has important negative implications on gender differences in economic outcomes. Women significantly suffer from the variation in likability and achieve overall worse economic outcomes than men," the study's authors report. "The likability factor may play a role in women earning lower wages than men, why women are less likely to be promoted to top management positions, and why women are underrepresented in higher levels of the corporate hierarchy."

The rest of this chapter will provide strategies to prevent a fall off the glass ledge and achieve the right degree of likability by toning down your obsession with people pleasing, setting appropriate boundaries, and embracing your femininity in a productive way.

LEDGE PROTECTOR #1: TONE DOWN THE PEOPLE PLEASING

A people pleaser is a person who has an emotional need to please others, often at the expense of their own needs or desires. It is a person who feels compelled to always say "yes" and bristles at the mere idea of saying "no." Sound familiar?

Psychotherapist and blogger Ilene Strauss Cohen describes her own struggle with this behavior: "I didn't know where other people ended and I began, and my decisions were based on what would make other people happy or comfortable. Little did I know that it really just made me lost, confused, and pretty unlikable."

She adds: "For most of my life, I used people pleasing in the same way other people use drugs, alcohol, food, or shopping—as a way to avoid the discomfort of others' disapproval. A few years ago, I realized that the only authentic way out was to become aware of my own internal world, recognizing that the only person I could change was myself."

People pleasing is common, even for leaders. My friend and longtime mentor Fran Hauser, a former president of Time Inc. Digital, a startup investor, and the author of the appropriately titled *The Myth of the Nice Girl*, told me that when managers people please, kindness stops being an asset and becomes a liability. "One strategy to strike the balance between being authoritative and likable is to embody a mentorship mentality. That means pointing out when expectations have been missed or performance needs to improve, but doing so from the perspective of how you can work together to close the gap," she says.

So many of us are on this journey. It often takes us a while to see that by abiding by outdated expectations to be obedient, small, and self-sacrificing for the sake of being liked, we are holding ourselves back. But we are not alone, and we can do things differently! In addition to the introspection that can increase your self-awareness and help you get to the root of your people pleasing, there are practical strategies you can use to stop doing it as much in the here and now. Here are some of them:

Buy yourself some time

As I was writing this chapter, I was in the middle of a negotiation for the potential acquisition of my company. It was one of the most stressful events I went through in 2020 (and that says a lot!). During the deal-making process, I was constantly put in the position to have to make a quick decision, even when I felt conflicted. I felt pressured to say yes to terms I didn't feel comfortable with in order to "make it easy" on the other party. I was so busy trying to avoid being perceived as difficult that I didn't properly negotiate and advocate for my terms early on in the process. To stay true to my own needs, I simply took more time with each contract, email, and proposition. Yes, the other party labeled me "slow" and "always behind." At first, it crushed me to hear that, but I quickly reminded myself that the Iman of today is more concerned with protecting her interest and speaking her truth than being universally liked. Ultimately, I held strong to my convictions and made the right (but tough) decision to pass on the deal.

As this example illustrates, most people pleasing occurs in the moment when the natural default is to comply. So delay giving a response until you've carefully thought it through. For instance, say: "Can I get back to you tomorrow?" or "I need to check my schedule" or "Let me consult with my spouse/adviser/boss," etc. If you do end up saying yes to a request, it won't be because of a knee-jerk reaction that leaves you feeling angry at yourself and resentful of the other person.

Take the path of least resistance

I don't often advocate that people do the easy thing, but

when you are trying to recover from people pleasing, it's far less difficult to deliver a "no" answer via text or email instead of turning someone down when they're standing right in front of you.

The written format also allows you to provide a diplomatic and coherent explanation for your decision.

Balance giving and receiving

As Cohen pointed out, doing too much hurts rather than helps relationships.

When you overfunction in your relationships, it leads others to underfunction, and that's when relationships become ineffective.

So while I'm not suggesting you keep score of everything you do for another person or in your department, it may make sense to maintain a ballpark sense of whether things like tasks, favors, check-ins, and other supportive actions at work or home are spread evenly.

According to my friend Kim Fulcher, a serial entrepreneur and motivational coach and author, the need to be liked manifests in layers and often starts with your family. "What women's parents, partners, and children think first dictates what we will do to be likeable, because that's our survival and connection," she told me. "Next, we worry about other people in our orbit, like friends and colleagues. Then, it's the external world—we want people to think we have it all together, but we don't want to sparkle too much because they might not like us."

Like Fran, Kim shared that the dance of likability—and the giving and receiving that go with it—grows more complex as women progress in their careers. "I always want to give to other women, because we don't have to defend our territory like our mothers did when there was only one spot for a woman," Kim says. This type of generosity doesn't necessarily ensure likability, though. "I have noticed that higher-ranked women are sometimes less liked than lower-ranked women because the higher-ranked ones are breaking gender stereotypes, and this makes women who haven't quite made it look harder at themselves," she says.

Kim has chosen to go on celebrating other women's potential and successes, whether or not they show that they like or appreciate her in return. "I'm going to be fifty next year, and it has taken me two decades to speak in my outside voice without being overly concerned what other people are going to think about it."

Consider others' judgments

We will spend more time in this book looking at why other people judge us, and we them—but when we are trying to recover from people pleasing, it's useful to think about what might be happening for the person we are trying to please (and might not be able to please). We are often assessed for likability and deemed "less than" because of the other person's negative judgment. That person might be judging against us because they are intimidated by us, afraid of their own shortcomings, or simply wish they were more like us. If this is the case, no amount of people pleasing will make that person like us, and giving up the pursuit to make them like us might be the healthiest thing to do.

Accept that some days will involve conflict

People pleasers go to great lengths to avoid problems with others. They say yes all the time solely because they fear the implications of saying no. But when humans interact, occasional friction is inevitable as one person's needs come up against the needs of another. We will look at this more closely in chapter 5, but for now, suffice it to say that conflict doesn't mean the other person doesn't like you or that you can't resolve it.

When Kim Fulcher ran the marketing department at an educational technology company, she found herself actively sabotaged by a male peer. Although the man made passive-aggressive comments in meetings and took credit for Kim's ideas, Kim did not stick up for herself. "I wanted everyone in the group to like me, and I thought if there was conflict, they wouldn't," she explains. "Except every feeling you keep inside has to be expressed in a different way. One day, during an offsite team meeting, I just blew up at him, and this undermined my position. Looking back, I should have been willing to confront him in a private conversation when issues first arose. I could have outlined what was acceptable. But by skirting the conflict because I wanted to be liked, I was tacitly telling him his poor treatment was okay."

◆Ledge Work: Understand the Circumstances That Lead to People Pleasing

Think about the type of situation that prompts you to excessively people please. For example, maybe you are afraid of disappointing your boss, so if her feedback on a project is mixed, you might immediately jump in and offer to do the whole thing over. Or maybe you agree to postpone your vacation because your sister needs help with her yard sale and one of your core beliefs is family first.

Recall the last time you people pleased at the expense of your own time, energy, and/or emotional well-being. Answer these questions about that time in your journal.

What was the situation, and have you noticed a pattern with similar situations?

What negative emotions did you feel just before you went overboard to fix the situation? For example, did you feel anxious, sad, or self-recrimination?

What's another way you might have coped with these emotions besides people pleasing?

What might you say to the other person the next time you're facing a similar scenario?

LEDGE PROTECTOR #2: CREATE HEALTHY BOUNDARIES

"You need to set better boundaries."

It's a piece of advice most of us have heard before—and yet, establishing boundaries that lead to respect rather than doormat-driven likability is not as simple as hanging a sign on yourself that says: "Please respect my boundaries."

Boundaries are commonly known as guidelines or limits that an individual uses to inform others about safe and appropriate ways to behave around them. Boundaries also dictate how the individual will respond if someone steps outside those guidelines or limits. If another person touches you in a way that makes you uncomfortable, that's an example of a physical boundary violation. If a person verbally attacks you, and it negatively impacts your mood and leads you to question your value, that's an emotional boundary violation. If you say yes when you want to say no in order to avoid conflict or rejection, that too is an emotional boundary issue.

When you allow your boundaries to be violated, the desire to be liked is often the culprit. If you can put this desire aside and focus on creating and maintaining healthy boundaries, ultimately you will improve your self-esteem, your ability to take care of yourself, and the quality of your relationships.

Boundaries are personal and vary from individual to individual. They are shaped by our heritage, where we live, how we were raised, our life experiences, and our personalities. If you don't know what your boundaries are, psychotherapist Judith Belmont suggests starting with basic rights. For instance, you want to be able to

- say no without feeling guilty
- be treated with respect

- attend to your own needs
- walk away from people who have unreasonable expectations or who are abusive

Rely on your intuition to inform you when to consider establishing a new boundary. For instance, if a colleague stands too close to you and you feel your chest becoming tight in response, you might need a boundary around physical proximity. Or if your partner spends your paycheck and you don't find out until you're fuming at the ATM, you might want to set a boundary around the handling of finances.

With more people working from home, many find the boundary between their personal and professional lives being trampled by managers or others from their workplace. You can protect yourself, however, with solutions such as setting a cut-off time for answering work-related communications, putting on your out-of-office message when you're on vacation or taking PTO, *actually* waiting to respond to emails until you return to work, and placing your phone on "Do Not Disturb" during an important conversation or work session.

Identifying your boundaries is only half the battle: the other half is communicating them effectively and, very importantly, reinforcing them. You want to be clear and firm without apologizing. If the person is upset by your boundary, that's *not* your concern. And even though it can be tough when you want to be likable, try to adhere to your set boundaries consistently; don't send mixed messages about the behavior you are not willing to accept. This will take practice, so do the best you can.

Early in her career, Fran Hauser fell into the same trap a lot of junior employees find themselves in. She said yes whenever someone more senior asked her for a favor or to stay late. "I wanted to be seen as a team player, so I always volunteered to make the client's last-minute revisions or to take notes in a meeting. I was happy to do these things because they felt strategic, and I believed extra tasks would prime me for a promotion. But by consistently being eager to take on more, I set a precedent with my boss who expected me to always be available. And when I had to cancel dinner plans with my friends for what seemed like the tenth time, I started feeling resentful. And I was starting to learn that being the default doer or go-to person doesn't always lead to a promotion, whether you're a junior employee or an executive," she shared with me.

Fran realized she needed to create boundaries, but she still wanted to come across as considerate and helpful. So she didn't start saying no to every request: "I created my own rule: if someone asked me to do the same task outside my job scope more than three times, I would say something. So, when my boss asked me to stay late again, I replied: 'I've been struggling with how to talk to you about this. Over the past two weeks, I've had to change my personal plans three times to stay late. I wonder if this is a good opportunity for someone else to pitch in.' Turns out, he didn't even realize the dynamic we'd created. It was just easier to have Fran do it because I always did. Shining a light on the issue was enough to take the extra work off my plate."

Remember too that

boundaries can be fluid. What's necessary in one instance may not apply in another, and your preferences may change over time.

If your boundaries are too rigid or you don't take the time to revisit them periodically, you may unnecessarily isolate yourself from people.

LEDGE PROTECTOR #3: IF IT WORKS FOR YOU, USE FEMININITY IN A PRODUCTIVE WAY

As I mentioned in the introduction, people fall along the gender spectrum in terms of how they identify. We all have different ideas about what we consider feminine and masculine or whether that distinction is even "a thing." So, I hope you'll bear with me as I share what femininity and masculinity mean to me.

I've never been the overly authoritive type of leader. My leadership style is about alignment, excitement, enthusiasm, and giving people a platform to excel. I always think back to a former job, which I felt I had to quit because my boss micromanaged me so severely. It made me feel less competent because it seemed he didn't trust I was doing the work and didn't believe in my capabilities—and the last thing I want to communicate to my people is that I don't trust them.

My femininity has been a huge asset in creating the positive work culture and environment I want at SWAAY. Because I'm naturally more nurturing, it's easy for me to see why someone is not performing. I feel that I can understand who I'm working with, which means the employee can get the best experience and we can get the best results. Bonds are formed *and* goals are met.

I find that in most cases masculine leadership is very transactional and uniformly focused on solutions and metrics. Occasionally, as in investor meetings or corporate partnerships, I need to lean in to this style to get what I want and need from the situation. But most other times, it helps to leverage what I consider my feminine energy.

Joan Williams is the author of the book *What Works for Women at Work* and a *New York Times* columnist. In her 2019 piece "How Women Can Escape the Likability Trap," Williams describes her interviews with two hundred women for her research on gender and the workplace.

"More than forty years of research by social scientists have shown that Americans define the good woman as helpful, modest, and nice. In other words, as focused on her family and community rather than working in her own self-interest," Williams writes.

She says the most likable female leaders mix authoritativeness and warmth. As one of her CEO interviewees told her, "I got feedback I was intimidating, so I would make sure that I got to know people, and before a meeting I would share something personal to make myself more approachable."

Williams recommends that women concerned with likability try doing something masculine in a feminine way. "Think of femininity as a toolkit and choose something that feels authentic to you," she says. "You might, for example, soften your negotiation approach (e.g. 'It wasn't clear to me whether this offer represents the top of the pay range') and use metaphors to recode traditionally masculine behavior in a more feminine context ('I don't think of sales as hunting; I think of it as gardening. I like to grow things.')."

Anna Rova, a coach, founder of girlskill.com, and host of the podcast *Claimed*, wrote the article, "True Feminine Power and Why Modern Female Empowerment Has Got It All Wrong," which is a provocative commentary on why blatant femininity isn't always a bad thing. "A little-known fact that is not spoken about today is that women actually have held power and influenced households and local and global events since the dawn of time, without having to demonstratively spin the world in their hands or wear the red cape. If you're a woman who understands her true feminine power and uses it to her own advantage, you know exactly what I mean."

Rova qualifies this feminine power as "the willingness to please you and win your attention, time, and presence" and the "magic that lures him in that he can't even explain." She says that while masculine power involves what we can see and touch and what we can do with physical force, feminine power is the opposite. It is invisible, intangible, and subtle. The power of a woman "fills in the blanks: fluid, flexible, dynamic, and robust. When she is connected to her instinctual self, she can sense and see things that give her perspective and deeper knowing."

Rova suggests that

because both masculine and feminine power are essential in our world, men and women should embrace feminine energy rather than diminish it.

Instead of competing with men, we can partner with them. We can work on believing we are enough outside the masculine definition of what it means to be powerful. We can spend more time in our hearts than our heads through meditation or quiet contemplation, and we can surround ourselves with uplifting people and ideas.

This is not to say we need to use our feminine wiles to manipulate people or to lose sight of our own masculine-oriented power. However, I do believe Williams is on to something when she says that feminine softness can occasionally be a useful tool for likability.

Voices from the SWAAY Community

Is Smiling a Prerequisite for Likability?

Mita Mallick

"And you should smile more often," he said, leaning in. As if he was sharing with me the secret to my advancing in the organization. "You should just smile."

That was the feedback I received early on in my career. Impromptu words of wisdom from a well-meaning male colleague. It would seem as though smiling would be the key to my success. Not smiling was clearly holding me back.

On one occasion, when I was sitting, tapping away quietly at my keyboard, someone came up to me and said, "What's wrong? Is something wrong?"

No. That was just my resting face. I was concentrating on an email. I wasn't smiling.

Another time I was walking down the hallway on a mission to make it to a meeting on time. "What's wrong? Is something wrong?"

No. I was wearing heels that are too high. I was developing a blister on my heels. I wasn't smiling.

And a third time. I was listening intently in a meeting, taking notes and following the conversation. "What's wrong? Is something wrong?"

No. I was just paying attention and thinking about next steps for the project. I wasn't smiling.

Throughout the course of my career, I inevitably started to smile more. I was conditioned to smile more. I smile often. I smile to make people feel welcome. I smile to disarm people. I smile and even throw in a laugh to cut the tension in a situation. I smile when given tough feedback. I smile when others are angry. I smile when I am angry, sometimes growling through my teeth. I smile often and smile plenty.

"You should smile more often. Just smile." But when is the last time we ever asked a man to smile more?

If a man doesn't smile, it's okay. We never question, never doubt. He's commanding. He has a presence and gravitas. He's a leader. He's a visionary.

He's someone we can follow. He will lead us to where we need to go. Follow that man!

When we don't smile? The narrative can quickly go in another direction.

Then we are cold. Lack empathy. Lack emotional intelligence. People just can't seem to connect with us. We make people uncomfortable. We appear aggressive, sometimes threatening. People wonder if we like them, if we approve of them, if we can lead teams. If people will follow us. If we can make an impact. We just don't have that warmth, that energy, that charisma—those intangible qualities that make that next great leader.

It would be so much simpler if we just smiled. So why don't we?

Because maybe like our friend Kim Kardashian, we don't want wrinkles. Because we don't feel well that day. Because we have blisters on our feet from heels that are far too high. Because we are just intently listening, planning what action we have to take next. Because we are fed up with the comments, the jokes, the daily attack of microaggressions we women face in our lives.

Because some of us just don't like to smile, because we don't have time to smile. We aren't here to make friends. We aren't here to smile and show off our happiness and make everyone else comfortable. We are here to make moves and make things happen, just like our male colleagues. We are here to make as much of an impact as humanly possible.

So what does smiling have to do with anything?

Next time you are in a meeting and someone questions why she doesn't smile enough, why she's so aggressive, why she's so calculating, why she doesn't collaborate, why she's difficult.

Ask yourself and the others in the room, would we use the same words to describe a male leader? And doubt his capabilities?

And for the record. I do love to smile. I have a great smile. I smile often. Because life is good.

But please don't ask me to smile. Unless we are taking a selfie. Unless we are out enjoying a glass of frosé. Unless I am with my children, snapping a photo, and we all shout "Cheese!" Then I will smile on command.

"Please Don't Ask Me to Smile" by Mita Mallick was published on SWAAY.com. Mita currently serves as the head of Inclusion, Equity, and Impact at Carta and is the former head of Diversity and Inclusion and Cross-Cultural Marketing at Unilever, where her efforts to build an inclusive and gender-balanced culture have been celebrated.

LEADERSHIP SPOTLIGHT

Most people dread having to give direct reports and constructive feedback on the way others perceive them. It's tricky. A friend of mine, now in her forties, told me recently that she's still traumatized by her boss telling her, "Your teammates don't like you," when she was fresh out of college.

There are effective ways to communicate to a female employee or mentee that her likability may be an issue and to help her improve. You can, for instance, gather feedback from other people, but don't hit her over the head with it; instead, share the consensus in a gentle and supportive way. You can say something like, "One of your colleagues is concerned that you aren't a fan of hers because you come across uninterested in your interactions."

Team meetings can be a useful setting for your employee or mentee to observe how she acts in comparison to others. For example, if she pays attention, she might notice that while everyone else starts the meeting with small talk and banter, she wants to get right down to business. While it's not necessarily bad, this behavior might negatively impact her ability to connect with her colleagues as people.

If your employee or mentee is worried about her likability, she might tend to isolate herself when she should actually do the opposite and surround herself with open, gregarious people who can serve as models. If she finds herself at a loss for words around these people, she should try to speak up anyway, because quiet individuals can be perceived as indifferent or uninterested. Encourage her to share a sincere and specific compliment or to ask a question that invites the other person to talk about themselves (because when other people feel like you are interested and listening to them, they are more likely to like you).

Finally, your employee or mentee can work on mastering the give and take of conversation—with both people participating equally. She can also work on showing her vulnerable side. This might involve admitting she doesn't have the answer to a problem, has made a mistake, or struggles with an insecurity. These behaviors will increase her relatability, and by extension her likability.

CUE THE REAL WORLD

Our ledge protectors in this section have hopefully provided useful guidance for a healthy relationship with likability. Now use the following prompts to write in your journal how you might leverage what you've learned.

- Do a quick life review and think about whether you have received repetitive messages about what isn't acceptable in the name of likability. For instance, were you told as a little girl that you were too loud and therefore less likable?

- If you learned to suppress certain behaviors to be more likable, how might you gradually bring them back in a way that works for you first and others second?

- Are there any areas in your life today where you are feeling resentful? Is there a boundary you need to set to feel better about the situation? If so, how will you go about identifying and communicating this boundary?

LIKABILITY LEDGE REVIEW

- Likability is the combination of personality traits that engages another person in an **emotional relationship** with you. Key traits of genuine likability include captivation and hope, authenticity and relatability, protectiveness and reliability, and compassion and perceptiveness.

- It often takes us a while to see that abiding to outdated expectations to be obedient, small, and self-sacrificing for the sake of being liked is holding us back. By getting to the root of our need to **people please**, we can start doing things differently.

- When you allow your **boundaries** to be violated, the desire to be liked is often the culprit. If you can put this desire aside and focus on creating and maintaining healthy boundaries, ultimately you will improve your self-esteem, your ability to take care of yourself, and the quality of your relationships.

- While we don't want to use our feminine wiles to manipulate men and don't want to lose sight of our own masculine-oriented power, **feminine softness** can be a useful means for likability.

- There are effective ways to communicate to a female employee or mentee that her likability may be an issue and to help her improve. You can, for instance, gather feedback from other people and **share a consensus** in a gentle and supportive way.

"I won't be taken seriously because of my appearance."

∞◇∞

"If I wear form-fitting clothes, they will think I am asking for it."

∞◇∞

"I don't have enough physical appeal to land my dream job."

∞◇∞

"I don't look like an executive, so how can I think I'll get the promotion?"

∞◇∞

"I'm just a scientist. I shouldn't put too much effort into my appearance!"

∞◇∞

"I am a mom now. I can't dress up like I used to."

∞◇∞

"My body features aren't flattering. I should just stick to loose clothing."

∞◇∞

"I want to be X, but I don't look like one."

∞◇∞

"I've worked way too hard for my career, but people assume things fall into my lap because of my looks."

∞◇∞

Chapter Three

PRESENTATION

I f you've been keeping up with the #metoo movement, you probably recall the time Tony Robbins, a world-renowned motivational speaker and self-help guru, was publicly called out for his tone-deaf comments about the revolutionary movement. During an eleven-minute exchange with an audience member, Robbins shared the story of a man who passed over a highly qualified woman for an executive position because she was "very attractive" and therefore "too big of a risk" for his company.

Typically, I just glance over these screw-ups and move on. But this time, I was livid. Robbins's conversation brought back a toxic memory of an investor claiming I was "too pretty to be a CEO." I'd sacrificed everything to achieve my purpose, and yet only my appearance seemed to matter.

I admired Robbins's work but felt his comments about the #metoo movement were damaging. As Tarana Burke, founder of the #metoo movement, says: "We have a hard enough time trying to shift the narrative." And a lot of that narrative starts and ends with our appearance. We know that looks matter, but few of us realize how much.

As a childhood tomboy, I hid behind loose clothes and made myself as invisible as I could. I loved playing sports and hanging out with the boys—somehow that made me feel less insecure about my looks. Growing up in the 1990s, in a country like Morocco, I felt the restrictions of being a girl. In Muslim countries, women who dress conservatively are safer and more respected. Although the rules weren't as intense within my liberal family, I was aware of them and as a result never cared to explore my feminine side. My self-esteem back then was tied to my accomplishments rather than my appearance. Today it's tied to both, and there's nothing wrong with that.

My traditional mother ultimately grew tired of seeing her only girl not be as in touch with her "feminine side"—whatever that meant. So while I was in Germany on a post-college research internship, she responded to an impromptu invite from the Miss Colorado USA state pageant and signed me up. Upon my return from Germany, I received a letter of acceptance to my very first pageant. You can imagine the look on my face: "Me? Competing in a pageant? Like with heels and a swimsuit and everything? On stage for thousands of people to judge?"

I told my mom to forget it. "Is this how much you love me? You want to see me make a fool out of myself?" I said jokingly as I ripped up the letter in front of her.

"This isn't about being pretty or girly; it's about building the confidence to show up on that stage as who you truly are and owning it," my mother replied. "This will be an amazing experience to push yourself outside your comfort zone. Plus you could use a new hobby."

She had a point there, for I didn't have much of an identity outside my academic prowess at the time. What was waiting for me outside my comfort zone? Who was I meant to become? What would happen if I started caring about my presentation and self-image? These questions couldn't be answered if I took the easy path.

It was a serendipitous moment, and it would change my life for the best. I took my mother's advice and walked blindly into my first pageant. Was I a nervous wreck? Heck yeah! Did I regret doing it? Absolutely not. In fact, I ended up competing every year after that. I went on to win the title of Miss New York US in 2015 and was the second runner-up for Miss United States that same year.

We've all watched *Miss Congeniality*, right? At some point, a lot of us thought about how cool it would be to be a badass *and* a beauty queen like Gracie Hart. When I first watched the movie with my mother, I secretly fell in love with the pageant process. I mean who doesn't love a good makeover scene or watching another woman successfully reinvent herself and build her confidence? Every year approximately 2.5 million women and girls throughout the United States participate in beauty pageants. But many are concerned that pageants objectify women and damage our self-esteem.

The truth is, preparing for a pageant requires an insane amount of self-discipline and perseverance. During my five years of competing, I dedicated every waking moment to building self-awareness, practicing my stage presence, perfecting my communication skills, studying for interviews, identifying my strengths and weaknesses, training my body, and sharpening my mind. I was challenged to physically and mentally reinvent myself in a way that aligned with the woman I aspired to become.

This changed me. I developed a new lifestyle that helped me stay on top of my game. Learning how to get the judges' and audience's attention helped me overcome my stage fright and become a more assured public speaker. When I looked in the mirror, I no longer saw an insecure tomboy trying to hide. I saw a confident and attractive woman with a strong presence, a loud voice, and a lot of potential. Taking care of my physical appearance and becoming comfortable with others' judgment have opened many doors in my career. And it wouldn't have been possible without the self-discovery I gained from my pageant journey.

As I've gotten older, I've realized that if we women want to be self-sufficient and accomplished, we must care about how we present ourselves. And there shouldn't be any shame or guilt associated with admitting that we want to look and feel good. To be clear, I am *not* advocating that women pursue plastic surgeries or extreme diets, try to look like other women they deem attractive, or keep up with unrealistic and unhealthy beauty standards. I am also *not* suggesting that we seek to dress in luxury brands or keep up with fashion trends we can't afford. I am simply saying we shouldn't be afraid to present an authentic image that represents how we want the world to see us. Pageantry taught me that just as we work to develop our professional and technical skills, the visual image we present is also part of our personal brand. Every now and then I stop and ask myself, *Is the leader I want to become properly represented in how I show up every day?*

Newsweek columnist Jessica Bennett said it best: "In this economy, looking good isn't just vanity, it's economic survival. Trying to look good because we know it helps us out professionally shouldn't necessarily be shunned, nor should we be plagued by personal guilt."

While writing this chapter, I looked up and saw Kamala Harris on TV delivering her acceptance speech after she became the first woman and first woman of color to hold the title of vice president of the United States. Watching Harris celebrate her victory in her dazzling, modern white suit brought forth a complex feeling. Was it pride? Joy? Hope? All of it?

As a woman of color myself, that moment was meaningful. Harris reminded me of my mother, and I admired her. She carefully matched her appearance and individual style to her powerful message and shining personality. We live in a time when image-conscious female leaders in politics and business bear influence beyond their achievements. They have become the new style icons.

I'm relieved. For so long, we have tiptoed around talking about the importance of self-presentation as a female leader. I never understood why women who loudly embraced beauty and style were perceived as not business-minded or not smart. The underlying perception is that women exist as an either-or, while men can have it all. I will never forget the time when I was asked by a male judge during my first pageant: "If you had to choose between being pretty or smart, which would you pick?" Or the time a male investor commented that I was "too pretty to be a CEO." Proving that a woman can be both pretty and smart has been a continuous struggle for many of us as we push boundaries and challenge the status quo. "Smart" and "beautiful" are not mutually exclusive, yet when it comes to women's labels, we often treat them as such.

This frustration is what led me to launch SWAAY, a forum that could take women beyond these damaging perceptions of passive sexuality or entrepreneurial ineptitude. SWAAY's diverse voices showcase women's competencies in spearheading innovation and political and cultural movements, and in tackling the greatest issues of our time. At the moment of victory, Harris proved to herself and the world that women from all backgrounds can shatter barriers—and look like the best version of themselves doing it.

In the rest of this chapter, I'll share why it's not a bad thing to embrace appearance as another tool in the arsenal. Your appearance is not something you must give up to be taken seriously. First up, I'll talk about chivalry and how it relates to the visual expression of who we are. Next, I'll delve into the costs of "appearance discrimination" and how not to perpetuate the cycle of hypocritically evaluating others by their appearance only. The right balance between individual style and work-culture appropriateness can be found.

LEDGE PROTECTOR #1: ACKNOWLEDGE WOMEN'S MIXED ATTITUDES ABOUT CHIVALRY

In a Medium article about modern chivalry, Shamontiel Vaughn admitted to the contradictions inherent in how women feel they should be treated and show up when they engage with men:

"After my Toastmasters meeting every second and fourth Saturday afternoon, off I scurry to lug a bin, cloth banner, and a T-banner stand from my club's lobby area. I am asked the same question by at least a handful of taller and bigger men: 'Do you need help with that?' or 'Where is your car?' And my response is always the same, 'Nope, I got it.'"

She adds: "I've convinced myself that it is counterproductive for someone to carry something *for* me that I can physically carry *myself* without breaking a sweat. My arms work just fine, thank you. Yet I also stand there expectantly waiting on one of those same taller, bigger men to hold the door for me. I would judge them if they didn't immediately do so."

Vaughn continues, "I come from a family of men who thoroughly enjoy being men—chivalry included. They hold doors. They lift furniture. They grab grocery bags without being asked. Sometimes I mind. Most of the time I don't. Meanwhile I often hog the driver's side of the car. I have no interest in anyone pulling out my chair or putting a jacket over a puddle. I'm a bag of chivalry hypocrisy." Vaughn concedes that not only is her individual behavior confusing to men but that things get even more complicated when you factor in that every woman has different expectations from her interactions with men and that every woman presents herself physically with varying degrees of traditional femininity.

Chivalry has been around since the Middle Ages, when it was a term used to describe how a knight should honorably help those weaker than himself. According to research at Cambridge University and Columbia University, modern-day chivalry is alive and well—and not just for men. In the study, researchers conducted behavioral experiments designed to test how individuals react to the notion of harming another person. In one version, participants were asked if they would push a person into the path of an ongoing trolley if it meant they could save the lives of five others. Some subjects were asked to push a male bystander, while others were asked to push a female or gender-neutral bystander. Results showed that participants of both genders were more likely to sacrifice a male or gender-neutral bystander than a woman, indicating an overall aversion to harming women. "There is indeed a gender bias in these matters," said Dean Mobbs, one of the researchers who is now director of the Caltech Brain Imaging Center. "Society perceives harming women as more morally unacceptable."

In short, even as our powerful psyches bristle against it, we women may be socially conditioned to expect men to protect us and admire our femininity. And I'd be remiss if I didn't admit that this hypocrisy occurs with my friends and me. We expect men to pay and hold the door open on a date, but we get offended when a man acts like he needs to take care of us. We want to be treated with kid gloves at work, but we also want to be taken seriously.

Women's ambivalence and tendency toward hypocrisy can be especially insidious in the arena of self-presentation.

If we lean too far in either direction or expect others to adhere to conflicting standards, it's off the ledge we go!

Working with my own hypocrisy, I've found it helps to give people the benefit of the doubt. If a person does something I think is wrong or inappropriate, I consider that they might see it differently or that the situation might be ambiguous. I try to remember that I'm not privy to the other person's internal world and that I cannot understand the exact combination of forces and circumstances that led to the behavior.

Over the years, I've also worked on being humbler. By increasing my self-awareness in all the ways we're discussing in this book, I have more opportunities to see that I'm not ethically or morally perfect either and that sometimes I even justify my less-than-stellar behavior. When I give advice to others, I take a step back to make sure I'm drinking my own Kool-Aid and take the time to fully comprehend my own beliefs so I can be consistent standing by them. If I suspect I'm being hypocritical and trust the person I'm interacting with, I might ask them what they think. The first time someone admitted, "Yes, Iman, a little bit," it hurt—but it really helped me avoid that hypocrisy going forward.

LEDGE PROTECTOR #2: UNDERSTAND THE COST OF APPEARANCE DISCRIMINATION AND AVOID JUDGING OTHERS' APPEARANCES

When I was a junior at Colorado State University, I landed a part-time job in a women's clothing store at the mall. It was a perfect situation for me, because unlike my other day job as a research assistant in the biochemistry lab, it was public facing. It allowed me to meet new people and regularly interact with other women.

One day when I was working the register, a young woman walked into the store, shopped around, and then headed over to me to pay. I was as helpful and welcoming as you'd expect a store employee to be, which prompted the woman to say: "Wow, you're actually really nice!?"

I asked why she was surprised.

"Honestly, when I walked in, I thought you'd be a bitch," she said.

I froze. "What? Why would you think that? Did I do something to offend you?"

"No, no, no. It's just that you have exotic facial features."

I must have looked confused because she followed up. "Well, it's because you're pretty, that's all. You should take it as a compliment."

I smiled, handed over her new bag of clothes, and said thank you (while pondering *Is that people's first impression of me? A bitch?*). I then proceeded to reach out to my friends and ask if I really looked like a bitch. Down the Google rabbit hole, I even found a book called *Most Pretty Girls Are Bitches* by Simon Manny Doyle. I had never experienced appearance-based categorization so directly—granted it was harmless and I apparently won that woman over!

Conventional wisdom says that it only takes seconds to make an impression on a new person. In their research at Princeton University, Alexander Todorov and Janine Willis found that the window is actually much shorter: it takes a tenth of a second to form an impression of a stranger based on their facial appearance. And being exposed to the stranger for longer doesn't significantly alter that first impression.

The Princeton study asked participants to evaluate strangers on specific traits and determined that they were able to judge strangers most quickly on attractiveness and trustworthiness. This appears to be an evolutionary phenomenon, because the ability to form such rapid judgments evolved as a mechanism for our ancestors to survive threatening environments.

This ability is present from a young age. According to research at Harvard University, published in the journal *Developmental Psychology*, young children judge others based on facial features as much as adults do. By the age of five, children make fast and consistent judgments of others based on features such as the tilt of the mouth and the distance between the eyes.

"Our study showed that children from age five, but not younger, appear to consistently use facial features in deciding how they should behave toward a person as well as their expectations of the other person's behavior," said lead author Tessa Charlesworth. "In other words, children's judgments from faces do appear to have consequences for behavior."

Overall, children three years and older almost always (88 percent of the time) made the stereotypically expected character judgments of the faces. They selected the trustworthy-, submissive-, and competent-looking faces as "nice," and the untrustworthy-, incompetent-, and dominant-looking faces as "mean." Additionally, children age five and up paired faces with stereotypically expected behaviors (e.g., selecting the dominant-looking face as the person who would "pick up heavy things").

A second set of experiments examined how children would behave toward people based on facial appearance. The participants looked at pairs of faces that were perceived to be trustworthy- or untrustworthy-looking and dominant- or submissive-looking and were asked which person they would rather give a gift to—for example, "This is Edgar, and this is Martin. If you had only one cookie, which person would you give it to?" By age five, children were consistently above chance in giving their gifts to the trustworthy- or submissive-looking faces.

In this book, we've talked about the wage gap for women in the US, but as Mindy Isser wrote in a 2020 blog for *In These Times*, there is another gap for women workers that involves the silent expectation around their appearance—the grooming gap. "If you purchase the right clothes, makeup, and haircut, higher wages are more within reach," Isser writes. "But grooming costs for women can be extremely expensive, and the grooming gap also results in the loss of 55 minutes each day for the average woman."

Isser cites a fascinating case study from Sara Nelson, president of the Association of Flight Attendants-CWA, an industry that is nearly 80 percent women. "The expectation around appearance literally interrupts your sleep. Flight attendants get minimal rest between flights, and the rest time is further shrunk because they are expected to appear perfectly coifed before their next flight," Nelson told Isser.

"The grooming gap's effects are compounded for women of color," says Isser. "According to Restaurant Opportunity Center, restaurant owners look for workers who are clean-cut, have good hygiene, or a professional appearance. Black women spend $473 million on relaxers, weaves, and other hair care, in part because of racist ideas that natural Black hair is not professional or attractive."

More than one in four employees have experienced discrimination because of their looks, and most often, it happens to women. Appearance-based discrimination occurs when a person is evaluated differently based on how they look. Research has consistently shown that workers and job candidates are often perceived and rated by how closely their features resemble typical masculine and feminine physicality.

Interestingly, a Harvard study found that when people try too hard with their appearance, it can backfire. "Women who wear some makeup to enhance their beauty are considered more likable and competent—but those with glamourous makeup are not," writes ABC News reporter Kellie Scott. And in the male-dominated STEM world, "Some studies have shown that more feminine-appearing women are less likely to be considered scientists even when they are scientists." I can attest to this as I was considered less of a scientist at the beginning of my career because I was also competing in beauty pageants.

It's maddening—and so very easy for the issue of appearance to send us careening over the glass ledge. Because it's sometimes easier to see a problem from another perspective, let's start addressing this issue by examining our own judgments of others' appearances.

As we've seen, judging others is something that's often done automatically, without any conscious thought or the time to explore alternative scenarios. I once attended a lecture where the speaker showed up looking quite disheveled. My first instinct was to think, *Maybe he's not taking this event as seriously as he should.* I later found out that the speaker had his flight canceled in a snowstorm and had driven all night to get there in time for the lecture. I felt immediately guilty and was glad I had the opportunity to learn the facts.

Forming a judgment about someone's appearance is a normal first reaction, but it's up to you what you do with that thought. Ideally, you pause and sit with the thought for a few moments. Instead of allowing your judgmental notions to conflate in your mind—or worse, acting on them—consider the possible reasons you may feel less than positive about someone's appearance. Maybe it's an unconscious bias. Maybe the person is your subordinate, and you're worried about how they'll be perceived. Maybe you're assuming the person is just being lazy.

Or maybe it's you. Ask yourself if it's possible that you're projecting insecurities about your own appearance onto this other person. Consider whether you have any negative emotions associated with your own experiences of being judged by your appearance. For instance, perhaps when you were younger, you were passed over for a job because you couldn't afford the "right look." You may now subconsciously judge a twenty-five-year-old colleague whose wardrobe choices don't follow the rules. Either way, remind yourself that someone's appearance is never the full story, and seek to understand who that person really is.

By coincidence, I began writing this chapter while judging the Miss Teen USA pageant in Memphis. In this situation, I really had to take my own advice and approach my evaluation from a holistic point of view. If my experience in pageantry has taught me anything, it's that winning a pageant is about mastering the art of impressions. Picking the next Miss Teen USA is about the overall feeling you get from a young woman. It's never about her facial features or how toned her body is. Among other things, judges must consider her ambitions, achievements, personality, speaking ability, body language, and overall confidence for a complete and accurate picture. To this end, let's move on to an exercise that will help you evaluate others in a multifaceted way.

◆ Ledge Work: Move Past Others' Initial Presentation

For better and worse, we instinctively make incorrect judgments about other people. Think about the last new person you met, and in your journal, write your first observations on each of the characteristics listed below. Provide a few details explaining your rationale. Place a checkmark next to the ones that were most memorable. Finally, note the overall impression you have of the person now that some time has passed.

- Facial Appearance

- Dress and Accessories

- Body Language

- Mannerisms

- Speaking Voice

- Articulateness

- Intelligence

- Friendliness

Has your initial impression changed now that you know the person better? In what way? What can this experience teach you about evaluating people based on first impressions?

◆

LEDGE PROTECTOR #3: STRIKE THE RIGHT BALANCE WITH YOUR OWN PRESENTATION

Whenever I have doubts about my self-presentation or think my appearance is too loud, I ask myself, *What would Bozoma Saint John do?* "I've always wanted to wear what makes me feel powerful," Bozoma told *Vogue's* Chioma Nnadi. Even the *Vogue* editors were blown away by her style—and she doesn't even work in fashion.

Bozoma is one of the best-known tech executives in Silicon Valley, making her mark as chief brand officer of Uber and currently as chief marketing officer of Netflix. As *Vogue* described her: "It's hard to imagine anyone standing taller or with more swagger than Saint John in the buttoned-up world of corporate America—or anywhere else for that matter."

The idea of a conventional nine-to-five wardrobe is fundamentally at odds with the way Bozoma operates. "I remember the one time I tried to fit into the corporate dress code," she told *Vogue*. "I wore khakis with creases down the front when I first started at Pepsi. But I didn't feel good; therefore my ideas weren't good, and my personality couldn't shine. It's why I think it's crazy when people say fashion is superficial, because I think it's part of what makes me comfy in my own skin."

Bozoma's attitude is not unique, and

in most workplaces today, there is an emphasis on inclusivity and belonging. Some people take that to mean they can wear whatever they want because their organization wants them to "be themselves." Although this is mostly true, when it comes to presentation, we also need to be the best version of ourselves.

There is a fine line.

My friend Mita Mallick, whose essay appeared earlier in this book, is the head of inclusion, equity, and impact at Carta, a financial technology company. I met her when she was an executive at consumer-goods giant Unilever and have since admired how her appearance and style reflect her powerful position in business. As the daughter of Indian immigrant parents, Mita is transparent about the impact of self-presentation. "Look, women are judged by their appearance," she told me. "My brownness is identified and processed before I open my mouth. I want to stand out wearing dresses and heels because I'm short, and also my confidence in how I show up comes from my style. The downside is when I don't dress up as much, people question it. They'll say, 'You look really tired.'"

Going to work, and in fact going anywhere in which you are meeting new people, requires some advance consideration of how you're presenting yourself and whether your choices gel with the environment. Many office settings have one of several dress codes, including these:

- **Business Professional:** Routine in industries like banking and law, this style involves tailored suits, dress flats or short heels, and simple jewelry and accessories.
- **Business Casual:** This look is not really casual, as it incorporates collared shirts or nice sweaters with slacks, khakis, or pencil skirts. Shoes are closed-toed.
- **Casual:** Once the domain of California-based technology companies, casual and its slightly upgraded sister, smart-casual, are now more common across all types of organizations. Appropriate casual wear for the office includes solid tee-shirts, clean denim, and clean sneakers. Avoid flip-flops and revealing blouses.

Well-groomed hair and nails are important in every environment. And yes, even if you are seeing colleagues and clients exclusively on Zoom, your style should still fit into one of these buckets while staying true to yourself.

You may be asking, "But why do companies still care about this?" There are several reasons. First, image breeds confidence, and as we've been talking about, first impressions matter a lot. If an organization is paying you, it wants to be certain your look is a positive reflection of the company's values and presents you as a credible professional. Second, consider why school uniforms are still a thing. In an environment where everyone is dressed similarly, it's easier to evaluate people according to their character, contributions, and results. And finally, because not everyone is a fashionista, dress codes take the ambiguity out of what to wear to work and when. Organizations want to make their expectations clear to avoid subjectivity around what is and isn't appropriate.

Allow me to share some personal experiences with this issue. Prior to launching my own company, one of my favorite parts about working in the corporate world was experimenting with my own corporate style and sharpening my professional visual identity. At first, I saw dress codes as limiting, an attack on individual style, but I gradually started challenging myself to embrace it and get creative with the guidelines. Every night before going to sleep, I browsed my saved outfits on Pinterest for inspiration and carefully picked out a few items to style for the next day, taking into consideration my schedule and responsibilities. Some days required more dressing up and more effort than others, but weaving this practice into my night routine made dressing for my job far more exciting. I was also better prepared, without a lot of rushing around in the morning. This simple habit played a big role in my developing a professional image that aligned with the woman I aspired to be.

In today's world, it's possible your organization has no dress code, which can be daunting and confusing. Longtime career expert Alison Doyle recommends that you select clothes and accessories that make you feel confident while expressing your personal style. "The key is an individualized look that appears polished and put together," she says. "Incorporate prints, textures, and patterns. You can even wear exercise clothing to the office if styled tactfully."

When in doubt, consider dressing up rather than down, especially if you are attending a job interview or meeting a client or senior executive. It also never hurts to ask someone in the organization for some basic appearance guidelines. These may be unspoken, so observation of the people in your work environment is critical. Through understated creativity, you can create looks that stand out in a refreshing rather than an alienating way. For instance, if you notice that most people wear chinos in a neutral shade, you might wear the same type of pants in pink or deep purple, with an eye-catching belt.

According to my friend Kim Fulcher, who you might recall is a women's empowerment guru, it's a tightrope. "Beauty is a power, and it opens doors," she told me. "I'm all for being feminine, as in well-groomed and aware of how you are presenting yourself. You want to look put-together and professional. When you are at your physical best, people respond to you better, and the more you put energy into taking care of yourself, the more it says about your worth. Plus a good hair day can put you in a great mood!"

Kim added: "Women can make mistakes being over the top. My first job was as a model, and I got into the habit of leading with that. Winning with your sexuality means your respect from other women will be nonexistent. Few want to see your boobs, and if they do, it's going to undermine your value."

Leadership adds an additional dimension to the conversation. When I started SWAAY, I became my own boss and ran my own schedule so dress-code guidelines didn't apply, and sometimes I was too inconsistent with my appearance and presentation simply because I could be. I realized that this took a toll on my confidence and self-perception. If anything, being my own boss meant I needed to manage my professional image more closely, because if I didn't, others would do it for me. My pageant background also put me at risk of being negatively stereotyped before stakeholders even met me, so I had to find the right balance to be perceived as capable and powerful.

Referring to leaders who don't fit the traditional mold, Laura Morgan Roberts, a professor at University of Virginia's Darden School of Business, says: "Members of negatively stereotyped identity groups may experience a threat known as devaluation. People are constantly forming theories about your competence, character, and commitment, which are rapidly disseminated throughout your workplace. It is wise to add your voice in framing others' theories about who you are and what you can accomplish."

And let's not forget the old saying that beauty is in the eye of the beholder. After all, the definition of beauty is a combination of qualities—such as shape, color, and form—that pleases the aesthetic senses, especially sight. Notice there's nothing there about having long hair or being rail thin!

Most of us want to look appealing, but exactly what that encompasses is different for every person. Maybe you like to dress in a traditional masculine or androgynous style. Maybe you are embracing your passage into your elder years and love your grey hair and wrinkles. Maybe you like

to wear makeup, and maybe you don't. As long as you are authentic in your approach, you can and should express your style in your own way.

In every environment, we need to embrace our unique style and put effort into our image, because at the end of the day, presentation is really about self-respect. Buddhist teacher Chogyam Trungpa Rinpoche asked his students to show up to class with care for their appearance because it was an expression of their dignity. A well-tended appearance showed a student was devoted to themselves and the teachings.

If the pressure to be conventionally beautiful weren't such an oppressive force, we wouldn't need to spend so much time talking about it. So I want to leave you with this: appearance-related decisions are a balance. At the end of the day, we take guardrails into account and then find ways for our individuality to flourish within them.

Voices from the SWAAY Community

What "Professional Dress" Actually Means

Jeanne Rihm

If you needed to hire a professional to, let's say, cater a dinner, head your marketing department, or perhaps act as an expert for you on a legal matter, how would you expect them to dress?

I will take a guess here and say you imagine each person with a different look and vibe, presenting themselves in unique ways. If their style fell short of what's perceived to be acceptable within their industry, you may even underestimate their skill set. You may question their ability to be trustworthy, confident, or knowledgeable.

You've probably already heard the phrases, "Dress for the job you want, not the job you have" or "Look good; feel good." But there's a lot more to appropriate styling for the workplace than those two outlooks alone.

We, as professionals, must ask ourselves, "What should I wear?" Some may reach for a suit and tie or heels and a dress, while others simply throw on jeans and a sweater. But though the latter might be an appropriate style for certain industries, it might not be for others. It is important to understand that different markets often have a distinctive (and often unspoken) unofficial dress code. Be cognizant of the environment, and if you're unsure how to dress, ask your human resources department what is generally considered appropriate.

One last point: dress authentically. You should wear clothes that make you feel confident, clothes that represent who you are intrinsically and professionally. Power up your sleeves, take control of your future, and move forward.

"How You Dress Is Your Calling Card" by Jeanne Rihm was published on SWAAY.com. Jeanne is a personal fashion stylist who specializes in helping women understand their unique body so they can dress with confidence.

LEADERSHIP SPOTLIGHT

As women managing others, we want to help our employees channel their own Bozoma Saint John. We want to support their feeling expressive and powerful while remaining respectful of the expectations in our workplace.

Sometimes, though, doing this involves a tough conversation. One such conversation involves providing feedback to an employee about their appearance not meeting the organization's norms. I've not yet had to do this, but if I did, I'd want guidance from Joseph Grenny, coauthor of *Crucial Conversations*. In an interview with *Harvard Business Review*'s Amy Gallo, Grenny suggested that leaders prepare in advance. "Don't make this about right and wrong, decent and indecent," he told Gallo. "Focus on your intention to communicate that you want her to be as successful as possible." In the conversation with your employee, don't meander to the point. Rather, start off with something specific like, "You're so great at your job, and I'd like to share some guidance about your dress that can make your work even more impactful."

You might feel anxious about delivering this type of feedback, but try not to show it. The person may not be that bothered by the topic, but a nervous, negative attitude on your part could change that. If the employee is violating either stated or unstated norms that you've never communicated, take responsibility for that. Then go through them as clearly as you can, using examples like: "Our parent company requires that our nails be polished so we personally reflect the look we are selling to clients" (stated norm), and "The culture here prefers clothing colors that are more understated" (an unstated norm). Use praise where you can, and encourage the person to make adaptations that feel right for them. Inquire if the employee has questions, and then end the conversation on a positive note. You don't want them to leave with the message that because their blouses are too tight they are a train wreck of a professional, because that was never the point.

A few last but very important notes: first, remember that everyone chooses to express themselves in their own way, and your definition of what looks good might be inherently different from your employee's definition. Whenever you can, recall the earlier points about judgment and err on the side of inclusivity. Also, keep in mind that your employee might be going through something that impacts their appearance. For example, when my friend Tracy returned to work after having her first child, her boss told her she wasn't "looking attractive" or "professional enough." Tracy was enraged. She was not sleeping well, her clothes didn't fit postpartum, and she was leaking breast milk when a scheduled meeting did not line up with her need to pump in private. Tracy was barely keeping it together, and this single woman with no kids, who was dressed perfectly, was lecturing her on appearance? Of course this did not go over well! The woman's approach to the situation lacked understanding and was inappropriate given the circumstances.

As you explore appearance-related issues with your employees, remember that lots of women are spinning multiple plates in the air. Before you form a judgment, it never hurts to ask about the person's general well-being and listen carefully to the answers you receive.

CUE THE REAL WORLD

Now that you've explored the ledge protectors on presentation, think about how they can help you present the best possible version of yourself. Brainstorm answers to these questions in your journal.

- Describe your unique style. What clothing, accessories, and hairstyle make you feel most confident and professional?

- Do you think this style lines up with your industry? If not, what are some steps you can take to achieve a balance between your comfort and the industry/organization's cultural expectations?

- Consider whether you have recently been hypocritical or judgmental about another's appearance. What were your initial impressions, and how did you act on them? If faced with a similar situation next time, what might you do differently?

PRESENTATION LEDGE REVIEW

- To avoid **hypocrisy**, give the benefit of the doubt. If a person does something you think is wrong or inappropriate, consider that they might see it differently or that the situation might be ambiguous.
- **Forming a judgment** about someone's appearance is a normal first reaction, but it's up to you what you do with that first thought. Ideally, pause and sit with the thought for a few moments.
- Don't project insecurities about your own appearance onto other people. Consider whether you have any **negative emotions** associated with your own experiences of being judged by your appearance.
- In every environment, embrace your unique style and put effort into your image, because presentation is really about **self-respect.** Appearance-related decisions are a balance, so take guardrails into account and then find ways for your individuality to flourish within them.
- As women managing other women, we want to help our employees feel expressive and powerful while remaining respectful of expectations in the workplace. If this involves a tough conversation, **use praise** and encourage the person to make adaptations that feel right for them.

"I don't even know who my authentic self is."

⬦⬦⬦⬦⬦

"Being vulnerable is the new power pose."

⬦⬦⬦⬦⬦

"They have to think I am authentic in order for me to get the job."

⬦⬦⬦⬦⬦

"If I let them in on my true self, they won't like me anymore."

⬦⬦⬦⬦⬦

"I should tell my team that I have no clue what I am doing."

⬦⬦⬦⬦⬦

"When my emotions get the better of me, I feel so guilty."

⬦⬦⬦⬦⬦

"I was too authentic, and now they think I'm unhinged."

⬦⬦⬦⬦⬦

"I worry that when I try to be authentic, I end up doing the opposite."

⬦⬦⬦⬦⬦

"I'm a boss. I want to be approachable but not too approachable."

⬦⬦⬦⬦⬦

"If I don't know who I am, how can I persuade anyone else?"

⬦⬦⬦⬦⬦

Chapter Four

AUTHENTICITY

Tonight is about picking the most authentic candidate that will represent us in the most authentic way! You are not just looking for beauty or for someone with a PhD or for the most popular girl. A Miss Universe winner is someone who exudes authenticity," Paula Shugart, president of the Miss Universe Organization, instructed the selection committee. We were getting ready to judge the Miss Universe 2018 competition in Bangkok, and this briefing wasn't the first time I heard about the importance of authenticity. However, this time I also thought to myself, *What does that mean anymore? And why has authenticity suddenly become the gold standard for leadership?*

As in life, pageantry is about putting on a great show. It's about showing up as the best version of yourself, showing the world what happens when you work on yourself every day. So how can a person be truly authentic when they know they're being judged from head to toe? How can we be authentic when we rehearsed, prepared, and trained to fit a certain mold?

In a "fake it till you make it" meets "just be yourself" world, I constantly ask myself, *Should I pretend to be myself, or should I actually be myself?*

The concept of authenticity has received a significant amount of attention recently as people search for meaning and purpose, particularly in their work lives. Its buzzword status rose with social media influencers who attribute much of their success and achievement to being authentic. But

how a person chooses to live authentically depends on their perspective, and I fear that a superficial meaning of authenticity can sabotage our growth and diminish potential.

We define authenticity as being true to our own personality, spirit, or character. Notice that the root of *authenticity* and *author* are the same. In other words, being authentic means that you are the author of your own life and behavior!

In my early twenties, I embarked on a colorful path of self-discovery and enlightenment to uncover what that meant for me. Immediately after my undergraduate education, I moved to a foreign country (again) when I was recruited by a nanotech company in Munich, Germany. In graduate school, I joined the Students for Global Health organization and funded my own medical missions to South Sudan, Kenya, Ecuador, and Morocco. I landed a position as a lead scientist for a new cancer therapy startup. All the while, I competed in pageants. Then, without a plan or a network, I spontaneously moved to New York, won a pageant, landed my dream job, quit said dream job, and accidentally kick-started my entrepreneurial journey.

When I transitioned out of the corporate world and into the entrepreneurial world, my authenticity was constantly challenged. I had my podcast, *Women Who SWAAY*, which had the potential to turn into a lucrative media venture, but up to that point, I hadn't seen myself as a businesswoman capable of pushing a strong mission, building a community, and being a public spokesperson for my own brand. I *thought* being my authentic self was doing the scientific work behind the scenes. This new founder/CEO role required leaving my outdated sense of self behind. The entrepreneurial path required mature self-confidence, as well as a sense that I could take control of unpredictable situations, make difficult decisions, and hold my own with other powerful and strong-willed leaders. I didn't have any of those prerequisites. At twenty-five-years old, if I'd followed the trendy advice to "be myself," I would have jeopardized my entrepreneurial success. In this particular instance, I had to fake a lot of it until I became most of it.

Authenticity came a bit easier to my fellow entrepreneurs Sunny Bonnell and Ashleigh Hansberger because they understood it. They thought, and had in fact been told, that they were oddballs. The long-time friends dropped out of college and started Motto, a branding agency, with just $250. At a time when the advertising world was still governed by the *Mad Men* of old, Sunny and Ashleigh decided to bring their true selves to their clients—shaping campaigns that were rebellious, auda-cious, hot-blooded, weird, hypnotic, and emotional, which reflected their own very unique personalities. When their book, *Rare Breed*, became an immediate success, no one was surprised. Sunny and Ashleigh had long captured attention and admiration through their authenticity.

Then there's my friend June. Like Sunny and Ashleigh, June is an accom-plished businesswoman who also aspired to be an author. She was dead set on writing a novel about teen celebrities, and though she managed to inter-view several stars, her finished manuscript was missing something. "You don't really know this world you're trying to inhabit," her agent told her. "What world do *you* know?" June knew the corporate world, specifically what it was like to be a high-achieving student who came to her first job with none of the diplomacy skills she needed to succeed in a cutthroat, highly political environment. June eventually got promoted, but hers was a long and arduous journey. She decided to write a book about it. It was a bestseller. In this case, June's authenticity paid off.

When we are authentic, we know what it means to be our whole and complete selves and are willing to show this to others. We've given substan-tial thought to who we are and who we are not, to who we were in the past and who we are now. Sunny, Ashleigh, and June stood out because in an image-obsessed world powered by social media, authenticity born out of careful consideration is rare. To fit in and get along with others, most of us simply present ourselves according to what society says we should be like.

Depending on the circumstances, the strong emotions associated with authenticity can spur negative reactions in others. Because women fall off the glass ledge when they are misguided in their pursuit of authenticity or when they give in to it too much or not enough, we need to explore how to have the healthiest possible relationship with our full selves. In order to de-velop a relationship with our authenticity that supports us, we must touch on how to handle difficult emotions effectively, how to harness outbursts to improve rather than sabotage our relationships, and how to shift our attitude so a positive self-definition *is* the authentic self.

LEDGE PROTECTOR #1: DEVELOP HEALTHY AUTHENTICITY

SWAAY columnist Liz Elting is a New York–based philanthropist and businesswoman recognized by *Forbes* as one of the richest self-made women, with an estimated net worth of $390 million. She is known for her outstanding entrepreneurship and her focus on developing women business leaders. She cofounded TransPerfect and served as co-CEO for over twenty-five years. TransPerfect is the world's largest provider of language and business solutions with over $800 million in revenue and more than five thousand employees in more than ninety cities around the globe.

Liz's decision to start a translation company was a result of her journey to find her authentic self, following an unsatisfying career after business school. "It was the early Nineties, and I was an arbitrage broker in the trading division of a large French bank," she told me. "But finance wasn't where my heart lay, and even as a stepping-stone, the job felt like a dead end for me as a woman in that time and place."

As Liz searched for what she was meant to do, she kept coming back to her first job out of college, working in the translation industry. "I've always loved language. My family traveled a lot, so I've lived all over the world—the US, Canada, Portugal, Spain, and Venezuela. It's been a life-long fascination, and I'd worked to gain fluency in Portuguese, Spanish, and French, and had studied Latin." Liz says that while working in translation in the 1980s, she saw a clear gap. "Translation was more or less a one-and-done affair. You needed a document translated, so you hired someone to do that. There were no comprehensive services for companies looking to do business internationally. Everything in my life up to that point led me to believe I was the person to fill that need. My background, my family, my interests, my education—they all played a role."

In cofounding TransPerfect, Liz pursued a career that fully aligned with her authentic self, and it made her the successful and powerful change-maker she is today. "Even if I hadn't been successful, I can say without a doubt that I'd have no regrets," she says.

Liz was fortunate to possess the keen self-awareness that's essential for building authenticity. According to psychologist Tchiki Davis, who writes about authenticity for *Psychology Today,* honing your authenticity requires observing yourself objectively. "Watch yourself in the present moment," she says. "Practice noticing which responses to pressure and challenges feel authentic and which feel inauthentic. Courageously explore the truth of what makes you who you are and ways to start living your values."

Davis suggests that we have two selves: the Adaptive Self and the Authentic Self. The Adaptive Self helps us function through difficult and confusing times, while the Authentic Self helps us feel whole, real, and self-confident. We need to dialogue with both of them to identify their motivations. For example, the Authentic Self may be afraid of rejection and therefore afraid to come forward, and the Adaptive Self may be protecting us from the ways in which we've been hurt in the past.

To build your authenticity muscle, you must understand the discrepancies between your beliefs and your actions and pay attention if you doubt what you're saying or doing.

Extreme uncertainty can be a clue that you're ignoring your Authentic Self—and it wants to be heard. (If you'll recall, this advice is similar to my ideas about hypocrisy.)

In May 2020, when the COVID pandemic was in full swing, I put my belongings in storage and temporarily moved home to Denver. My anxiety skyrocketed, and at first I wasn't sure why. After all, I was very lucky to be healthy and financially secure. As I dissected my thoughts in therapy and through an anxiety journal, I realized there was a discrepancy between how quarantine was affecting my Authentic Self and the actions of my Adaptive Self in response to the unprecedented personal and professional challenges that arose with the pandemic.

In this challenging time, I found it helpful to journal not only about my anxiety but also about my goals and how I was progressing in my overall life purpose. I also became more deliberate about how I spent my energy and who I kept in my company. I was on the lookout for misalignment.

Rather than rushing to judgment or making impulsive moves because it was easier for me or another person, I've learned to take my time and think through actions and decisions that feel authentic and serve my purpose.

Allowing the Authentic Self to take over can be scary, and inevitably you will not want to hear everything she has to say. Her viewpoints might be unpopular, inconvenient, or otherwise at odds with the conventional life you or others have set up for yourself. So don't pressure yourself to be 100 percent on board right away, and practice self-compassion if you occasionally find yourself ignoring your intuition about what's authentic for you and what isn't.

We must also realize that our sense of authenticity and how we express it will likely shift as we age and take on new roles. Allowing this to happen is essential for growth. As Herminia Ibarra wrote in her article "The Authenticity Paradox" for *Harvard Business Review*: "The only way to avoid being pigeonholed and ultimately become better leaders is to do the things that a rigidly authentic sense of self would keep us from doing." Ibarra explains: "The notion of adhering to one true self flies in the face of research about how people evolve with experience, discovering facets of themselves they would never have unearthed through introspection alone. And being utterly transparent—disclosing every single thought and feeling—is both unrealistic and risky."

Stanford psychologist Deborah Gruenfeld describes this dilemma in presenting one's true self as managing the tension between authority and approachability. "To be authoritative, you privilege your knowledge, experience, and expertise over the team's, maintaining a measure of distance," she says. "To be approachable, you emphasize your relationships with people, their input, and their perspective, and you lead with empathy and warmth. Getting the balance right presents an acute authenticity crisis for true-to-selfers, who typically have a strong preference for behaving one way or the other."

I've been there. There have definitely been times in which I made myself *too* approachable, and it undermined my ability to assert my ideas as a capable leader. I needed to hold more distance from my employees and stakeholders to gain their confidence and get the job done.

Authenticity should be a vehicle to build trust, not to lose credibility. I've learned that when contemplating whether I should express myself, I should always ask, *Will being authentic in this situation help me build trust, or will it cause people to question me?* As an example, my Authentic Self would have angrily told male investors who acted inappropriately to piss off, but instead I pointed out their unfitting behavior and respectfully walked away. Protecting my fledgling business and my reputation were more important than my need to be authentic in that moment.

Becoming a more authentic human doesn't happen overnight. It takes a great deal of introspection and possibly assistance from a therapist or a coach. It's also not something you can do once, because as I've mentioned,

the authentic you at twenty-five is very different than the authentic you at forty-five. Developing healthy authenticity means knowing how to monitor yourself and decide what feels best to you at a given point in time.

◆Ledge Work: Visualize Letting Inauthentic Beliefs Go

Think about a time recently when your authenticity alarm went off. Perhaps you let someone push you into something you didn't feel comfortable doing, or maybe you sold yourself out in some way at work. In your journal, write about the situation and what your actions at the time tell you about your Adaptive Self's beliefs.

Then sit in a quiet room, either in silence or with some relaxing music. Close your eyes and imagine a bubbling stream with lily pads meandering across the water. On each lily pad, place a belief that's no longer working for you, and then watch that pad float away until you can't see it any longer.

Sample Situation: You agreed to lie to your VP about a project mishap because your boss asked you to cover for her.

Sample Inauthentic Belief to Release: Approval is everything, even if what I'm being asked to do is wrong.

LEDGE PROTECTOR #2: MANAGE DIFFICULT EMOTIONS

In 1986, well-known psychologist John Gottman and his colleagues built an apartment laboratory at the University of Washington known as the Love Lab. Here, they discovered the basis of intimacy and how it relates to conflict. Over the course of seven long-term studies, Gottman and his colleagues discovered that based on the way couples fought and whether there was the presence of criticism, defensiveness, contempt, and stonewalling, they could predict eventual divorce with 90 percent accuracy.

It wasn't all doom and gloom, though. In fact, the Gottman team learned that regulating one's emotions in highly charged interpersonal interactions can improve relationship outcomes. For instance, in one of Gottman's studies, the team discovered that a twenty-minute break in which arguing couples stopped talking and read magazines instead helped them reconnect with their sense of humor and affection.

Toni Parker, a psychotherapist and Gottman practitioner, offers her take on why mindfulness can be beneficial in expressing emotions in an authentic and nondamaging way. "Life is full of family, relationship, and work stressors, and as a result, difficult emotions like anger, confusion, fear, loneliness, and sadness can arise," she says on the Gottman blog. "By calming down and soothing yourself, you have space to reflect and thoughtfully respond rather than react."

This is a critical point, because whether we like it or not, emotional reactivity can result in a fall off the glass ledge.

Early in my career, I worked for a biotech communications agency in New York City. I spent countless hours on a new business pitch presentation, gathering a focus group, researching the company's technology, and auditing its current marketing assets. I even put together a spreadsheet of investor firms and press publications that fit its mission and positioning. I was 100 percent prepared to land this new client.

At a team meeting the day before the pitch, my VP said that he'd prefer one of the other (male) account executives do the presentation. This colleague had been with the firm longer, and they wanted to send someone more "credible" and "experienced," even though he had no R&D experience or a science background. Not to mention, he wasn't as prepared as I was.

My vision went dark, and I had a visceral reaction. I erupted. "This is total bullshit! Why should he get credit for all the work I put into this?"

My Authentic Self sure was in full force in that moment, but it would have been better to take a breather and gather my thoughts before expressing my disappointment. Not only was I hauled into the big boss's office, but by losing control and behaving unprofessionally, I broke my team's trust. Here are some steps, a paraphrasing of Parker's ideas, that you can take to avoid meltdowns like this.

Accept physical signs
Notice where you are feeling negativity in your body. Maybe tears are fighting their way forward or your heart is pounding. Don't push these sensations away; rather, turn toward them. If you're afraid of losing your cool, take a break somewhere private so you don't say or do something you'll later regret.

Identify and label the emotion
Give a name to the emotional feeling behind the physical symptoms. But rather than saying, "I am anxious" say, "This is anxiety." According to Parker, this way you acknowledge the presence of the emotion while remaining detached from it. As with physical signs, don't deny the emotions. Simply sit with them as best you can and be compassionate toward yourself. As Parker suggests, think of a loved one who might be having a hard time. What would you say to them?

Recognize that emotions are impermanent
All emotions, even the most difficult ones, are fleeting. If you wait for the mood to pass, it inevitably will. In the meantime, you can ask yourself: *What do I need now?* or *How can I nurture myself?* If there is another person involved, you can try to see the situation from their side, to consider their point of view with empathy.

Investigate root causes
Once the emotion is behind you, it's helpful to investigate what triggered you. Perhaps you became upset because your manager didn't engage in the manner you expected. Maybe a friend's comment about your appearance prompted insecurity or self-loathing. If you can, recall the last few times you experienced this emotion. Do you notice a pattern?

LEDGE PROTECTOR #3: USE OUTBURSTS TO STRENGTHEN RELATIONSHIPS

Whether in the office or at the mall, public displays of negative emotion are generally frowned upon. Will we live in a kinder, gentler world post-pandemic? Perhaps. Still, when you lose your cool in front of people you don't know well, even if you're 100 percent in the right, you can injure your reputation. I learned this the hard way. Inevitably, witnesses won't remember how or why the situation escalated, only the loss of control that resulted.

I'm not saying you should suppress negative emotions. It's okay to have an emotional response. You should acknowledge those feelings. But when you're done feeling, it's time to start thinking. Harnessing your emotions strategically to get what you need is a superpower. It's possible to express them productively and authentically while adapting to the situation and without turning people off.

As an example, when I first felt passion about the fight for women's voices and equality, I immediately defaulted as a frustrated and rebellious type of advocate. Because that's how I truly felt. I thought those emotions would be more effective in driving change, but I learned that an incendiary approach immediately shuts down the conversation. I then worked on channeling my anger into the motivation to educate and influence.

I haven't been perfect. Sometimes my feelings get the best of me and emotional outbreaks happen, but when they do, it doesn't have to be the end of the world. Beating yourself up for a normal human reaction to a stressful or anger-producing situation won't help you move on; instead, it will keep you ruminating about the incident for days or even months to come. Owning your behavior will keep you from careening off the glass ledge.

How do you do this? First, remember that outbursts and emotionally charged conversations often occur when you feel offended, disrespected, insulted, triggered, or hurt. By using these upsets as an opportunity to validate, process, and articulate your emotions, you can authentically re-build trust with the people involved.

If you ever feel you need to apologize, make sure it's for inappropriate behavior rather than the feelings that led to it.

For instance, in the work pitch situation I shared, I later apologized, not for being frustrated but for the impulsive way I expressed that frustration. I went back to my team and said: "I want to apologize for inappropriately raising my voice earlier today and talking negatively about another colleague. It's not how I wanted to approach the situation. I strongly believe that I deserve to be the one leading the pitch meeting after developing all the material, and I let that anger control me in the moment." I went on to explain, confidently instead of offensively, why I would add greater value to the presentation than my colleague. My willingness to repair the situation partially restored my credibility and my team's compassion for me—and I got back the pitch meeting.

So if you've lost control in a situation, don't be afraid to acknowledge the incident. Although it's far easier to pretend nothing happened, the "sweep it under the rug" approach will not reflect well on your maturity. Addressing the issue upfront, in person, and one on one is admittedly awkward, so writing down your key messages in advance can buffer. Once in front of the person involved, be sincere and genuinely contrite about any inappropriate behavior. In an even and diplomatic tone, outline your position and what you would like to see happen next. Keep the conversation short, and close by thanking the person for their understanding.

Most likely, one meltdown will not end a career or oust you from a social circle, but you do want to prevent repeat performances. In that vein, follow the earlier advice on paying attention to the physical signs of negative emotions and understanding root causes and triggers. You can also practice how you might react if you find yourself in a similarly agitated state. For example, if you have responded angrily to project feedback in the past, it might be worth rehearsing what you'll say and do to stay calm the next time you receive such feedback. The preparation will also help you confidently project the best aspects of your Authentic Self.

LEDGE PROTECTOR #4: SHIFT YOUR ATTITUDE TOWARD THE POSITIVE

Of course, it's easier to manage emotions that are gentler, and when we can maintain a positive attitude, we often find that the negative side of our Authentic Self is thwarted. Several research studies illustrate the tangible power of positivity.

One such study, conducted at Kings College, showed that positive visualization could replace negative thoughts. Researchers asked participants in one group to generate mental images of positive outcomes to worrisome topics, in another group to generate verbal descriptions of positive outcomes to worrisome topics, and in a third group to generate positive images unrelated to current problems. Members of all three groups reported significantly fewer negative thoughts during the study period, and every individual reported less worry and anxiety overall. From this, the researchers concluded that doing any positive ideation decreases worry and increases joy.

To learn more about the benefit of a positive attitude, we can also look to the plentiful literature on happiness. Multiple studies cited in a roundup by the American Psychological Association have found that positive mood and optimism are associated with comparatively better health as measured by health problems reported, such as missed days from work due to sickness and hospitalization.

Taken together, the APA-cited studies illustrate that over time, positive thinking enables people to build social, physical, and intellectual capital and to create emotions such as happiness, joy, resilience, and contentment. This reminds me of the saying, "You get what you give." A positive attitude shows up in your interactions with others and prompts people to be positive in return. It also affords us the grace to weather life's crises and obstacles, so that we get over them sooner and return to more favorable circumstances.

But what if a positive attitude doesn't come naturally to you? As a naturally anxious person, I've been there. The good news is that it's something you can work on over time using these strategies.

Pay attention to your thoughts

While there are some situations that are unavoidably bad, like getting sick or losing your job, you can choose your response to such situations.

For example, it may be natural to feel depression after a breakup, but by focusing on the positive aspects of a relationship ending (like the opportunity to reinvent yourself), you can rediscover your light more quickly. You can create a reality of recovering and exploring rather than wallowing in heartbreak.

Repeat positive affirmations

Self-talk is a reoccurring theme in this book, and again it applies strongly here. By placing positive and encouraging sayings around your physical space and reading them out loud every time you pass by, you'll gradually come to believe them and align your Authentic Self. One of my favorite sayings, for instance, is, "If you don't like the scenery, keep looking out the window. Eventually it will change." This affirmation has helped me during many dark days, when it felt like my pain would last forever. To make working with positive affirmations less boring and more effective, I play them on YouTube every night before I fall asleep, letting my subconscious mind absorb them. This is now a regular part of my night routine, and it really does help me wake up more positive and grateful every morning.

Put yourself in feel-good situations

As you might have gathered from the story about my new business pitch presentation, I was a bit of a hothead when I was younger. I cringe remembering how comfortable I was being overtly confrontational and dramatic when I was angry at someone. I wore it like a badge of honor, but in retrospect, that kind of fire only alienated people. Eventually, I challenged that aspect of my Authentic Self and nurtured my Adaptive Self. I saw that not every frustrating situation requires a big reaction. I adopted a new mantra for myself: *When you feel disrespect, choose distance.* Today, when faced with negativity, I choose not to return the energy. I just remove myself and put myself in a feel-good situation instead.

Life cannot always be rainbows and sunshine, but you can help your Authentic Self be more positive by surrounding yourself with optimistic company and using conversation topics and language that bolster rather than sabotage your spirits. For example, it's tough to remain upbeat when your circle of friends is judgmental, critical, and gossipy. Regularly engaging in personal and professional pursuits that energize you and picking a form of exercise that boosts your endorphins will also help to sustain positivity over the long term.

Enjoy the support of other women

We have a whole chapter coming up about handling competition, and one of the strategies, "winning together," also reinforces a positive attitude. Fostering a community of ambitious and driven women at SWAAY, I've noticed that as a group we lift each other up and tend to be more creative and optimistic together. I've tried to create a culture in which authenticity means bringing your unique perspective to the table without worrying about whether someone will use it as an opening to co-opt the edge for themselves.

Seek inspiration from art, music, and literature

Especially in the past few years, both traditional media and online media have become quite polarizing. Watching too much political news or looking obsessively at your friends' pristine Insta feeds can wreak havoc on your positivity. At the same time, there are literally millions of books and songs that can get your thoughts flowing in the right direction, helping you discover the sunniest side of your Authentic Self.

My friend Nia Franklin has been a composer all her life. She has written over a hundred songs, including one she began performing at age five. Nia decided to fulfill her Authentic Self with an undergraduate degree in composition from East Carolina University, but during her freshman year, her father was diagnosed with non-Hodgkin's lymphoma. Nia became his stem cell donor. She also needed to pay for school, which led her to seek scholarships with the Miss America organization. Nia was crowned Miss Five Boroughs at the age of twenty-three and went on to win Miss New York 2018 and Miss America 2019. For the Miss America competition, Nia wowed the judges and audience with her unique rendition of "Quando me'n vo" from Puccini's *La Bohème*.

Now, Nia finds herself balancing her Authentic Self, a musician at heart, with the business opportunities available to her as a former Miss America. Even with such a high profile, it hasn't always been easy. "Authenticity is so important to me as an artist, and I have had to navigate being true to myself in a field where people don't often look like me," she told me. "As a Black woman, I can't deny the influences that are important to me. Even though I'm in the classical field, I also write music that is soulful. If someone doesn't like that, I don't worry about controlling how they feel."

Voices from the SWAAY Community

Embracing Your Inner Unicorn

Jenny Block

For as long as I can remember, people have told me that talking to me or spending time with me always makes them feel really good about themselves and how they are making their way in the world. The truth is most humans have two very basic desires that need to be fulfilled: they need to be heard, and they need to be a part of the herd. They need to be "a unicorn."

Being a unicorn is all about living authentically and unapologetically. The unicorn is herself, no more and no less. Being a unicorn is about learning how to take care of yourself, others, and the world at large without losing yourself or hurting the people around you. Life is not all ribbons and roses, and that's okay. Sometimes you're going to want to spend a whole Saturday in bed, and that's okay. You're always okay even if nothing else seems to be okay.

Too much of life, especially when it comes to work, is about leaning in or sucking it up. Too much is about always having to turn our hobbies into hustles. Too much is about either climbing over other people or never getting the promotion and the recognition we deserve. There's nothing in between.

Perhaps the hardest place to be a unicorn is at work. Even if you're one of the lucky ones who loves her job, work is hard. Otherwise, as the saying goes, it wouldn't be work. But not allowing yourself to be distracted by other people's less-than-unicorn-worthy behavior and instead going full unicorn yourself, even when you'd rather go the way of the snake, will help you to feel good about what you do.

My dad says I've never gotten a job for which I'm qualified, so I suppose I've always been a unicorn. I figure, with a little magic, I'll be able to figure it out. And so far, so good. A unicorn says, "Yes." A unicorn says, "I can do that." Sure, this won't work for being a brain surgeon or a commercial pilot, but there are a plethora of jobs for which it will work. And if you already are a brain surgeon or a commercial pilot, it can certainly get you to the next level in your career—whatever that might be!

Unicorns also tend to reinvent themselves. I've been an actress, a law student, a production assistant, a college professor, an artist's model, a dance teacher, a camp activities director, a speaker, and an author about sex. I wanted to do all of those things. I knew deep down that I could do all of those things. So I used my skills at one job to help me to get a position in another.

Working takes work. There's no getting around that. As with everything else, the only thing we can change is ourselves, our attitudes, and our reactions. So you have to ask yourself, "What's it going to be?" If your answer is the way of the unicorn, you're already on the right track.

"Unlock Your Inner Unicorn" by Jenny Block was published on SWAAY.com. Jenny is the author of *The Ultimate Guide to Solo Sex* and *O Wow: Discovering Your Ultimate Orgasm.*

LEADERSHIP SPOTLIGHT

In an article for *Harvard Business Review*, executive coach Ron Carucci describes a client who went out of her way to develop a work environment where people feel safe sharing their emotions. As a result, Tim, one of the client's most talented designers, was comfortable admitting his insecurities to his team. Eventually, though, Tim's bottomless need for reassurance rubbed people the wrong way. "I don't want to lose his talent," Anna, Ron's client, told him, "but I don't have the energy to manage him."

Carucci explains that there are several ways employees can be emotionally needy, including asking the same questions, needing constant affirmation, oversharing, and struggling to receive and cope with feedback. This might be better described as too much vulnerability rather than too much authenticity. Vulnerability in the self-improvement realm nearly always has an emotional component (i.e., being susceptible to emotional wounding), whereas authenticity doesn't necessarily involve such emotion (i.e., authenticity is more about understanding your true self and being willing to show it to others). I want to make the distinction that being authentic doesn't mean you are also vulnerable.

Even in a chapter that's mostly about authenticity and not vulnerability, this is a good place to explore what you might do if you are a leader and an emotionally needy employee is bringing the rest of the team down.

According to Carucci, emotionally needy people often don't realize the degree to which they drain others because their strong feelings are the norm for them. To learn about their awareness of others' boundaries, schedule a one-on-one meeting. "Use this time to ask them questions and gauge if they are aware of the impact their behavior is having on their peers," says Carucci. "Back up your questions with specific behavioral examples, and be proscriptive, drawing clear distinctions between which emotional expressions and needs are appropriate, which are problematic, and why."

Some leaders abandon their efforts after this first conversation, but entrenched behaviors die hard. If you want to see change, you may have to revisit the issue. For example, Carucci's client told her employee Tim: "I'm not sure how else I can reassure you about the quality of your work. What I need you to do is reflect on why the reassurance I've offered hasn't worked. I'd like you to be especially curious about where your need for extra reassurance is coming from so you can be more self-sufficient when you're feeling insecure."

If the emotionally needy employee is trying to take your feedback, continue to demonstrate that you're in their corner. Reiterate that you care about them and your relationship, and don't let other team members talk behind the person's back. Tolerating a stream of gossip and complaints about the person in question will jeopardize the psychological safety of your whole team.

Remember, while a leader's job is to understand each employee's needs and adjust their approach to an employee's unique temperaments, there is a limit. It is not your job to be an employee's therapist. If you find yourself slipping into this role, gently extricate yourself. Whether your employee requires professional intervention or practice learning to care for themselves, familiarize yourself with your company's employee assistance resources so you can recommend them. This is what they are there for!

CUE THE REAL WORLD

Now that we've discussed authenticity from a variety of angles, let's explore how to use the ledge protectors in this chapter to validate your feelings and encourage a positive response from others. Write your ideas in your journal.

- Describe your Authentic Self and your Adaptive Self each in a few sentences. How do they differ, and are any of the gaps problematic?

- Have you ever allowed a negative emotion to get out of control? What was the result? How might you handle such a situation differently after reading this chapter?

- Describe a time in your life when it was difficult to maintain a positive attitude. What strategies did you use then, and what new strategies do you think you could add?

AUTHENTICITY LEDGE REVIEW

- The **Adaptive Self** helps us function in difficult and confusing times, while the **Authentic Self** helps us feel whole, real, and self-confident. We need to dialogue with both of them to identify their motivations.
- When we are authentic, we know what it means to be our whole and complete selves and are willing to show this to others. We've given substantial thought to **who we are and who we are not** and to who we were in the past and who we are now.
- All emotions, even the most difficult ones, are fleeting. If you **wait for the mood to pass**, it inevitably will. In the meantime, you can ask yourself, *What do I need now?* or *How can I nurture myself?*
- Harnessing your emotions to get what you need is a superpower. It's possible to **express your emotions productively** and authentically while adapting to a situation and not turning people off.
- If you've lost your cool, **practice how you might react** if you find yourself in a similarly agitated state in the future. For example, if you have responded angrily to project feedback in the past, rehearse how you'll stay calm the next time you receive feedback.

"Let's just kiss and make up."

"I'm just going to stay out of this."

"Do I really need to make this into a problem?"

"The worst thing about work? The difficult people."

"It's easier not to bring it up."

"I'll just do a workaround to accommodate this person's limitations."

"I could never tell them how I really feel! They'd be crushed."

"When it comes to confrontation, I'll do anything to avoid it."

"If I talk to someone in charge, it'll come back to haunt me."

"But I want to have the last word. I'm right!"

Chapter Five

CONFLICT

can't believe I have to do this, but I have to let you go. I can no longer afford to pay you."

I felt like I was about to throw up. They all looked at me, completely surprised and confused. My team knew our fundraising process was a challenging one, but it seemed they hadn't considered that it would come down to this moment. And truthfully, neither did I!

"Wow, so that's it? All this hard work for nothing? So am I given two weeks then? You know, so I can find another job?"

My shareholders were urging me to lay off most of our staff to keep the business afloat while figuring out the fundraising hurdle. I was running out of capital, and there was no way I could pay my staff for the following two weeks.

"I am sorry, but your termination is effective immediately. Today is your last day."

Prior to this moment, I had never "fired" anyone, and as an up-and-coming leader, I didn't feel great about handling conflict and unpleasant situations because I wanted to be liked.

The conversation escalated, and the next thing I knew, one team member was crying, bemoaning what she was going to do next, and blaming me for the challenging scenario she was now in.

My team had worked just as hard as I had to get the business off the ground. Letting them go felt horrible. I had failed them, the first people to believe in what was once a simple idea. As soon as I got home, I vomited. My stomach was in my throat in the weeks that followed. That scene played over and over again in my head. Was I too soft? Too harsh? Should I have been more assertive and unemotional?

And to think that I had once dreamed of a diplomatic career. I didn't know I was nowhere near ready for that role because my approach to conflict needed major work. As an aspiring entrepreneur, I also needed to get comfortable being uncomfortable. But I found that I had a built-in resistance to conflict that would take a lot of practice to break down.

In an article for Quartz, journalist Josie Glausiusz wonders if the world would be more peaceful if there were more women leaders. The answers she received from experts are surprising.

Political scientists Mary Caprioli and Mark Boyer counted ten military crises in the twentieth century involving four female leaders. Studying four centuries of European monarchs, professors Oeindrila Dube and S. P. Harish found that countries ruled by queens were 27 percent more likely than kings to participate in interstate conflicts. One notable example? Catherine the Great, who became empress of Russia in 1762 following the assassination of her husband Peter III, led military campaigns that extended the borders of Russia by 520,000 square kilometers.

Given the small number of women leaders throughout history, it's difficult to answer Glausiusz's question definitively. And there is plenty of research to support women as peacemakers.

For instance, Glausiusz notes that states are more likely to achieve lasting peace post-conflict when women are invited to the negotiating table. Women make up a tiny number of diplomats, but their impact is significant. The US nonprofit Inclusive Security researched 182 signed peace agreements between 1989 and 2011 and found that agreements were 35 percent more likely to last at least fifteen years if women were included as negotiators, mediators, and signatories.

Throughout this book, we've looked at women's communication strengths, and these are certainly in play here. "Women succeed as mediators and negotiators because of qualities traditionally perceived as feminine and maternal," writes Glausiusz. "In Northern Ireland, Somalia, and South Africa, female participants in peace processes earned a reputation for fostering dialogue and engaging all sides. They are also often seen as honest brokers, more trustworthy and less threatening, because they act outside formal power structures."

Taken together, this research tells me that

women can be powerful participants in conflict when we want to be, and acting like men doesn't necessarily help us to be more effective.

Instead, we must recognize that conflict is an inevitable reality in the human experience. It's everywhere, and smoothing over difficult situations to avoid confrontation doesn't always serve us.

Conflict can be especially damaging in the workplace. The CPP Global Human Capital Report found that US employees spend more than two hours a week engaged in disagreements that disrupt the flow of work. This translates into an unbelievable $300 billion paid hours or 400 million workdays. Among the other findings:

- Nearly 30 percent of employees deal with conflict almost constantly.
- Nearly 50 percent of conflict is a result of personality clashes and warring egos.
- 27 percent of employees have witnessed conflicts lead to personal attacks.
- 25 percent of employees have seen conflict result in sickness or absence.
- Nearly 10 percent of employees have seen workplace conflict cause a project to fail.

In his well-known theory of competition and cooperation, social psychologist Morton Deutsch maintains that there are two attitudes we can choose when presented with conflict. In choosing the competition attitude, someone has to lose if I am going to win. Conflicts defined by this attitude include impaired communication, obstruction, stonewalling, and repeated disagreements and typically result in diminished performance.

On the other hand, an attitude of cooperation promotes conflict as an opportunity to achieve shared goals. Conflicting interests don't have to lead to war if we think of them as a mutual problem to solve. If we approach the problem in a way that benefits everyone—through respect, helpfulness, trust, and coordination of effort—we all win.

The attitude of cooperation requires that we acknowledge conflict, though.

But we women would sometimes rather accept all the responsibility than risk making the people around us uncomfortable.

We might avoid addressing a small disagreement until it grows into a relationship problem. As evidenced by the #metoo phenomenon, we often fail to stand up against harassment because we think our personal and professional lives will suffer for it. Or worse? We might not want to put the perpetrator's career or personal life at risk.

Indeed, conflict represents an especially sharp edge of the glass ledge. Let's now delve deeper into how to resolve conflicts objectively, how to deliver bad news or "hurt someone's feelings" while being kind and direct, how to cope with abusive people, and how to know when it's best to disagree and move on.

LEDGE PROTECTOR #1: RESOLVE CONFLICTS PRODUCTIVELY

When I had to pick a sport, I chose tennis because I wouldn't have to deal with team conflicts. When I launched SWAAY, I wanted to do it as a lone founder for the express reason that two or more people going into business together often resulted in—you guessed it—conflict. I was confident in my vision and values and didn't think a cofounder or partners were necessary.

But a few years ago, while going through a rough patch with the lack of capital, I confided in one of my closest friends who also founded a tech start-up. She understood what I was going through, as she'd been there herself. After spending a lot of time together, we thought it made sense to join forces and potentially bring our respective businesses together under one roof.

She stepped in as an official shareholder and partner, and under her leadership and mentorship, SWAAY had one of its most successful years. We worked well together, and for once I thought I could fully trust someone with my business: the good and the bad.

Over time, though, I sensed a misalignment was growing in how we perceived the value of our respective brands within the merging organization. There were both conflicts of vision, interests, and leadership style. For months I ignored my true feelings about the situation and tried to rationalize my lack of excitement and satisfaction with the proposed deal. I wanted to make this work so badly so that my friend and I could both be happy.

I sat through a series of legal calls in which I felt undermined. I told myself I was being an egotistical founder, that this was a good opportunity for SWAAY. In trying so hard to avoid a conflict with another person, I ran into a more damaging one, a conflict with myself. The more my intuition and logic fought with each other and the stronger the inner voices grew, the more I tried to see the situation for what it wasn't. I talked to my legal counselors, my financial adviser, and a few shareholders. I delved more deeply into the paperwork. I wanted to be as impartial as possible, knowing that in saying no to the deal, I might also lose a friend and a mentor. But in the end, I simply asked myself: *What's more important, following my gut to protect my interests or ignoring it to protect another person's interests?*

The answer led to an honest conversation with my friend about why her proposed structure and offer didn't work for me. At that point, she made it clear there was no room for negotiation, and we decided to part ways. Although it was an amicable separation, there's no denying how emotionally difficult the process was for me.

When faced with a situation like this, or even one that arises more suddenly, the worst thing you can do is react in a way you'll regret later as a result of avoiding the discomfort of conflict. Therefore, the first step in resolving conflict productively is to take a time-out. Take some deep breaths, scream into a pillow, or vent to a friend if you need to, and when you've calmed down, try to reflect objectively on the situation.

Few are as skilled at conflict resolution than project managers. After pausing your initial knee-jerk reaction to a conflicted situation, Natalie Semczuk—who writes for the Digital Project Manager website—suggests you next consider the best way to proceed. "If the conflict was part of a larger dynamic (a meeting involving several people, a flurry of emails, or a small conflict within a bigger discussion), it might be best to wait to address this until later," she writes. "Acknowledge that there is conflict on the table, that it should be returned to after a period of time, and move on."

Your next move is to address the conflict in private because you want the parties involved to feel free to express themselves in a safe place without commentary from the peanut gallery. This private conversation can take place in person, via video chat, phone, email, or instant message. If you want to ensure a diplomatic discussion, a written format allows you and the other to think through responses before sharing them. The method you choose depends on individual preferences. My personal advice: always keep a paper trail, or as the cool kids call them these days "receipts." Receipts are especially important if the issue is workplace related.

It's difficult to broach a conflict, but try not to let your discomfort stop you from initiating a response. "Frame the conversation by stating that a conflict occurred, and reinforce the fact that everyone should have a chance to express their understanding and feelings about the situation—and then allow them to have that chance," advises Semczuk.

Note that initiating a response should not include going around the person with whom you have the conflict. Have you ever worked or been friends with a woman who would complain or gossip constantly to you about someone else rather than going directly to the source? It was irritating, right? Not only will this approach fail to solve the conflict, but it may also cause you to lose respect from the other person or people you've now involved in the situation.

My dearest friend Michelle McClean has been a model since she was thirteen, and in 1992, at nineteen, she won the world's most prestigious pageant: Miss Universe. We met in 2018 when we both judged Miss Universe in Thailand, and ever since I've been so inspired by her background, charisma, and success. She's had many diverse opportunities, from hosting a TV show and directing a property company to launching a jewelry business and consulting in solar energy for her home country of Namibia.

We reconnected at the Miss USA 2020 pageant while I was there to judge the teen competition. We caught up over drinks and talked all things business and pageantry. At the time, I was knee-deep in passive-aggressive emails and never-ending legal negotiations pertaining to my company's potential merger. Michelle offered some valuable advice: "I approach every personal and business scenario with the mindset of putting myself in the other person's shoes first. I always try to think, *How would I like to be approached?* I'll be honest and transparent about my point of view, then give them an opportunity to share their thoughts and suggestions."

She was right. Up until then, I hadn't thought much about the other party's point of view. With that perspective shift, I could navigate the conflict with more openness and empathy. I chose to see my friend and her company in a positive light because of the opportunities they'd brought to the table rather than an entity that was out to get me. Instead of dreading the back-and-forth emails, I thought of them as a way to preserve healthy communication between the two sides, no matter the outcome.

In your conflict situation, once the other person or people have had their say without interruption, it's useful to repeat back to them what you heard to make sure you fully understand their viewpoint. Resist the urge to immediately fill in any silences, because although these can be awkward, they can also mean that people want to respond thoughtfully. Respect the silence.

Hopefully, clearing the air will kill the conflict on the first try, but even so, it's wise to follow up. After everyone has had a chance to consider the resolution, reach out again, thank the involved parties for their collaboration, and communicate that you are open to continuing the dialogue.

"It's about compassion first, and then objectives," Michelle told me. "I want to get buy-in so people end up being excited and passionate and willing to support me and each other." I'm so grateful to Michelle for helping me turn a potentially destructive conflict into a constructive one. Not only were my friend and I able to move on peacefully, I learned important lessons along the way.

◆ Ledge Work: Change the Way You Think About Conflict

Conflict can be an opportunity, opening the door for something new and even better to come into your life. Think back to a recent conversation about conflict in which you shared your needs, boundaries, and common goals that led to an improvement in your relationship or workflow with another person.

What was the situation?

What was your strategy for broaching the conflict successfully?

What was the outcome? How do you feel about the situation now, and how has your personal or professional relationship with the person involved fared over time?

How can you shift the way you think about conflict so the next time you're in a similar scenario, you view it as an opportunity rather than an obstacle?

◆

LEDGE PROTECTOR #2: COMMUNICATE UPSETTING NEWS WITH DIGNITY

No one ever wants to deliver a message another person doesn't want to hear. But refusing to do so or taking so long that the person or people get the news from somewhere else, when it should be coming from you, is how we fall off the glass ledge. It undermines our power and influence and makes us appear wishy-washy. The most effective way to reduce your fear is to prepare for the situation in advance. An extemporaneous conversation may feel more authentic to you, but you run the risk of saying something that could make the situation worse.

Remember what we discussed in the previous chapter? Authenticity isn't always your best friend. It's a good idea to script your remarks, including a brief and honest explanation of what's happening and a justification for any unpopular decisions. Whether said decisions were your call or not, you should be able to communicate why your news reflects the most appropriate course of action.

For instance, if you have to tell a friend why you can't go to their wedding or an employee why you have to lay them off, you want to make sure the other person understands that you did your best to look at all possibilities and that the decision weighs heavily on you.

In an article for *Forbes*, Alina Morkin of Voices.com recommends that you are also clear about what you don't want to say or can't say. "Sometimes more detail can confuse the issue unnecessarily," she says.

Once the initial script is complete, anticipate the other person's reaction. Might you be accused of unfairness or nefarious motives? Might the conversation grow antagonistic? What questions can you expect? Think through how you will maintain control, showing compassion for the other person while also being as direct as possible. How can you acknowledge the person's frustrations and validate any negative feelings without being overly apologetic? And while no one likes a sugar coater, you don't want to be a soulless machine either. There's a reason we still prefer humans for these discussions!

Keep in mind that people receiving upsetting news may try to negotiate. If there isn't room for this, say so.

Giving someone false hope and having to backtrack later is a surefire way to permanently damage the relationship.

If you handle it properly, being the bearer of unpleasant news doesn't mean you are severing ties or even that relations between you will be embarrassing for all time. In most situations, everyone involved will eventually move on. "In my experience, if you give customers, employees, and anyone else the feeling that the situation is treated with transparency, responsibility, and accountability, and if you are forthcoming and honest, it will lead to renewed trust," says Pini Yakuel of Optimove in *Forbes*.

LEDGE PROTECTOR #3: COPE (AND MAINTAIN YOUR SANITY) WITH ABUSIVE PEOPLE

Gretchen Carlson grew to be a household name as a result of her time on morning television, but before that she was also Miss America. That whirlwind year in 1989 should have been the most exciting of her life, but instead it was traumatic. While Gretchen should have been traveling around the country, freely celebrating her achievements, she was suffering silently from unwanted sexual advances by high-powered executives.

Years later, Gretchen became one of the first women to shatter the notion of "socially acceptable" sexual harassment. In July 2016, she filed a lawsuit against Roger Ailes, chairman and CEO of Fox News. Fox fired Ailes and paid Gretchen a $20 million settlement. She went on to write a book, *Be Fierce*, and launch the Gretchen Carlson Leadership Initiative, which offers advocacy training to underserved women. She also founded the nonprofit Lift Our Voices to eradicate silencing mechanisms in the workplace (such as forced arbitration clauses and nondisclosure agreements) that protect harassers, and she has lobbied Congress with her bill to end forced arbitration in workplace contracts.

I first learned about Gretchen when I picked up a copy of *Time* magazine in October 2016, two days after I officially launched SWAAY. Tearing up as I paged through the article, I read how Gretchen handled one of the biggest conflicts in her life, one that would go on to become a catalyst for the #metoo revolution. Her courage to stand up to one of the biggest and most powerful men in media gave me the strength and hope I needed to assert myself when dealing with abusive potential investors.

A few months later, my adviser Fran Hauser (whom you met in chapter 2) introduced me to Gretchen. She loved SWAAY's mission and immediately became an investor and mentor. To this day, whenever I find myself in uncomfortable situations with men who abuse their power, I ask myself, *What would Gretchen do?*

And when it comes to difficult people, we've all been there. A neighbor who willfully disturbs the peace. A friend who tells you to lose weight every time you see them. A boss who lets loose on you in a meeting. An unappreciative client who oversteps your boundaries. We'd like to think that after surviving childhood, we've left bullying behind. Unfortunately, adults can be cruel too. But how can you decide if a certain behavior is abusive versus simply annoying? And what can you do about it?

Let's start with verbal abuse.

Generally speaking, another person is abusive if they make comments that are meant to intimidate, degrade, or humiliate.

Instances of verbal abuse might include spreading malicious gossip or lies, screaming or cursing, making damaging accusations, and threatening someone's safety or livelihood.

If you are dealing with an abusive person in your life, how you proceed may depend on whether the abuser is breaking the law. In the workplace, for example, the Equal Employment Opportunity Commission describes harassment as "unwelcome conduct based on race, color, religion, sex, national origin, age, disability, or genetic information." Verbal offenses like insults, slurs, and jokes are included under this umbrella, and according to InHerSight blogger Abbey Slattery, if you're unsure whether verbal abuse is subject to legal action, ask yourself these four questions:

- Have the incidents been unwelcome?
- Has the discrimination targeted me based on a protected characteristic?
- Have the comments happened multiple times over an extended period of time?
- From both an objective and subjective point of view, have the incidents been hostile?

In the event of workplace abuse, many organizations have human resources (HR) departments, or at least an HR representative, that can assist. In addition to verbal abuse that meets the above criteria, you might consider approaching HR if any of the following are relevant:

- You witness or are asked to participate in an illegal act, such as stealing from the company or distributing proprietary materials.
- Your office space is unhealthy and/or your management isn't taking proper precautions to keep you safe (as was sadly the case with many employers during the COVID pandemic).

- A manager or a coworker has harmed you physically or sexually, has intimated that they might harm you physically or sexually, or has made sexual innuendos or comments that make you uncomfortable.
- You experience overt discrimination, such as a supervisor who only promotes certain team members despite equal accomplishments and skills.

Prepare for your HR meeting by compiling written documentation of the abuse, including a description of each situation, when and where it occurred, and what was said.

If a manager or a coworker is simply mean or making it somewhat difficult to do your job, the decision to go to HR is a little murkier. While sometimes HR representatives can help with basic interpersonal conflict, there are risks. If it's in the best interest of the business, your rep may side with the more senior person in the conflict. At the very least, you should expect that your complaints will get back to the abuser and you may experience retaliation. Factor this into your course of action.

Gretchen Carlson had some terrific advice for me on this exact subject. "Oftentimes what happens is women put up with it for a long time, and then they suddenly decide one day, 'I'm going to do something about it,' and they go complain but they don't have a plan. You can't put the genie back in the bottle once you speak up. You have to document everything as well as tell trusted friends, so you have alibis and evidence. That's number one." Gretchen also warns to be careful of HR, preferring instead that women approach an ombudsman or an outside, independent resource. She recommends the website BetterBrave.com to link up with an attorney if necessary. She also advocates for companies to truly conduct independent investigations of all toxic workplace issues to avoid the inherent conflict of interest when HR handles the claims.

The stress of ongoing conflict will take a toll on you psychologically and physically, so it should be addressed in some manner. If the issue is in the verbal abuse category, you could try to work it out with the abuser. Done effectively, talking to the person directly might resolve the problem, whether the context is work, home, or community. It's surprising how many people lack self-awareness, and it's quite possible your abuser doesn't realize their behavior is harmful. Schedule a meeting—in person if you can manage it—when neither of you is too busy nor surrounded by other people. In the conversation, be as diplomatic and approachable as you can. Briefly outline why you are there, using "I" statements to prevent defensiveness and avoiding blanket comments about the person's motives or intentions. For instance, say:

> "I don't feel valued during our team meetings when you dismiss my ideas before I have the chance to elaborate."
> Instead of: "You're jealous that I have more ideas to present, and you are threatened by that because you think you're better than me."

Or

> "I feel anxious coming to you with performance issues because I worry you'll take it personally."
> Instead of: "Every time I give you feedback, you think I'm out to get you."

If you and the other person still don't see eye to eye, it can't hurt to get a second opinion. An objective third party, such as a coworker, a friend, or a family member who knows both of you, can offer insights.

LEDGE PROTECTOR #4: LEARN TO DISAGREE AND MOVE ON

This protector approach is my personal favorite of late. As a former depressed adolescent who dealt with anger through therapy, I learned the benefits of letting go. There are scenarios in life that require tense conversations, even if not outright conflict. Being able to listen to another point of view, discuss an issue civilly, and agree to disagree without having the last word are all important skills. So let's say you need or want to present an argument to a person you know or suspect has a different point of view. Take note of these tips.

Decide if it's worth it

Before you engage in a debate, think through what you're hoping to accomplish. If your goal is to seek understanding, that's one thing. But if you won't feel vindicated unless you change the other person's mind, try to evaluate that likelihood realistically. While some people thrive on contentious conversations, others shrink from them. Bringing up a hot-button issue could do more harm than good.

Make a factual case

Disagreements only become problematic when people allow their emotions to get the best of them. Don't lead with unfounded opinions, and express your ideas using logic and wisdom. It's critical you keep your tone even and approach the person in conciliatory (versus attack) mode, using neutral examples that won't set off an immediate explosion.

Inquire about the other perspective

According to *Today Show* source Holly Weeks, the author of *Failure to Communicate: How Conversations Go Wrong and What You Can Do to Right Them*, you can open with something like: "I know conservatives have strong opinions about X issue, but I'm not as familiar with why they feel this way about Y issue." While it's appropriate to ask questions and fully listen to the answers (as opposed to simply waiting for your chance to respond or tuning out ideas you believe are incorrect or offensive), there's no need to apologize for your own beliefs.

"Legitimize their point of view (yes, I understand that you want to spend more money now and invest in a higher-quality couch we'll have for a while) and then explain why you disagree (but if we do that, we'll have to use some of the money we've set aside for travel this year)," says Weeks. "It helps put edges around the problem and focus on which problem you need to solve."

Look for the good

Rarely will you disagree 100 percent with another person's ideas. There has to be something there with which you can get on board. As Muse.com writer Kat Boogaard suggests, you can say something like, "I definitely think you're on the right track in saying that we need to improve our customer response time. But what if we did it this way instead?" Here the idea is shared in a way that's friendly and collaborative and not at all accusatory. While you're at it, I would go a step further and suggest avoiding the word *but*. Acknowledging a point is moot when you follow your "yes" with a "but."

Accept a stalemate if you must

The other person may not come around, and unless they are your child or work for you directly, they probably don't have to.

"Perhaps one of the most important pieces of respectfully disagreeing with someone is knowing when you need to just call it quits and move on," says Boogaard. "No, it's not always easy to swallow your pride and walk away—particularly when you feel strongly about your side. But sometimes it's the best thing you can do." Try not to hold the difference of opinion against the other person and instead focus on the aspects of your life or work you can control.

I have known Cate Luzio for a few years now. We met when her publicist reached out to SWAAY about a feature story on her newly launched venture, Luminary. Cate's company is a collaboration hub for women to grow professionally and expand their networks. I was thrilled not only to get a hard-hat tour of her space in Manhattan but also become a member when Luminary officially opened its doors in late 2018. A former banker turned entrepreneur, Cate has been in a lot of situations where she's had to confront those with different perspectives. "Even if you know you don't agree, be transparent," she advises. "And sooner rather than later. Don't let it fester, because there will be long-term pain for you, the other party, and those around you. Communicate openly, and think through the other person's point of view before you respond. It may not always work out the way you want, but nine times out of ten there will be a resolution."

Even if there isn't, being proactive will improve your outlook. And approaching a conflict or a disagreement isn't always about winning. "I recall asking a former boss for a raise and being told no," Cate shares. "I went back to him after that conversation, summarized what I'd heard, and laid out a plan for getting the extra money. Ultimately, he still didn't agree, but at least I articulated my points well."

Now that's a boss move!

Voices from the SWAAY Community

Finding Your Own Voice in Conflict

Dr. Nikki Goldstein

Recently, I was helping a friend through a breakup. It was sad, as they are both great people, but I struggled to understand sometimes exactly why she wanted to end her long-term relationship in the first place.

It felt as though she knew what she wanted but just didn't have the right words. As she continued to pour her heart out to me, I had a moment of realization. After nine years, she didn't have much of a voice in her relationship. And now that she was speaking up and speaking up louder, her concerns, needs, wants, desires, and dreams were not being truly heard, and maybe never were.

When thinking about the number one thing women are doing that can hurt them in a relationship, this is the one thing I feel commonly comes back to bite us, especially in heterosexual relationships.

As common as it is, it's also not completely our fault. From a very young age, women are taught to be pleasing. Little girls are demure and gentle princesses, while boys are encouraged to be rough and tough. We are progressing away from these backward and limiting gender stereotypes and moving toward a more inclusive society, but I still often hear the reasoning "because he is a boy" or "because she is a girl."

Our birth sex should not determine how we act and relate with people. I often wonder if these traits excuse or encourage a gender in the way they behave. But is it a matter of DNA or social conditioning? And when it comes to young girls being passive and pleasing, social conditioning is what I fear the most.

Women are often valued for being in a relationship, as though they are worthy because someone chooses to be with them. We also commonly teach women not to be too aggressive, too bitchy, too demanding, a ball breaker—if she is in a relationship with a man. But often in these messages, what we do is tell women they should be the ones to compromise for the sake of a relationship.

Women are expected to compromise more because they are the ones who are "supposed" to be nurturing, soft, and more pleasing—maybe even putting their family first before they have even had one. But what about what a woman truly wants? When do we tell a woman to use her voice, to speak her mind, to rock the boat, even to be direct or stern?

If only we taught young girls from the start that their position and role in a relationship has nothing to do with their gender. That you should make compromises but so should the other person. That you should speak up, even if it causes conflict. I see so many women, just like my friend, compromise too much, not speak their mind, and then get to a point where they crack.

In relationships, we can get in an automatic mode—into a routine with daily stressors, with lots to consider and think about. We might talk about surface wants and needs, but the deeper things can go left unsaid for quite some time. It's never truly about who is doing the dishes or who is putting the rubbish out, but rather about someone asking for more help around the house and being more considered.

It might sound simple: someone should speak up and the other person should listen. But often, after years and years of feeling like your voice isn't truly heard, isn't listened to, or is second best, the hurt, anger, frustration, and resentment can feel like too much.

I might not be able to help my friend patch up her relationship, but I can encourage more women to find their voice, and hopefully more from the start. If you are dating someone and something makes you feel uncomfortable, speak up. If you have needs that are not being met, tell the other person (and that goes for sex too). It doesn't have to be aggressive, but it does need to be said in whatever way you feel it needs to be said.

When I was thinking about this article and using my friend's experience as an example, I also had a realization of my own. As strong a woman as I am, I have not been speaking up as much as I should. And really, this is no one else's fault but my own.

My partner is not domineering, controlling, or ignorant to my wants and needs. But I had been the one not speaking up about them. Maybe because I feared possible consequences or conflict or because I am the nurturing one in the relationship who is good at making compromises and giving to another—a trait I sometimes wonder how much is truly me and how much is socially conditioned due to my gender. So, then I spoke up some more.

I must admit, it wasn't so pleasant at first, but more because I think I was annoyed at myself that I hadn't been more direct about some of my wants and needs sooner. But we got through to the other side. My partner even asked me, "Why didn't you just tell me that's what you wanted?" I didn't at the time because I didn't want to rock the boat or cause an issue. I now look back and feel sad that I felt that way about voicing some of the things I truly needed with my partner.

Start speaking up, but also make sure that you listen in return. If you can start doing this in your life overall, you might set a pattern where you do this in a relationship one day too. Relationships are about two people's wants, dreams, and needs. It's not just up to one person to compromise but for both people to ensure each other's voices are heard and each person to ensure their voice is listened to.

"The Number One Relationship Mistake Women Make" by Dr. Nikki Goldstein was published on SWAAY.com. Dr. Goldstein holds a bachelor's degree in psychology, a postgraduate diploma in counseling, and a doctorate in human sexuality. She appears regularly across various media networks in Australia, the US, and New Zealand and has become a respected go-to authority on love, sex, relationships, and dating.

LEADERSHIP SPOTLIGHT

If you are a leader in your personal or professional life, there will be times when you will oversee two or more individuals who disagree or are otherwise engaged in conflict. In this situation, you'll have to manage your role carefully. Your first instinct might be to stay out of the issue entirely or to make a unilateral decision that puts out the fire right away. Truthfully, though, the best course of action is mediation. Why? You want to model and encourage diplomacy, and you also want the arguing individuals to be encouraged to use their voices and take ownership for resolving the problem. Although it can be difficult to jump in, especially if no one has asked for your opinion, you should do so at the first sign of trouble. Putting off involvement might result in an escalation that's tougher to address.

Ask the parties involved what's going on, and make sure you stay even in your line of questioning. You might think one person is right, or (because you are human) you might like one party better than the other. It's okay to acknowledge these feelings (to yourself), but try not to allow them to get in the way of treating both sides fairly.

Next, meet with both sides. In an article for *Harvard Business Review*, Northwestern University Kellogg School of Management Professor Jeanne Brett and Northwestern University Pritzker School of Law Professor Stephen Goldberg cite sound advice based on their research on mediation and negotiation:

"In the initial meeting, explain that you see your role as helping them to find a mutually acceptable resolution to their conflict but also to ensure that the resolution does not have negative implications for the team. Make clear that deciding whether a particular agreement is acceptable requires their buy-in and yours. The goal of the initial meeting is to have them leave with emotions abated and feeling respected by you, if not yet by each other."

Brett and Goldberg suggest that subsequent meetings get to the heart of each party's position. What do they want and why, and what are their top priorities? "Reformulate what you think you understand about one colleague's interests and make sure the other colleague is hearing them."

The goal is for the parties to actively propose resolutions that meet their own and the other's interests. And sometimes, adversaries can simply put the past behind them and mutually decide on a new course of action. But if tension lingers or uncertainty is still a concern, Brett and Goldberg recommend trying one of these types of agreements:

- **Limited duration:** Try something for a limited time and then evaluate before continuing.
- **Contingent:** Agreements that depend on a future event *not* happening. If the future event does happen, an alternative agreement takes effect.
- **Nonprecedential setting:** Parties agree that a settlement now will not set a precedent should a similar conflict arise in the future.

It's important to accept that things might not always work out perfectly. You may have to step in with your authority, or there may be lingering animosity. However, at least you can say you did your best to preserve relationships and act in the best interest of the group.

CUE THE REAL WORLD

In these ledge protectors, we've examined conflict from several angles. Now let's think about how this chapter's conflict-resolution strategies could help you take better control of uncomfortable situations and respond effectively. Write your ideas in your journal.

- Recall a personal or professional situation in which conflict was allowed to fester because no one spoke up. What were the consequences?

- Consider a time when you had to let a relationship go. Did you end things with as much kindness as was possible, and if not, how could you have framed the conversation better?

- Describe a recent scenario in which you agreed to disagree with another person. Were you actually able to let the issue go; if not, why not?

- Imagine you are overseeing a committee for a volunteer organization in your community. Your co-chair consistently berates you for the actions you take on the committee's behalf but does not offer additional suggestions or contribute to the work. You are hurt and upset and resentful that a volunteer post is causing you so much emotional turmoil. The organization's president asks you how things are going. What do you tell them?

CONFLICT LEDGE REVIEW

- The first step in resolving conflict productively is to take a **time-out.** Take some deep breaths, scream into a pillow, or vent to a friend if you need to, and when you've calmed down, try to reflect objectively on the situation.
- The most effective way to reduce your fear of communicating upsetting news is to **prepare for the situation in advance** and think through your remarks.
- Sometimes abusive people don't realize their behavior is harmful. Before you go higher up, consider scheduling a conversation to talk about the matter; be friendly and approachable to **prevent defensiveness.**
- There are scenarios in life that require tense conversations, even if not outright conflict. Being able to listen to another **point of view**, discuss an issue civilly, and agree to disagree are all important skills.
- When you are in the middle of a conflict, the best course of action is **mediation.** You can model and encourage diplomacy, while the arguing individuals can own the resolution.

"Why would they want to hire me? I don't have enough experience."

◇◇◇◇◇◇

"It's okay, I didn't want it anyway."

◇◇◇◇◇◇

"I just don't have it in me to do that."

◇◇◇◇◇◇

"Don't mind me. I'm just being my usual clueless self!"

◇◇◇◇◇◇

"Why should what I have to say matter?"

◇◇◇◇◇◇

"I can't start this if I don't know how it's going to end."

◇◇◇◇◇◇

"Just thinking about speaking in front of people makes me ill."

◇◇◇◇◇◇

"I might deserve it, but that doesn't mean I can achieve it."

◇◇◇◇◇◇

"I'm afraid to express my needs. What if others ignore them?"

◇◇◇◇◇◇

"What makes me so special?"

◇◇◇◇◇◇

Chapter Six

CONFIDENCE

After more than five years in pageantry, six years of higher education, four years of medical missions, ten years in the corporate and business world, and thousands of dollars spent on life coaches, I thought I had built my self-confidence for good. I spent most of my early twenties studying myself, learning about my weaknesses and strengths, my insecurities and beliefs, my dreams and ambitions. I've taken massive risks, countless psychological assessments, and had perspective-changing experiences. Pageantry and the chances I took in venturing out in a world I didn't understand were the foundation for building my self-esteem, and my risky and not always successful entrepreneurial career has been a crash course on confidence—not to mention life!

I developed incredible self-awareness, and no one would dare tell me otherwise. Hell, I even perfected "the power pose." Given all this, I told myself, *If I could walk on stage in a bikini in front of thousands of strangers, keep calm through a civil war during one of my medical missions in South Sudan, and start a successful business with no experience, then I can do anything.*

Fast forward to a few years later. I'm now in my early thirties, and sometimes I find myself back at square one, feeling like I haven't made much progress at all. So what am I missing? How is it that I have spent years trying to feel unstoppable only to find myself low on self-confidence once again?

Early in my career, the guidance I received on confidence aimed to mold me from the outside-in. I was taught how to speak confidently, how to walk confidently, how to dress confidently, and how to act confidently. Did it work? It gave me a temporary boost. Was it sustainable? Not always.

When the COVID pandemic hit, I was overcome by self-doubt and didn't know how to pick myself up. This was driven by uncertainty and unexpected change in both my personal and professional lives. Like many, I started questioning a lot of things, with the extra time spent at home leading to uncomfortable self-reflection and taking inventory of meaning. I no longer experienced the exciting feelings I previously had collaborating with my team and meeting the SWAAY community in person. I broke off a seven-year relationship because it no longer felt we were on the same page. I gave up the apartment I lived in for years. I said goodbye to New York and moved back home to Denver to surround myself with family, only to find out my parents were stuck in Morocco for the entirety of the pandemic. Even my brother got COVID.

Because my anxiety caused me to develop more self-sabotaging habits, like procrastination and isolation, I began seeing a therapist regularly. I wanted to reframe my thinking, properly process some of the changes, and cope with the pain the world was going through. I wanted to leverage my time at home to journal more and put in the self-work needed to bounce back and address my confidence issues. This time, the key to reconstructing my self-confidence involved building it from the inside-out. For a year, I put aside who I thought I was supposed to be and allowed myself to take a step back. I put my ego on time-out and instead focused on re-identifying my values, seeking mental support, and reframing my thinking.

To be clear, I feel extremely grateful and lucky. The pandemic affected millions of lives in far more extreme ways, especially women in the workforce who had to balance homeschooling and their careers, women who had to navigate layoffs and start over in an unfavorable economy, women on the front lines working long hours, and women who were sick or cared for sick loved ones or lost their loved ones. I admire these people more than I can say, and while my experience doesn't compare to theirs, it did impact me.

That summer, I went out with one of my closest friends, Reem Edan. Reem had been making huge strides in her career as a stand-up comedian. I admired her courage to drop everything and pursue a vocation that very few understood. When she asked how my business was going and what other projects I had going on, I happily shared that I'd signed with a book agent and had submitted my first proposal to a few publishers. Reem's face lit up: "Congratulations! It's all happening. I am so excited for you!"

"Thanks," I replied, "but I mean, it's too early to tell. I'm not sure I have what it takes to write a book."

She paused. "Yeah, you know, you might be right. I don't think you're ready for it. If you think about it, you don't have many interesting experiences to draw from."

I reached for my drink and frowned. "Excuse me? What do you mean?"

Leave it to Reem to use her sarcasm and reverse psychology to prove a point. "See how offended you get when someone else discounts your capabilities? But when *you* doubt yourself, somehow you're okay with it," she told me. "The next time you put yourself down, think about how you'd feel if someone else said those same things to you. You need to normalize the act of speaking highly of yourself."

She was right. My visit with Reem then turned into an interesting conversation about how confidence fits into comedy. To be a comedian, one has to possess a lot of confidence. Shows often sell out because of jokes based on self-deprecating humor or a tendency to disparage or undervalue oneself. One of the most well-known examples is Jerry Seinfeld, who made hundreds of millions peddling East Coast neuroticism. It's just the way it is: self-loathing makes people laugh.

In an article for Inkline, Aisiri Amin points out how Australian comic Hannah Gadsby is different. In her Netflix special, *Nanette*, Gadsby doesn't spend much time poking fun at her herself as a lesbian growing up in a small Tasmanian town where homosexuality was illegal until 1997. Instead, she uses the forum to talk frankly about sexuality, gender, childhood trauma, and feminism—and to send a message. According to Amin, Gadsby's show "carefully illustrates how self-deprecating humor distorts and destroys one's sense of self and constantly pulls them down in their quagmire of self-hate." In her special, Gadsby explains that a joke has only two parts, the beginning and the middle. No one is interested in the end because the end inevitably isn't that funny. "For the longest time, Gadsby hadn't been telling her story right because the punchline had become more important than the story itself. She's made a bold choice not to go with the conventional flow, but to flip the comedy scene to be more empowering," Amin writes.

When I asked Reem about this, she had some interesting insights. "For younger comics, self-deprecation is usually the first stop on your comedic journey. Why? Because it's easier (and less disruptive) to point out the obvious and make yourself the butt of the joke," she told me. "Think of it as both an offense and a defense strategy: poking fun at the lowest common denominator in order to control the narrative (i.e., I'm letting you laugh *with* me because I'm in on the joke)."

Reem once used self-deprecating humor in her sets. She loved to tell the story about growing up as the fat kid in an Iraqi family who had no choice but to be funny. Like Gadsby, however, Reem now uses this material sparingly. "At the root of comedy is truth, so today I ask myself, 'Do I really believe in what I'm saying with this joke?' If my punchline is simply the lowest hanging fruit, I'll think of a more authentic and nuanced joke. You don't want to bully yourself because then people feel sorry for you."

"I've come to learn that true and lasting confidence is not gained by poking fun at yourself, but by taking the leap and proving you can do something that scares you," Reem told me. "For me, that was getting onstage. For other women, that can mean speaking up in the big meeting, starting a business, whatever. Be your own biggest cheerleader. Earn the real laugh—all the way to the bank."

In academic research on self-deprecating humor, Brad Bitterly of the University of Michigan's Ross School of Business and Alison Wood Brooks of Harvard Business School found it can be an effective method for neutralizing negative information about oneself. "When individuals add humor to a disclosure, counterparts view the negative information as less true and less important," they write in *Harvard Business Review*. For example, their study found that job candidates who revealed their limited math ability in a humorous manner ('I can add and subtract, but geometry is where I draw the line') were perceived as better able to do math than those who disclosed the information in a serious manner ('I can add and subtract, but I struggle with geometry'). But Bitterly and Wood Brooks admit that self-deprecation can backfire if the trait or skill in question is an essential area of competence: "A statistician can more safely make self-deprecating jokes about her spelling than about her statistical skills," they write.

In a chapter on confidence, it's critical that we address self-deprecation that can turn into self-sabotage. Invalidating every sincere compliment with a self-deprecating response or dominating every conversation with self-directed zingers may point to a larger self-confidence issue. Not only might you make others uncomfortable but also you might just start believing your own negative hype and talk this way to yourself even when you're alone! We are programmed for self-deprecating humor and negative self-talk because that's what society expects from us, and because it's easier. But the constant barrage of criticism in our heads pushes us to neutralize and deflect positive information about ourselves, and while we're "just trying to be funny," we go careening off the ledge.

Before we go further, let's define a few concepts that are often used interchangeably. *Self-esteem* is the belief in one's own value and worth. *Self-confidence*, on the other hand, refers to whether one believes they can succeed. Just because you think you deserve good things (self-esteem) doesn't necessarily mean you think you can achieve them (self-confidence).

Of course,

when you've spent a long time being controlled by low self-esteem and/or low self-confidence, you might have ingrained, self-defeating patterns of relating to others.

So the ledge protectors in this chapter will address this, providing guidance on communicating assertively, expressing opinions effectively, and managing a fear of failure. Later in the book, we'll also look at how self-confidence relates to professional growth specifically.

LEDGE PROTECTOR #1: PRACTICE ASSERTIVE COMMUNICATION

Maria Daniela Pipas and Mohammad Jaradat recently authored one of the most widely cited works on assertive communication. They define assertive communication as the ability to speak and interact in a manner that considers and respects the rights and opinions of others while also standing up for your own rights, needs, and boundaries. Assertive communicators speak up for themselves so effectively that they reduce the types of conflict we talked about in the last chapter.

They also experience greater self-confidence, reduced depression and anxiety, a greater ability to manage stress, and a reduced likelihood of being coerced or exploited.

Many situations in today's world trigger our need for assertive communication, including discriminatory actions at work, demanding family members at home, and disrespectful behaviors in public or on the road. In these instances, it's tempting to resort to aggressive communication to ensure our voices are heard and our needs met.

There are key differences between assertive and aggressive communication. While assertive communication is controlled, calm, and open to collaboration, aggressive communication is rigid, agitated, threatening, and manipulative. Assertive people solve problems with their communication style, whereas aggressive communicators tend to create more problems.

The opposite of aggressive communication is passive communication, which involves a pattern of not sharing what you think and want, overlooking your needs, and allowing others to take advantage of you. There's also passive-aggressive communication, which involves refusing to express yourself directly and instead manipulating others to get what you want. Passive-aggressive communication is common among those who lack self-confidence because it allows them to play the victim and avoid confrontation.

Throughout my career, I've been guilty of both passive and passive-aggressive communication, and I've also lacked assertiveness to the point where another person had to speak up *for* me!

Throughout this book, I've talked about the mistakes I made in my early days as an entrepreneur. When I talked to investors, I'd present myself as the underdog, which undermined my confidence and highlighted the ways I was underqualified to receive the funding I needed. This became obvious the day my brother, Adil (SWAAY's chief technology officer at the time), attended a meeting with me.

Adil had been sitting quietly while I gave my pitch, until he could not remain silent any longer. "Look, I know Iman likes to joke about her lack of business and media experience, but I'll point out that she also has acquired leadership and risk-taking skills from medical missions around the world," he told my audience. "She's been a change agent in our community through pageantry and public speaking, she led preclinical trials before the age of twenty-five, and most importantly she has rallied and empowered a global audience of women on her podcast. These activities directly relate to the vision we're pitching today."

Are you thinking what I was thinking?

Though I was grateful to Adil for giving a great speech that led to one of SWAAY's first significant investments, this was my company and those were my accomplishments. I *should* have been the one to communicate assertively about them. If your little brother has to stand up for you in a meeting where you're pitching *your* company, you need to rethink your self-esteem and self-confidence. And that's exactly what I did. (And thank you, little brother, for having my back!) Since that meeting, I've made it a point to hone my assertiveness, starting with these building blocks:

- Address disagreements at a time when others can be receptive.
- Make direct eye contact.
- Stand up straight.
- Take up your proper space; don't shrink to appear smaller.
- Maintain a neutral or friendly facial expression.
- Speak in an even, audible tone, without worrying about being too loud.
- Clearly express your point using specific examples.
- Use "I" instead of "You" statements. (Note, though, that too many statements starting with "I feel" or "I think" can actually undermine your assertiveness and authority).

- Avoid blaming yourself or others.
- Accept compliments and avoid undermining yourself or your experience.

To better illustrate these guidelines, let's look at an aggressive, a passive, and an assertive way of responding to a situation where a friend scheduled a party for a date you'd already said you wouldn't be available.

- **Aggressive:** "You did this even though you knew I couldn't make it. You never take my schedule into account. You're inconsiderate. Maybe we shouldn't hang out anymore."
- **Passive:** "I guess it's okay. I'm so hard to pin down anyway. Don't worry about it." (And then ruminating about what a bad friend she is until your resentment boils over.)
- **Assertive:** "I feel disappointed that you are having the party on the one date I said I couldn't make it. Next time, could we please try to settle on a day that works for both of us?"

Alternatively, what about a scenario in which a family member asks you to travel cross-country to provide childcare or eldercare, but it conflicts with important meetings you have at work?

- **Aggressive:** "You know I am extremely busy with work these days and can't take time off. I can't believe you're guilting me into doing this."
- **Passive:** "I'm worried I'll get fired if I take that much time off of work, but maybe it's wrong to prioritize my job over family. Let me get back to you." (And then hoping they'll simply forget they asked.)
- **Assertive:** "I feel conflicted over this. I want to support the family, but I don't think I can swing a trip right now. What are some things I can do to be helpful from here?"

One of my most popular podcast guests and recent friend, Evy Poumpouras has taught me a lot about assertive communication. After getting her start in law enforcement in the NYPD and surviving the Twin Towers collapse on 9/11, Evy went to work for the Secret Service. Evy was not only one of just a few women in the Service, but she was also tasked with interviewing intimidating figures about potential criminal activity. "During my work in three presidential administrations, I learned that effective communication is a more powerful weapon than anything you might carry," she told me during our podcast interview. "You can't demand respect, and you can't make people listen to you, even in law enforcement. The minute you use force, it goes downhill. I was always most effective when I got into the mindset of what mattered to the other person and was thoughtful and deliberate in trying to get the information I needed. If you talk to people like they're garbage, you'll get garbage in return. Instead of being aggressive and calling someone a liar, it's better to say something like: 'You're not being entirely truthful with me. Are you holding something back?'"

Evy admits that being this measured wasn't always easy. "There would definitely be times when people would act crazy and curse me out or spit on me. But I learned I didn't have to mimic them or let my ego get in the way. I'd mainly just listen, because the person who talks the most ends up revealing the most and has the least power," she told me. "And even now, when I feel myself getting emotional about a situation, I'll give myself twenty-four hours to cool down."

Evy also agrees that assertive people carry themselves a certain way and that positive body language translates into confidence. "When you walk into a room, be present and think about how you're coming across, because people are sizing you up," she advises. "Always be aware of your posture and how you are standing. Take up space; don't close in on yourself. Take your time speaking and amplify your voice. Do a self-assessment: if I saw me come through that door right now, what would I think?"

For many of us, learning assertive communication is a lifelong pursuit, and no one is perfect.

The next time you have the opportunity to be assertive, don't shy away from it. If you're nervous, which is understandable, consider identifying someone in your life who

you feel embodies confidence. Talk to this person about your communication fears, and then practice role-playing assertive conversations with them.

Use both verbal and nonverbal communication techniques, and ask for feedback on how effectively you implemented these strategies. The more experience you get, the less intimidating these situations will be!

◆Ledge Work: Define Your Worth

In growing confidence, it's important to first define why you are worthy of achieving positive outcomes and then to emphasize these points to yourself over and over. Complete these sentence prompts in your journal. Place the most impactful ones in a place you'll see every day, such as a mirror or a device screen. (Mine are written on my closet mirror, where I see them every morning and every night.)

- I am unique because . . .

- At work, I am the best person to . . .

- My friends appreciate when I . . .

- I'm the person in my family others look to for . . .

- I have succeeded in life because I am . . .

- I am loved by . . .

- I feel most confident when I . . .

- Others admire me when I . . .

◆

LEDGE PROTECTOR #2: EXPRESS OPINIONS EFFECTIVELY

Related to assertiveness is the art of knowing when to chime in with your point of view and when to keep your thoughts to yourself. And it's important that when you do keep your thoughts to yourself, it's not because you lack the self-confidence to express them.

As a CEO, thought-leadership mentor, scientist, pageant judge, friend, and family member, I am asked routinely to give my opinion on issues large and small. Whether I'm advising an employee how to respond to an email inquiry, a pageant contestant how to prepare for her interview, a friend how to navigate career opportunities, or an aspiring entrepreneur how to start a business, I always want to ensure that my point of view is both welcome and helpful.

Lolly Daskal, author of *The Leadership Gap: What Gets Between You and Your Greatness*, says that those with a reputation for wisdom are asked for their opinion often—and that's a good thing. There are, however, a few parameters when it comes to giving your opinion and actually being heard. First, when you're an authority on a subject, you might become accustomed to offering your opinion whether it's solicited or not. Be careful of scenarios in which no one directly asks you what to do. "Make sure the situation warrants an opinion," advises Daskal. "There are many cases where silence is the wiser path." Even if you are asked, it's not a foregone conclusion that you're the best person to provide an answer. If your opinion is ill informed or biased, know when it's better to recommend that someone more qualified address the issue.

Daskal also suggests listening to the whole story before jumping in. "You'll know exactly what's being asked of you, you may learn more about the issue in the process, and the person doing the asking will be more engaged and receptive." Especially if you are providing an opinion out of the blue or the issue at hand is sensitive, think through your approach before speaking. Consider the data and facts at your disposal and formulate some specifics to support your opinion. By building a case and using a clear, straightforward approach and an even tone to explain it, you'll increase your credibility and the likelihood of a positive outcome.

Daskal recommends some useful sentence openers for sharing your opinion:

- In my opinion . . .
- From my point of view . . .
- I would say . . .
- My impression is . . .
- Speaking personally . . .

When it comes to opinions, you want to be empathetic. Put yourself in the other person's shoes and ask yourself: *How would I feel if someone expressed this opinion to me? Will this person receive the opinion well? Will my ideas help them?* You also want to be confident. As I mentioned before, prefacing too many of your statements as opinion is overkill. Sometimes, you just need to take a firm stand.

Finally, remember that your opinion is just that, your opinion. Others will feel differently based on their unique backgrounds and experiences. As we talked about in the last chapter, different perspectives should be expected, allowed, and embraced.

Being appropriately self-confident means knowing the line between speaking up and forcing someone over to your point of view.

LEDGE PROTECTOR #3: MANAGE FEAR OF FAILURE

In her native Puerto Rico, Julixa Newman, an inspiring woman I interviewed on my *Women Who SWAAY* podcast, was a single mother at sixteen years old. She started working as a hotel housecleaner and ended up the founder of her own successful company. It's the American dream, but Julixa was told "no" more times than she can count. While pregnant with twins, Julixa saw that few products on the market were designed for parents of multiples. She started her own line of funny tee-shirts with only $150, eventually sold her TwinTrexx baby carrier to major retailers like Walmart, and launched Stuff 4 Multiples, an e-commerce store with over 1,800 products.

"Throughout my life, I've learned that you can get back up, no matter what the circumstances might be. There were nights when I slept in parking lots and cried my eyes out because I'd spent my last $5 on milk for the baby," she told me. "When I first left Puerto Rico for Orlando, I interviewed for a front desk position at a hotel. The general manager told me I was better suited for housekeeping, so I took the job and basically insisted on moving up."

Even as her company exploded, Julixa faced failure and rejection as she struggled to get her niche business off the ground. "As a woman running a startup, you aren't given much of a chance," she says. "I was given a lot of excuses, like, 'Your minimum order has to be ten thousand.' But I didn't give up, I just searched for manufacturers overseas."

When it was time to market her products to retailer buyers, Julixa faced more obstacles: "I was often ignored until I realized I got more replies when I sent emails using a male name. In countries like Saudi Arabia, I had to approach many, many people in purchasing. Sometimes they were other women and sometimes men who were more receptive to working with women. It took a lot of hustle, perseverance, and confidence that I had good products that people needed."

Anyone who wants to accomplish big things has to, as Julixa put it, be willing to prove themselves a bit more. "If you have one million-dollar idea one week and then another the next week, business ownership may not be for you. You have to stick with your project and keep selling and improving your product," she told me. "Not all approaches will succeed, and inevitably someone won't like what you have to offer. And while no one likes to hear their baby called ugly, you take the lows with the highs."

But most people, including Julixa, are a little afraid of failing. If you are facing a challenging situation and you aren't a little scared, it means you don't know enough to be afraid or you're in denial about what's in front of you. Fear of failure isn't a problem unless you let it stop you from acting. And I'll be honest, I see this all the time. Maybe you succeeded early in life and you are afraid you can't top previous accomplishments, so you don't try. Maybe you've succeeded all your life so you can't envision another outcome. Maybe your organization or your boss doesn't reward risk-taking or experimentation, so you are encouraged to play it safe. Maybe you suffer from impostor syndrome and don't think you deserve to be where you are (more on this in chapter 10). Some people fear failure because of the way they were raised. For instance, if your parent was highly critical of you, and you grew up desperately trying to avoid disappointing them, as an adult you might seek constant praise and validation from others.

According to Lifehack CEO Leon Ho, people with true self-confidence know they won't always succeed, whereas a person who is more fragile avoids risks. "Failure becomes the supreme nightmare: a frightful horror they must avoid at any cost," he writes on his site. "The simplest way to do this is to stick rigidly to what you know you can do, protect yourself, work the longest hours, double- and triple-check everything, and be the most conscientious and conservative person in the universe."

And if this doesn't work? People who fear failure might use any possible means to keep it at bay. They might, says Ho, "falsify numbers, hide anything negative, conceal errors, avoid customer feedback, or constantly shift the blame onto anyone too weak to fight back." I've seen this happen numerous times to founders who were extremely ambitious about their startups and felt the pressure to inflate their numbers and conceal errors just to gain validation and approval for more funding. It's a compelling way to avoid failure, but it isn't sustainable. While "fail fast and often" may be the national mantra for the startup community, no one really wants to fail. Too much is at stake. I myself was very reluctant to hear any negative feedback early on in my pitch meetings—or from anyone really. I feared that if I internalized the rejection and criticism, I'd be kick-starting my descent to a potential bankruptcy and the social stigma that comes with it. However, a more nuanced perspective of fear can help you see it as a catalyst. Your fear can either inhibit, sabotage, *or* motivate you.

Regardless of where your fear of failure comes from or how it manifests, if you want to maintain balance on the glass ledge, you must use every tool in your arsenal to overcome fear or leverage it to reach your goals. If you don't, you will stifle your creativity and hold back your growth. Before we move on, let's examine a few techniques that can help.

Identify the source of the fear

What exactly are you afraid of? We've alluded to this in previous chapters; understanding where your feelings are coming from is the key to self-assurance. For example, are you worried that someone in your social circle will reject you or that you will appear incompetent? Do you fear your financial stability may be in jeopardy? Write down potential reasons for your fear in your journal, always attempting to dig deeper by asking yourself why. For example, "I'm afraid that if I quit my full-time job and pursue my artistic passion, then I will be less successful. Why does this scare me? Because I was raised in a household that believed job stability is more rewarding than the pursuit of creativity."

Reverse how you view the situation

When we think of failure, we usually imagine something big and bad, with little or no upside. But what if risking failure is actually a good thing because you'll learn something new in the process and will ultimately be better off with the lesson? Talk to yourself in these terms, emphasizing the positive things about yourself and the scenario. "In many cases, you believe what you tell yourself," says Ho. "Your internal dialogue affects how you react and behave. . . . Create a new mental script that you can reach for when you feel negativity creeping in. The voice inside your head has a great effect on what you do," he advises.

Envision what might happen

For many, the worst part about potential failure is the uncertainty. You don't know if your risk will pan out or not, so it helps to weigh the pros and cons and consider different outcomes. You might find that the benefits easily outweigh the drawbacks, which can lift your confidence. Along these lines, it's also useful to think through the worst thing that could possibly happen and then take steps to prepare for that outcome as best you can to remove some of the fear associated with the decision. "It never hurts to have a backup plan," says Ho. "Perhaps you've applied for a grant to fund an initiative at work. In the worst-case scenario, if you don't get the grant, are there other ways you could get the funds?"

Remember that even if you do fail, you won't do so in a bubble. There is something to be gained from every situation, even those in which you can't spot a ray of light at first. Look for the lesson. When you find it, keep it in your back pocket for next time. And keep your head held high.

If you don't have the confidence to at least try to grab that brass ring, you can be sure you will never reach it.

Remember the fear I shared with Reem at the beginning of this chapter? I was afraid I shouldn't write a book because I wouldn't have enough experience or valuable advice to share. While writing *The Glass Ledge*, I wondered whether I should push publication back a few years. But I decided to go for it, and I'm pleased to share that as I've moved along in the process, my confidence in the endeavor has grown. Not to mention, I've learned so much and gained more experience from this journey as a first-time author, which is the key to building more confidence.

Voices from the SWAAY Community

Detaching from the Outcome

Melissa M. Proctor

Open-mindedness and inclusiveness are what I project, even subconsciously. I have always been the nonjudgmental type, allowing people the freedom to be who they want to be and express themselves without fear of judgment. I can vibe with it or not, but I'm not the type to judge. Whether their sentiments echo my own or not, I never want to make others feel they have to suppress themselves around me.

That goes for both personal and professional relationships. Because of my own authenticity, I have inadvertently provided an environment for those around me to be their authentic selves. This, in turn, facilitates the establishment of relationships built on trust and transparency.

My desire to experience the fullness of the world and get the most out of this life and my willingness to be open to whatever God has for me have allowed me the freedom to enjoy experiences and opportunities I would not have been able to conceive had I been close-minded. I have navigated my career like many others, not always knowing how everything will unfold. Certainly there are things that I like and things that I don't, but openness and willingness have manifested so many paths in my life, from my marriage to my jobs to how I maneuver day to day.

Freedom is the ability to move in that way, the freedom from being constrained by thoughts we all have: *What if I fail? What if this doesn't work? What if the outcome is not what I expect?* Don't get me wrong, I am definitely a planner in some aspects. I'm pretty type A. I research, think things through, and weigh options. However, some people get so caught up and overwhelmed by the planning, they forget to enjoy the process.

Have you ever met someone who gets so stressed by trying to figure out what the final destination is that they've lost the excitement of the journey itself? Are you that person? If so, that probably transcends to other areas of your life. Sometimes you have to relinquish control and embrace the reality that you may not be able to determine the outcome, but don't let that stop you from showing up. Trust. I'm talking to me and to you. No one is perfect.

Even in corporate settings, people are sometimes afraid to take risks, wondering, *Well what if it doesn't work?* With my teams, I've always tried to foster environments that allowed room for mistakes. We tried it, and it didn't work. It's not the end of the world. We will try again and again if we have to. Be willing to take risks. Challenge yourself, and don't forget your principles. Remember, no one manages your career but you.

Even if you accept a challenge and it does not quite turn out the way you anticipated, the lessons learned through the process are invaluable. Plus now you know what you don't like. When you accept new challenges, your confidence will grow as you reach new heights. There is no such thing as failure, only new lessons learned.

Don't get it twisted. I am not trying to paint a picture of myself as this totally carefree being, living worry free while occasionally fitting in the necessary business meeting. I'm human. I doubt myself all the time. I am my toughest critic. I question whether I'm good enough, if I have what it takes, if I'm in the right place. Before any public-speaking events or an interview or a business call, I pray, "Lord, please guide my words, and don't let me say something whack."

With experience and time, I've learned to lean on faith; particularly during those moments of doubt, faith has sustained me. Faith helps to soothe my fears. I credit my mom with teaching me with her constant reminder that nothing beats a trial but a failure. Regardless of the outcome, whether the result turns out to be the crappiest thing ever, even if you see what you've just built crumble and fall, if you have done your absolute best, you can't do any more. Just get up and try again. Don't let the fear of failure stop you from stepping onto the court and playing the game.

"Lessons to Live By: When the Ball Is in Your Court, Get Open" by Melisa M. Proctor was published on SWAAY.com. Melissa is the executive vice president and chief marketing officer of the Atlanta Hawks & State Farm Arena.

LEADERSHIP SPOTLIGHT

You might think that once you get promoted or become your own boss, confidence shortages become a thing of the past. Now that you're a leader, you can finally fully trust your own abilities. In reality, this is far from the case. According to a recent Gartner survey, only half of 2,800 leaders said they were well equipped to lead their organization in the future. In part, this is due to their failure to recognize their own skills gaps and where they need help, as well as their organizations' unwillingness to provide the right formal training.

If you're a leader who doubts your own capabilities, it's useful to evaluate the situation objectively, which we'll talk more about in the upcoming chapter on growth and impostor syndrome. But Gartner has also suggested a new model of complementary leadership, in which professional development and management responsibilities are shared by others with similar skill sets. "Leaders today have more responsibilities than ever but are ill-equipped to take on their expanded roles," Gartner vice president Sari Wilde says. "Our research found that leaders are not always best-positioned to manage every responsibility they are tasked with; instead, the best leaders identify others who have a stronger grasp of skills at which they are weak and share responsibilities with them." Gartner's research illustrates that when leaders use the complementary model, their teams' performances increased by 60 percent and their own performance increased by 40 percent.

No one is perfect, and no one is ever finished learning, no matter how high they may climb. However, knowing where you need to improve and how to harness the resources to do so can boost your confidence significantly. And as a leader, when you approach your own development this way, you will serve as a role model for those you supervise.

CUE THE REAL WORLD

The ledge protectors around confidence focus on ways to increase your self-belief and express your thoughts in a manner that's conducive to better understanding. Write the responses to the following questions in your journal.

- Do you struggle with assertive communication in your personal life, professional life, or both? If so, what's one action you can take to practice honing this ability?

- Think about the last time you expressed an unpopular opinion. What was the response? Is there anything you could have done to make your approach more effective?

- Consider a high-stakes situation in your life that either took place in the past or is happening currently. How can you detach from the outcome in a way that doesn't leave you paralyzed by the fear of failure?

CONFIDENCE LEDGE REVIEW

- Invalidating every sincere compliment with a **self-deprecating** response or dominating every conversation with self-directed zingers may point to a larger self-confidence issue.
- **Assertive communication** is the ability to speak and interact in a manner that considers and respects the rights and opinions of others while also standing up for your rights, needs, and boundaries.
- If you are providing an opinion out of the blue or the issue at hand is sensitive, think through your approach before speaking. **Consider the data** and facts at your disposal, and formulate some specifics to support your opinion.
- For many, the worst part about potential failure is the uncertainty. What helps is to weigh the **pros and cons** of your risk and consider different outcomes.
- No one is ever finished **learning**, no matter how high they may climb. Knowing where you need to improve and how to harness the resources to do so, however, can boost your confidence significantly.

"These kind of hours are expected at my company."

ᴓᴓᴓᴓᴓ

"I don't have time to eat lunch, let alone date."

ᴓᴓᴓᴓᴓ

"I know I was sick last month. I just don't have a good immune system."

ᴓᴓᴓᴓᴓ

"Sure I want kids. But I'll just freeze my eggs, and it'll be all good."

ᴓᴓᴓᴓᴓ

*"I'm working from home; there's no excuse not to
respond to my boss within an hour."*

ᴓᴓᴓᴓᴓ

"I always have to be thinking five steps ahead."

ᴓᴓᴓᴓᴓ

"If I get promoted, I won't be able to spend time with my kids."

ᴓᴓᴓᴓᴓ

"If I want to be successful, I have to sacrifice my social life."

ᴓᴓᴓᴓᴓ

*"My parents are getting older. If I don't spend all my
spare time with them now, I'll regret it later."*

ᴓᴓᴓᴓᴓ

"Why even think about balance? It's a scam!"

ᴓᴓᴓᴓᴓ

Chapter Seven

BALANCE

When I was sixteen, I asked my dad why he and my mom gave up their careers in Morocco to move to a country where they would need to work twice as hard to earn half as much. His answer instilled a deep guilt that later fueled my overachieving tendencies.

"Life is about making sacrifices for the people and things you care most about," he told me. "One day, when you have kids, you'll understand."

And that was the moment that led to the huge "my parents didn't give up everything for me to be average" chip on my shoulder. By my early thirties, I'd accomplished everything I said I would. But the more I achieve, the more ambitious I get. There is always more work to do, more people to meet, more events to attend, more ideas to develop, more money to make, more books to write, more places to see—more excuses to go shopping. When I am not out conquering the world, I am strategizing and planning my takeover. There is no in-between.

In New York, the rat race never stops. It's wonderful and honorable to work hard and take pride in your professional growth. And as the saying goes, the devil finds work for idle hands. But work is only a part of life, not all of life.

While writing this chapter on my balcony in Morocco, I was staring at the ocean. The birds were chirping, and there was a hot cup of coffee at my side. I'd never felt more at peace. I also reflected on all the times I've been on the verge of a nervous breakdown, trying to convince myself that all the sacrifices were worth it. My mother once told me: "You're really good at managing your career and your business, but you're horrible at living. You always cared about health and you wanted to have a big family of your own, but since you started working, you've lost sight of those values. You need to find a balance."

That statement has been living rent free in my head ever since. My mother was right. When the COVID pandemic hit, it forced some of us to slow down and consider how we are living our lives. The constant running around with unnecessary commitments and commutes came to an abrupt halt.

During that time, I started doing an exercise where I would ask myself, *Who am I?* I'd answer with statements that aren't linked to my work or my accomplishments, because my work and my accomplishments are what I do, not who I am. At first, it was difficult to come to the realization that outside of my work achievements, I didn't really know how to define myself. But the exercise encouraged me to connect more with who I am as a woman and who I aim to be. I decided to commit to less doing and more being.

With that new perspective and mindset, I started shifting my attention and focus to the other parts of my life I had neglected in the name of "hard work." When I turned thirty-one, I consulted a fertility specialist to understand my options. I had my egg count tested and planned for freezing procedures, should they be necessary. I've been nervous throughout these processes. Although I may still not be at a point where I can balance work and family, it has been refreshing and helpful to talk so openly about the topic. The traditional silence around it leads many high-achieving women to feel they have to choose between a long-lasting career or children. The discussions have allowed me to clarify my intention, which is to prioritize building my own family regardless of my professional commitments.

Time magazine contributor Arghavan Salles understands what I'm going through. She is a surgeon who practices at the prestigious Washington University in St. Louis. At the age of thirty-eight, Salles visited a fertility clinic to inquire about egg freezing. For all of the years she was training to be a doctor, Salles spent most of her time in hospitals with little time left to search for a romantic partner. "I prioritized my career over my personal life, and when I was younger, this tradeoff felt worth it," she writes in *Time*. Sounds familiar? But once her career was finally in the bag, Salles wasn't so sure. Not only had she subjected her body to nights on call, irregular exercise habits, and too much stress, all the steps she'd have to go through to have a biological child now seemed overwhelming.

Egg freezing involves multiple injections, blood draws, and ultrasounds over a period of several weeks. Retrieving mature follicles carries the risk of injuring major blood vessels or the intestines. Women experience headaches, bloating, and cramping. The procedures and the associated medications are incredibly expensive. And even after all that, the odds of success aren't great. At the well-known Shady Grove Fertility Clinic in Maryland, only 7 percent of retrieved eggs produce a live birth. To have a 50 percent chance of having one child, a woman in her late thirties needs to freeze at least fifteen eggs.

For Salles, this seemed like an unlikely number. It didn't stop her from trying, however. Once she started the process, she was invested in it, imagining her child's future in every follicle that appeared on the ultrasound. Salles proceeded with an underperforming cycle because doing otherwise felt like failure—perhaps the most consequential failure of her life. "Throughout the process I wondered: *What is the point of my existence if I cannot perform this basic human function: reproduction?*"

Salles isn't shut out from having a family. She can keep trying to retrieve enough eggs, do in vitro fertilization with donor eggs, or adopt. But the heartache of this process is not necessarily what she would have chosen. "I know I'm not the only one grappling with these issues," she writes. "It is now my mission to raise awareness among younger women to take advantage of their fertility when they have it—which might mean getting pregnant sooner or freezing eggs or embryos earlier in life. I am encouraging them to make a plan for their family and embarking on research to understand the burden of infertility on female physicians."

Young women doctors aren't the only ones working longer and longer hours to get ahead. In 2019, the time-tracking software company RescueTime analyzed 185 million working hours to determine just how prevalent overwork is. Among the key findings:

- 26 percent of work is done outside of normal working hours.
- American workers average *at least* one hour of work outside of working hours on eighty-nine days/year (and on 50 percent of all weekend days).
- American workers check email and messages every six minutes, on average, which can add anywhere from 50 to 100 percent more time to the workday.

Oprah Winfrey once said that you can have it all, just not all at once. And it's indeed impossible to excel at everything from marriage, children, and eldercare to careers, side hustles, and hobbies. But while there aren't enough hours in the day to place full focus on everything that's important to us, we fall off the glass ledge when we put all our proverbial eggs in one basket and neglect the others. Some ambitious women like Salles (and me for a time) pay the most attention to their careers, because that seems most pressing following a rigorous education. Remember chapter 2 on likability? Many women also put off advanced degrees or launching a business because we always want to say yes to our partners, parents, and children. We think self-care is selfish, so we neglect our physical and emotional needs until we are consumed with exhaustion and overwhelm. You don't have to be a surgeon like Salles to know that

equally balancing all the critical areas of your life will undoubtedly prove elusive and unrealistic.

And there are tradeoffs. Karyn Schoenbart is the chief executive officer of the NPD Group, a global provider of information and advisory services. Under Karyn's leadership, NPD became one of the *Fortune* 100 Best Companies to Work For in New York. While building an executive career, Karyn raised two children and maintained a happy marriage. And as if she wasn't already busy enough, she fulfilled her goal of coaching others to greater levels of achievement when she published her book *Mom.B.A.: Essential Business Advice from One Generation to the Next.*

Karyn is definitely a powerhouse I look up to, and she'll be the first to say that not everything in life works out perfectly and that she had to make sacrifices along the way. "I do wish I could have taken advantage of the opportunity to get an MBA. My company offered to sponsor me, free of charge, to attend Columbia University's executive program," she told me. "But that would have involved going to school in addition to working full time and raising two small children. Looking back, I would have made the same decision." Karyn's focus on family and career also meant that for long stretches of time she didn't exercise, keep up with the news, or hang out much with her girlfriends. "Once, I even forgot to feed my kids dinner, and another time, I left them at religion school. But I was able to be kind to myself when I couldn't be all things to all people, and in the end, things worked out okay."

We each have a finite number of resources to play with. So it's helpful to figure out how to direct your energy so that the various elements work together in the best possible way. Elisette Carlson writes in an article on SWAAY: "As a working mother of two children who runs a branding and marketing agency, is very committed to daily exercise, and juggles a handful of other professional and personal commitments, I've learned to accept that balance doesn't really exist. (And I know I am *not* alone!) The elusive work-life balance is BS."

I don't disagree. Therefore, perhaps the appropriate phrase is not "work-life balance" but "work-life integration." In addition to our careers, there are other areas of life we must attend to, including our health, rest, family, community, and joy. The exact definition of healthy integration depends on the person, but one thing is constant: we need to be continually monitoring the input and output in these areas to assess how well integration is working. For example, is our blood pressure at a healthy level? Are we feeling content or irritated most of the time?

I want to be clear that I'm not advocating that you pay too much attention to or obsess over this. We will talk more about the pitfalls of perfectionism later in the book, but it *is* possible to be too perfectionistic about healthy work-life integration. As an example, we all know people who bring their "always on the go" attitude to everything in their life, even activities that are designed to relax and bring pleasure. Can you imagine going to a meditation group just so you can check it off your list? But this happens all the time. If we really want to be centered, we have to cultivate a mindset of being in touch with what actually brings us life-sustaining energy, rather than what is supposed to.

I'm someone who has had to make hard choices about what to focus on and when, so I want to use the rest of this chapter to advise on strategically planning your life to move big dreams forward one small step at a time, understanding the benefits of living fully in the present, recognizing the toll of imbalance, and achieving optimal work-life integration in a challenging climate.

LEDGE PROTECTOR #1: STRATEGICALLY PLAN YOUR LIFE

I have a friend, Marie, who is about a decade older than me. When Marie graduated from college, she started a career in public relations. Working for a series of large agencies, Marie quickly climbed the ladder and before long was working seven days a week as a vice president.

When Marie got engaged, she knew she wanted to have a child in the next five years. She also knew she wanted the flexibility to spend a lot of time with her baby. Marie saw that her high-powered career as a PR executive wasn't compatible with her desire to raise children and that she needed to get out of it before she was forced to choose mothering over earning a living.

Marie wanted to continue to work, but she had to find something more flexible. She had a talent for making customized event centerpieces, so she gradually laid the groundwork for an online business while still working at the PR agency.

By the time Marie got pregnant with her first daughter, she had a thriving Etsy store that was earning about a quarter of her day job's income. By the time her daughter was a year old, Marie had her own website and a roster of regular customers and could afford to resign.

When her kids were still theoretical, Marie had the goal of being around for their childhoods. She accomplished this goal because she thought hard and ahead about what she wanted out of her life. She realized career changes don't happen overnight, so she took the necessary actions, one small step at a time. Fortunately, this is a process you can replicate, strategically planning your life as you would the future of a business. Here are a few steps to that end.

Step 1: Brainstorm your most important values

Ask yourself: What values fulfill me? What values do I want to practice in my life? Many individuals will choose values such as purpose, financial freedom, service, wellness, or creativity. One of Marie's values, for instance, is quality family time.

Step 2: Write your personal mission statement

A personal mission statement is a clear description of the person you intend to be in your life. For example, Marie created a personal mission statement that reads: "I am an educated, artistic, and entrepreneurial woman who wants to launch a business that will allow me to earn an income while raising my children." Note that it's okay to revisit and refine your mission statement, as it might change over time.

Step 3: Assess your skills

Before you set specific goals and plan certain activities, it's worth asking what you can do better than others or what things you can do that others might pay for. Marie had already designed centerpieces for several friends and family members, so she knew she had this talent and that there was a demand for her work. She also knew she was more self-driven and organized than most people and was likely to be successful managing the administrative tasks associated with a new business.

Step 4: Target your growth areas

For decades, people have set goals in the SMART format, which stands for "specific, measurable, attainable, relevant, and time-bound." Drafting and frequently revisiting SMART goals is a good use of your time because it holds you accountable for your own success. You can also use your SMART goals to ensure a more consistent focus on work-life integration. One of Marie's balance-related SMART goals reads as follows.

Goal: Launch an independent online presence in 2019
- **Specific? YES**
  - Secure funding for building an e-commerce website in Q1.
  - Hire a product photographer, site copywriter, and search engine optimization expert, and develop an execution plan for each in Q2.
  - Promote discounts to existing Etsy customers in exchange for ten testimonials to use on the website and other marketing materials in Q3.
  - Build out email list to 250 subscribers in Q4.
- **Measurable? YES**
- **Attainable? YES**
- **Relevant? YES**
- **Time-Bound? YES**

Achieving goals in the service of better work-life integration doesn't have to be difficult. The key is the size of the goal. Research at INSEAD, an organization that develops leadership programs for multinational companies, found that thanks to a quirk in the way our brain evaluates goals, people feel it's easier and more palatable to achieve a small, incremental goal than to maintain the status quo. This discovery contrasts with the popular belief that no change is easier than any change, and it means that when you set right-sized objectives rather than out-sized ones, you will actually be more motivated than if you do nothing at all.

Randi Zuckerberg is a technology entrepreneur, founder of Zuckerberg Media, a bestselling author, a Broadway singer, and an avid proponent of getting more young girls into STEM. She's also a mom of two boys.

When we were chatting before I appeared on her Sirius XM show a couple of years ago, Randi told me that navigating a packed schedule and a multitude of personal and professional responsibilities is built on a single notion: picking and choosing. In her latest book, *Pick Three: You Can Have It All (Just Not Every Day)*, Randi also explored goal setting in three critical lifestyle areas. Why three? "Not everything can be top priority, so instead of trying to do everything and winding up doing it all in a thoroughly mediocre way," Randi says, "it's always better to prioritize and show up for things 100 percent. I figured that there had to be a way to accomplish everything I wanted to do in terms of work, sleep, family, friends, and fitness, but in a way that was focused, mindful, and strategic. Having the discipline to do a few of these things really well every day has allowed me to take on many more projects than I ever dreamed possible, while feeling way less overwhelmed and frazzled (though of course I do still have my moments)!"

◆Ledge Work: Setting Incremental Goals

Incremental goals are a series of smaller objectives that contribute to the achievement of a big-picture work-life integration goal. In this example, notice that the larger goal and the incremental goals are also *smart*.

Larger Goal: Reduce cholesterol by 20 milligrams per deciliter by the end of the calendar year (six months from now).

Incremental Goals:

- Solidify the habit of consuming fiber by eating at least two servings of vegetables a day for the months of July and August.

- Download a diet tracker and record no more than 1,500 calories per day for the months of July and August.

- Read nutrition labels on grocery trips during September and October, and avoid purchasing any products with trans fats.

- Engage in physical activity (running or biking) at least three hours per week during the months of November and December.

In your journal, write down a larger goal with a six- to twelve-month timespan, as well as four or five incremental goals to help you reach the larger goal. Consider setting the larger goal in an area of your life you've been neglecting recently.

LEDGE PROTECTOR #2: LIVE FULLY IN THE PRESENT

Long-term integration is tough to manage if you don't set goals that facilitate it. But like other aspects of the glass ledge, goals can be taken too far. When we are too singularly focused on the future, we ignore the value of the present.

I recently read a life-changing book by Michael A. Singer called *The Surrender Experiment*. After a deep spiritual awakening, Singer decided to live alone in the middle of the woods, let go of himself, and embrace a life of solitude. He was surprised that when he surrendered and allowed the universe to call the shots, an array of rich opportunities for growth and discovery opened up without much effort on his part. His story taught me to reconsider how I am living life. I decided to stop chasing and start attracting. How do you start attracting? You set balance-oriented intentions and focus on your inner well-being while striving to achieve them.

In addition to pursuing these intentions deliberately, I now seek inner harmony with mindful attention. Mindfulness is a series of strategies designed to bring awareness to our present moment thoughts, feelings, and bodily sensations and to experience these without interpretation or judgment. For years, my therapist pointed out that my biggest struggle was harsh self-judgment. Sure, being self-critical pushes you to grow and improve, but without moderation, it can be damaging. Research from Harvard University and other research centers show that mindfulness is effective for reducing stress and encouraging an overall sense of calm. Best of all, it can be learned. The foundation for mindfulness is deep belly breathing.

To practice belly breathing, place one hand on your chest and the other on your stomach. Take a deep breath in (lasting four to five seconds) through the nose and feel your hand on your stomach move as you inflate your diaphragm with air. Slowly release your breath out of your mouth (again, lasting four to five seconds), and repeat this breathing pattern. Do this as many times during the day as you can remember, and before long, it will become routine.

When we are in pressure-filled situations that create imbalance, even short mindfulness exercises are helpful in calming the body's nervous and digestive systems. Some ideas include these:

- **Body Scanning exercise:** Bring your awareness to each part of your body, one part at a time. Pay attention to things like how your clothing feels against your skin, the sensation of your lower body touching what you're seated on, any tension that you have in a body part, etc.
- **Hold a Fruit exercise:** Hold a piece of fruit and pretend you've never encountered it before. Observe the way it looks, feels in your fingers, smells, and tastes.
- **Bell exercise:** Set your phone to ring a bell tone after two minutes. Close your eyes and listen for the tone. When you hear it, concentrate on the sound until it fades. If you have an Apple Watch, check out the mindfulness feature that prompts breathing and stretching breaks throughout the day.

Once you learn to be mindful, it's easier to see when the day is getting away from you, know when something you're doing doesn't feel right, or hear when your inner voice is telling you to slow down. Living in the present allows us to make the most of every minute. Life is precious but unpredictable, and we can never be sure how much time we have left for the things that really matter.

LEDGE PROTECTOR #3:
RECOGNIZE THE TOLL OF IMBALANCE

The law firm Wright Hassall recently surveyed two thousand UK professionals about the mental-health strain caused by overwork. More than a third of respondents said that extra hours were causing them anxiety, and more than a third reported increased stress. Nearly half of respondents said employers do not offer any form of mental-health support, and of those with employers that do offer it, nearly a quarter said the support is inadequate while 19 percent don't know how to access it.

In a 2020 Conference Board survey, nearly half of respondents said their work-life balance had decreased during the COVID pandemic, and the Organization for Economic Cooperation and Development's 2020 Better Life Index found that the US ranks thirtieth out of forty countries in time devoted to leisure and personal care.

We at SWAAY partnered with consumer goods company Unilever in 2020 for a virtual event series tackling COVID's effects on women in the workplace. Highly accomplished women on the panels shared their wisdom on many of the topics in *The Glass Ledge*, including prioritizing self-care, letting go of perfectionism, and helping companies to adopt and effectively implement women-friendly policies. At the heart of the conversations were these statistics: about one in four working mothers surveyed by McKinsey and LeanIn.org in the summer of 2020 indicated that they were considering downshifting their careers;

by the fall of 2020, nearly 2.2 million US women had actually left the workforce,

according to the National Women's Law Center. Although it's disheartening to learn that so many women left their jobs, at least they recognized they were burning out or that other parts of their lives needed to take precedence. Some of us have a harder time coming to that conclusion. Burnout is a state of chronic stress, and according to psychologist Sherrie Bourg Carter, it doesn't happen suddenly. "You don't wake up one morning and all of a sudden have burnout," she says. "Its nature is much more insidious, creeping up on us over time like a slow leak, which makes it much harder to recognize. Still, our bodies and minds do give us warnings, and if you know what to look for, you can recognize it before it's too late."

And what are the signs? Bourg Carter cites these:

- **Physical and emotional exhaustion**, including chronic fatigue, insomnia, forgetfulness or impaired concentration, chest pain, shortness of breath, gastrointestinal pain, dizziness, headaches, loss of appetite, and increased anxiety and depression.
- **Cynicism and detachment**, including loss of interest in activities you previously enjoyed, pessimism, isolation, and a general feeling of disconnectedness from others.
- **Feelings of ineffectiveness and lack of accomplishment**, including apathy and hopelessness, irritability, lack of productivity, and poor work performance.

I didn't know much about these signs back in early 2018 when my body began to give out on me. I was on my way to an important meeting with a potential strategic corporate partner when I felt nauseous and weak. I'd spent long hours preparing for this meeting, and at that moment, I couldn't remember the last time I'd had a full meal. I hadn't had much of an appetite, but I'd chalked that up to stress. Whatever this was, I was sure I could tough it out. But the universe had other plans. While the meeting was still going on, I had to excuse myself to the restroom. I was in such unbearable gastrointestinal pain I passed out, and my brother had to take me to the nearest clinic. The diagnosis? A massive kidney infection that had been building for months.

The partnership with the company didn't pan out. If I'd only listened to my body early on, perhaps that meeting would have proceeded differently. If you recognize burnout signs like mine, it's important to assess the cause. Should imbalance or poor work-life integration be the culprit, consider taking these specific actions to get back in alignment.

Set boundaries for yourself

In chapter 2, we've already looked at setting your boundaries with other people, but what about setting boundaries with yourself? It's up to you to create a workable schedule, factoring in what you are going to do when and for whom, your natural energy levels, your exercise habits, your sleep requirements, and family engagements. Even if your job is home based, set and adhere to a cutoff time when you will stop working and attend to other things. Blocking out space on your calendar can be helpful in this regard. I've made it a point to include my personal time and fitness schedule on my work calendar to help me respect those hours the same way I show up for work commitments.

Communicate with your managers and coworkers

With mental-health conversations becoming more mainstream, speaking up about the desire for better work-life integration is viewed more favorably. Before you engage in a behavior change, like ignoring work emails sent outside business hours, talk to your team about it. Explain your rationale and seek feedback on expectations. Make it clear that your commitment to the job has not changed and that you will continue to perform at a high level.

Revisit the division of labor in your household

Just because you are capable of doing everything—cooking, cleaning, household management, pet and childcare, etc.—doesn't mean you should.

If you have a partner, you should develop a task list that's as evenly distributed as possible between the two of you. Brigid Schulte, author of *Overwhelmed: Work, Love, and Play When No One Has the Time* and director of the Better Life Lab, suggests these exercises to help:

- **The Ruth Bader Ginsburg:** When the former Supreme Court justice's son misbehaved, school officials often called her. She reminded the school that her son had two parents and asked that they alternate between them. Parents can use this example as a jumping-off point to discuss the division of these types of responsibilities and how to take turns owning them.
- **The Leisure Cosponsor:** Each partner should make a list of something they would like to do for fun that week or that month and then develop an accountability plan to ensure each person gets their desired experience. This makes a clear statement that both partners deserve an equal amount of leisure and builds in support to ensure the time is taken.

Voices from the SWAAY Community

Navigating the Home Landscape

Nubia DuVall Wilson

The day I started writing this essay, I got in a spat with my husband while I was baking brownies with the kids. He didn't understand why I had doubled the recipe. Despite the fact that I announced this multiple times: because I wanted to make them thick like I did as a child. As soon as I poured the batter into the pan, he came in and said, "Ooh, that's going to be so thick! Shouldn't we split the batter into two pans?" I saw red. I lashed out at him, telling him how dare he question my nostalgia brownies and why not just say, "Thank you for doing this with the kids," and "I can't wait to eat them"? He looked at me like I was crazy.

Total transparency, I rarely bake, so this was a big deal. On top of that, because of my upbringing, I am hypersensitive to negative feedback when I think I am doing my best. Minutes later, I went to apologize with a spatula full of yummy raw brownie mix for amends, but he asked me to leave him alone. We were both having a rough day. Within an hour, we were saying sorry and laughing at the stupid fight. By nighttime, we were pigging out on my dessert, and my husband acknowledged that double-thick brownies are heaven.

Moral of the story? This pandemic is bringing out the worst and best of us.

Lately, my frustration and pent-up anger has come from observing that this lockdown has brought working mothers—those who normally had outside help—back ten steps with respect to work-life balance, domestic tasks, and what is expected of us when we are married with children. I can't do it all. I won't do it all. So what does that look like in my house right now?

Here's how we are trying to figure this crazy $h&% out!

Look at the Big Picture

Life is rough right now. Emotions and anxieties are sky high, and it is easy to get upset over trivial things. The things that were already annoying you about your partner (big and small) are now amplified. What is a trapped couple to do? Communicate! I've been in therapy since 2015 for PTSD, which has taught me the language and given me the courage to voice my needs appropriately. (Prior to that I didn't think I knew how to do so without yelling). It has taken many years to know how to feel my complex emotions, recognize where they are coming from, and then open up to my husband about what I need from him and why. We aren't perfect. Sometimes a voice will be raised here or there when we disagree or get frustrated, but the two of us know that communication will always be a work in progress. At the end of the day, we want to maintain a loving, healthy relationship—that is our priority.

Let Your Inner Voice Be Heard

Why didn't he pick up the laundry basket I left by the steps to go upstairs? Why did he leave his dirty dishes in the sink when the dishwasher was empty? Sometimes you have to take that inner dialogue in your head with all those complaints about your partner "not doing enough" and say it out loud productively and with respect. Instead of yelling at your partner about why they left dirty dishes in the sink, say, "I am frustrated today because I am feeling overwhelmed with my homeschooling duties while trying to accomplish my work. Can we talk about how you can help me during the day?" Your partner is just as stressed as you are, just about different things, probably. Sitting down and problem-solving together will make you feel supported and part of a team instead of it being about "him versus me."

Plan Ahead

Okay, I am going to say it: some men don't exactly plan in advance as well as women do. My husband admits this fact all the time! Instead of forcing him to figure it out on his own, I turn it into a team effort.

On Sunday, we ask each other what our week looks like, pointing out meeting-heavy days or stressful deadlines. Each night we review our schedules again, so we can cover one another, which prevents only one person becoming responsible for watching over the kids all the time. We tag-team who is responsible for being the "teacher" each day of the week. Sometimes we put Google Calendar invites on our work calendars as reminders for things like when one of us needs to be on a Zoom call and the kids can't be using up our bandwidth. Our short-term memory isn't the best these days, so constant check-ins are saving us.

What Can Each of You Own?

My husband always says how happy he is that I can "keep so many things straight," so he doesn't have to. But even I have a breaking point, and the onus can't always be on one person to remember everything. That's the mental load we all know about as mothers. What household or homeschooling to-dos can you two split up and each be accountable for? There are things your partner can manage, such as being in charge of a certain subject for homeschooling or planning the week of meals.

Sometimes I ask my husband to handle things that aren't on his radar. I may not have the time, but it will drive me crazy if it isn't done. For example, my son's school asked for a photo of him for the yearbook, and they wanted us to decorate a page for him. While I was catching up on my work at 9:00 p.m. after the kids went to bed, my husband worked on the yearbook stuff. Although not a huge priority, in the end, we wanted our son to be included in this memory book, and it was worth the few minutes spent for a lifetime of memories.

"How I Am Maintaining My Work-Life Balance During Quarantine" by Nubia DuVall Wilson was published on SWAAY.com. Nubia is an author, founder of Cielo Consulting, and advocate for survivors of child sexual abuse.

LEADERSHIP SPOTLIGHT

Because of their desire to serve others and lead by example, leaders can be vulnerable to overwork, especially during times of disruption and crisis. In these situations, it's critical to be a positive role model for effective work-life integration even if you are overwhelmed. Remember the airplane rule about putting your own oxygen mask on first. Leaders who burn out won't help the organization, the people who work for them, or their customers. An imbalanced leader is more likely to make poor decisions, miss important details, fail to delegate when appropriate, and neglect team members who are feeling burnout too.

Illustrate to your people through explicit examples how you are managing your health, your time, and your priorities. And if you don't want your people logging into the collaboration platform at 2:00 a.m., don't do it yourself. They may feel compelled to follow suit, leading to an internal competition for who can work the latest hours. Try to be flexible with how work gets done and receptive to new approaches and workarounds. Be transparent—within reason—about the juggling challenges you're facing at work and home.

During a crisis, the worst thing a leader can do is act out of touch with or in denial of current realities. Employees want their leaders to understand and have empathy for what they're going through.

Whether you work in an office or not, be visible and accessible to your team. Let people know when and how to reach you and what communication channels are most appropriate for different scenarios. Consider checking in with team members regularly about the status of their work-life integration efforts and schedule time for the team to get together and let off some steam via happy hours or games, even if they're virtual.

If you feel like you're losing control or your own burnout is worsening, freely reach out for advice. Your own manager, an HR representative, or a counselor are all good resources. Even if you've been a leader for a while, the past few years have brought unprecedented stress for everyone. In many cases, the most mature and upstanding thing you can do is ask for help.

Tai Beauchamp, whom I interviewed on my podcast, has been an inspiration when it comes to leadership and work-life integration. She made history as *Seventeen* magazine's youngest and first African American beauty director at the age of twenty-five. In addition to starting her own website, The Tai Life, which inspires women to be their full selves, Tai hosts TLC's *Window Warriors* and is a frequent media commentator on *The View*, *The Wendy Williams Show*, and *Bethenny*.

Since her start as an intern at *O Magazine*, where she worked sixteen-hour days, Tai wanted to become the editor in chief of a magazine. She credits early mentors for her rapid ascent and now tries to be the best leader she can.

As a high-profile executive, Tai told me, you're not sitting in some beautiful tower. "People at the helm of a major magazine are engaged socially. It's a privilege to connect authentically with and inspire people," she says. Post-publishing, Tai still leads in many areas of her life, and her secrets to effective work-life integration are knowing when she's burned out and needs to move on and being highly scheduled. She taught me a calendar trick I now swear by. "If it's not on the calendar, it doesn't happen," she shared. "I use scheduling to ensure I have time for the things I feel are important. I prioritize what's essential and I don't overextend myself." Tai models these skills for her teams through open dialogue and delegation. "I know the people who I can rely on and that I don't have to do everything myself," she says. By emphasizing this attitude, Tai protects herself well and keeps her balance on the glass ledge.

CUE THE REAL WORLD

Now that we've discussed some ledge-protector strategies around work-life integration, how might you move forward in finding the best mix for you? Use these questions as prompts to reflect on your thoughts in your journal.

- What wellness goals or enjoyable activities will you commit to each week? Examples of wellness goals include taking a fitness class, cooking a healthy meal, practicing an instrument, learning meditation, or spending quality time with your family.

- How will you ensure that you attend to these goals every week? For instance, can you block time on your calendar, have an accountability buddy, or pay for a course?

- How does each of these goals fit into your life's strategic plan and help you achieve better work-life integration?

BALANCE LEDGE REVIEW

- While there aren't enough hours in the day to place full focus on everything that's important, we fall off the glass ledge when we put all our proverbial eggs in one basket and **neglect the others.**
- Achieving goals in the service of better work-life integration doesn't have to be difficult. The key is **the size of the goal.** People feel it's easier to achieve a small incremental goal than to maintain the status quo.
- **Mindfulness** is a series of strategies that bring awareness to present-moment thoughts, feelings, and bodily sensations without interpreting or judging them.
- If you recognize **burnout signs** in yourself, assess the cause. Should imbalance or poor work-life integration be the culprit, consider taking specific actions to get back in alignment.
- Remember the **airplane rule** about putting on your own oxygen mask first. An imbalanced leader is more likely to make poor decisions, miss important details, and fail to delegate when appropriate.

"If I'm too competitive, they'll see me as the enemy."

◇◇◇◇◇

"Society wants women to tear each other down."

◇◇◇◇◇

"I don't want to compete. I want us all to win."

◇◇◇◇◇

"I feel obligated to help out other women whether we're aligned or not."

◇◇◇◇◇

"There's only room for so many of us at the top."

◇◇◇◇◇

*"It's easier to compete against myself than
stand out against someone else."*

◇◇◇◇◇

"I can't help being jealous. Everything is so easy for her!"

◇◇◇◇◇

"If I can't be number one, I might as well quit."

◇◇◇◇◇

"Stepping into the ring when I want something feels greedy."

◇◇◇◇◇

*"I can't show my competitive side because
women take everything so personally."*

◇◇◇◇◇

Chapter Eight

COMPETITION

I was raised to be competitive. Growing up under Moroccan and French school systems, it wasn't just about passing or failing the classes. It was about ranking number one across the entire curriculum—and outshining my classmates was my number-one sport. My parents signed me up for extracurricular activities and expected me to excel in those too. By the time I was a teenager, when I wasn't competing for good grades, I was competing in tennis. Every year I listed the names of the people I needed to beat on a corkboard in my room.

When we moved from Morocco to Colorado, I made my high school's women varsity tennis team and ranked first in doubles. I loved competing, whether it was against my teammates or other teams. It was one of the very few hobbies that helped me release my unresolved teenage depression while settling into life in a new country. Channeling my competitive spirit this way also brought back a sense of belonging.

I've always been comfortable competing with both boys and girls, men and women. I've never been ashamed to admit that winning is an essential part of the game of life. My competitive spirit drove me to become the best at what I did, and I enjoyed competitor camaraderie.

This is probably why I was attracted to pageantry. Beauty pageants and the women who compete in them have an outdated reputation for cattiness and hostility. If I had a dollar for every time someone asked me if women backstage sabotage each other or snatch the crown from the winner out of jealousy, I'd be writing this book from my beach-front mansion. Is it a competitive environment? Yes, absolutely. But in the seven years I competed, I never sensed aggressiveness in it. I never witnessed women being manipulative or mean to get ahead. In fact, pageantry was the first environment where I found competition and sisterhood integrated in a nonthreatening way. Many of the women I initially perceived as rivals have become the people I most admire and support—and vice versa. While healthy competition is welcomed among pageant contestants, comparison *is* the enemy because it can lead to envy and feelings that are ultimately self-sabotaging. The pageant management knows this and encourages contestants to build friendships and community throughout the competition.

In an article for Quartz, Diane Barth writes that while competition is alive and well among women, it doesn't have to be a bad thing. "The feeling many women have that competition is shameful actually makes the results of jealousy and envy worse," she says. "To the contrary, finding a way to integrate competition and rivalry with loving, admiring, and nurturing feelings toward the same person can be difficult but extremely rewarding." Amen! It's as if Barth was at those pageants with me.

In the business world, though, this healthy attitude toward competition isn't always present, even as we extol the virtues of "women supporting women." Jessica Knoll started her career working at *Cosmopolitan*, a job thousands of twenty-something women would do for free. Although she rose to the position of senior editor, Jessica never stopped feeling insecure. Her experience led her to write two novels, *Luckiest Girl Alive* and *The Favorite Sister*, which both explore the theme of women's competition.

"On the surface, there's a change happening. Women are recognizing the power of putting all of our voices together," Knoll told Melissa Batchelor Warnke in an interview for Girlboss. "But I'm also seeing people getting behind that message who don't live it." Knoll says that once she started thinking about women being pitted against each other, she started seeing it everywhere. "I was watching a celebrity news show, and they were talking about how Kate Middleton was probably miffed that Prince Harry and Meghan Markle's wedding date would take place so close on the heels of her giving birth so she'd have to squeeze into a dress. The hosts suggested she wasn't really happy for them. This was all speculation; there was absolutely nothing to suggest that this was really going on." Knoll went on to say in her interview that, "When we're fed bullshit about women, it's important that we view it with a critical eye and a critical ear. This isn't really how these two sisters-in-law are looking at each other; that's just spin. I've started stepping back and saying, 'I'm not catty, I'm not jealous. You put me in this position.' We can find an empowering response: 'I refuse to let this culture define me or define my relationships with other women anymore. I'm going to be the one to define them,'" Knoll asserted.

I'm disappointed by a culture that promotes this "women *only* tear each other down" angle. When we view women as backstabbers, we reinforce the mindset that we must watch our backs with each other. The media has conditioned me to think that every woman I meet is out to get me, even though most of my experiences have been quite the opposite. In reality, men are much more likely to aggressively compete than women. Research indicates that women are actually reluctant to compete with anyone other than themselves. In a study by the University of Pennsylvania, George Mason University, and the German Institute for Economic Research, among 1,200 participants in a question-and-answer game, 58 percent of the men chose to receive greater rewards for competing against others compared to only 38 percent of the women.

More intriguing? Only 22 percent of the women chose to compete against another woman, and women who were told their opponent had the same ability chose to compete only 30 percent of the time. "Our study and others suggest that women tend to underestimate their own ability relative to their opponent," coauthor Coren Apicella told Medical Daily. "If women are underestimating their ability, then they are less likely to compete, and consequently, they may be less likely to improve their performance or get that recognition from winning."

Is this research evidence that the pendulum might be swinging too far in the other direction? As women's movements like Girlboss, Lean In, and #metoo have taken off, some are now embracing the idea that women must band together in *all* circumstances and should be shamed for doing otherwise. But why must we sacrifice our competitive spirit for collaboration? Why do we internalize that it's (sometimes) okay to compete with men but feel we must restrain our competitive side with other women?

If we want to stay balanced on the glass ledge, we must design positive beliefs around healthy competition with both men and women and embrace these as a growth strategy—so long as we play fair! To that end, the rest of this chapter will explore how to use competition to improve yourself, how to manage jealousy and envy, and how to form positive relationships with "competitors."

LEDGE PROTECTOR #1: USE COMPETITION TO IMPROVE YOURSELF

Several years ago, in the service of self-growth, I spontaneously decided to move to New York. This was just after I "lost" (I placed first runner-up) at the Miss Colorado USA pageant to the girl who was dating the guy I liked. She not only won the guy's heart but also snagged the crown for which I had worked so hard. Although heartbroken that night, I felt more driven than ever. Her triumphs pushed me to finally take a leap of faith and go after all four of my dreams at once: move to New York City, land my dream job, fall in love, and win a New York State pageant title. I achieved all four within six months of taking that leap of faith. To this day I am thankful for that competitive moment. We were both winners that night!

Humans have had to compete since the beginning of our existence. After all, if we didn't pull our weight and pull it well, our tribe might ostracize us, and we'd be vulnerable to predators. Many people still feel that instinctual competitive fire in their bellies. "Competition activates the prefrontal cortex area of the brain," explains Colin Robertson in an article for WillPowered.com. "It gives us a rush of willpower and focuses our mind on doing whatever it takes to get there."

As Robertson points out, competition does not have to involve losers. In tribal days, "natural competition did not originate from jealousy or hatred of one another. It stemmed from an inner desire to be the best."

So how can you develop your competitive spirit if it doesn't come easily to you? Robertson has a few good suggestions, the first being to literally look in the mirror. "Something odd happens in our brains when we look at ourselves in the mirror. Rather than seeing who we are, we see who we want to be. Having this ideal self in mind triggers our competitive response and helps us find the motivation to be our best." Next, keep in mind that

a sense of healthy competition is easier to cultivate when you care about the thing for which you're competing.

"We must have something that we want to be the best at so badly that we will work toward it even when we're stressed and tired," says Robertson. "Don't try to force this purpose. Find the thing you're willing to fight for and devote yourself to that. This will allow you to tap into your true potential." Finally, Robertson advocates having a benchmark for success: "Our competition drive is highest when we know exactly what we are competing against. Athletes, for example, measure their current performance against the performance they need in order to win."

Your benchmark doesn't have to be official or shared with anyone else as long as it's clear, detailed, and achievable. Smart competitors know when they have the chops to compete and when to let others have the niche or the spotlight.

As an example, Rachel Drori, a woman I admire and have interviewed on my podcast, stepped into a crowded market for her company when she founded Daily Harvest a few years ago. "When I was getting started, Blue Apron and Hello Fresh already existed," she explains. "I was grateful for the competition because it helped me understand that there was an appetite for direct-to-consumer food. I learned from their experience, namely that it was pretty difficult to deliver everything fresh. A meal kit would sit rotting in my fridge because I hadn't had time to make it."

By studying her competition, Rachel went to market with a variety of prepared frozen smoothies and parfaits. "Freezing actually maintains the nutrients, and by telling consumers this, we had them looking at frozen food in a new way. We tried to create something different, and to this day we don't have any competitors that do the exact same thing."

I have my own experience here too. When I entered the women's digital media space, I was told constantly that the space was too crowded. Advertising dollars were lacking, and readers were overwhelmed by too much content. It took studying the shortcomings of my competition to identify white spaces for SWAAY's business model, structure, and platform offering. While other women founders in my space were raising more money than I was, I read every article I could find about their successes and used them as inspiration to improve my own product. Without the news of how these women founders broke barriers, I wouldn't have continued to believe in what I do and the possibility of growing SWAAY to millions of readers.

Like everyone else, I've had to navigate my feelings of envy along the way and learn to be truly happy for others' accomplishments. And it has been worth it, because when it's done the right way, competition can be energizing, rewarding, and even fun.

LEDGE PROTECTOR #2: LEARN TO MANAGE JEALOUSY

Jealousy is one of those sentiments that definitely evolves with age. "A number of women said that they felt less competitive as they got older," writes Diane Barth in Quartz. "But many told me that they had learned to find other women who were comfortable with who they were; they didn't try to outdo one another or hide their successes." There's truth to this. When I was younger, I could barely contain the green-eyed monster, but as I get older, I've learned more strategies to make it easier.

Here's the first one. Regardless of how old you are or where you are in your life, you must come to terms with the fact that there's always someone better than you.

No matter how brilliant, talented, lucky, or gorgeous you are, you're bound to come across someone who is more brilliant, more talented, luckier, and more gorgeous.

Comparing yourself to others and hoping you'll end up on top is a losing proposition.

Being jealous of others also takes up a lot of energy. It's a negative feeling that distracts you from doing what you need to do to achieve your goals. Jealousy can also lead you to behavior you'd normally think abhorrent, like sabotaging another person's success, embarrassing the person in public, or burning bridges.

Poor self-awareness is why we tumble from a lot of glass ledges. Jealousy is definitely a hurdle to overcome. It may manifest as dislike, so if the other person hasn't done anything to offend you, consider whether jealousy might be the culprit and if you are being catty in response. "Ask yourself if you are running in a pack of cliquish, catty friends," writes engineer and former US Navy leader Jenn Donahue in an essay for SWAAY. "The mean girl, after all, rarely hunts alone. Instead, remain committed to the high road and find others to join you. If you are part of a cruel clique, try reaching out to work with someone outside your club. You can still receive recognition for your contributions while acknowledging others when they do something well. And if you see other women being catty toward each other, become an active bystander and step in."

If anyone knows how to take the high road, it's Jenn. She built a bridge in the middle of an Iraqi war zone and constructed combat outposts in deserts filled with insurgents. Known as "Earthquake Doc," Jenn spearheaded earthquake and tsunami reconnaissance missions in Samoa and Japan, designed the seismic plans for a bridge over the Panama Canal, and served as the seismology expert at five nuclear power plants. She certainly didn't have time for jealousy or cattiness on these missions!

Lastly, keep in mind that if you are jealous of someone because their life seems perfect, the reality may be far different. I'm a prime example. There was a time if you looked at my life-reel—having a pageant title, running a meaningful business, maintaining a happy long-term relationship, being in the press, speaking at high-profile events, and judging Miss Universe—that I seemed to have it all together. But behind the curtain, I was consumed by anxiety, stress, and overwhelm. There were weeks when my business was so short on capital that my bank account was overdrawn by $3,000 and I was behind on my own bills. When I keynoted the Harvard Women in Business conference alongside billionaire makeup guru Huda Kattan and finance veteran Sallie Krawcheck, some of the audience members told me they were jealous of my career and financial freedom. Meanwhile, a few days earlier, I wasn't sure I could afford my train ticket to the event. So it's important to remind yourself that successes and struggles aren't always what they seem, and in the age of social media, you might actually be further along than most of the people you feel jealous of.

The best way to combat peer jealousy is simply to compete directly and fairly. As Jenn advises: "Focus on your own growth and achievable milestones. But don't get frustrated if the change is slow. The way we learned to compete is a habit, and habits don't change overnight."

◆Ledge Work: Getting to the Root of Envy

As Diane Barth writes in her Quartz article, "The more directly we acknowledge competition, the less likely it is that we will resort to underhanded or manipulative behavior when they emerge—sparing us toxic feelings and damage to our self-esteem and our friendships."

Admitting, even to ourselves, that we are jealous of another person can be difficult to do. Consider a person in your life who has something you want. It could be greater career success, a doting boyfriend, a supportive family, an innate talent, or a more beautiful physical appearance. In your journal, note how you feel when you see or hear from this person. For example, have you noticed physiological symptoms like a racing heart or shortness of breath? Have you felt a vague sense of hostility or resentment even though the other person did nothing to deserve it? How have these feelings impacted your relationship?

Now consider a person you don't know in real life who has something you want. You might feel a twinge every time you see them on your social media channels. In your journal, note whether this person's name or image triggers you, and speculate why you might feel the way you do.

◆

LEDGE PROTECTOR #3: ENCOURAGE POSITIVE RELATIONSHIPS WITH COMPETITORS

In 2015, I met an amazing founder who was as passionate about uplifting women as I am. Let's call her Amy. When I had the chance to interview her as one of the first guests on my podcast, we immediately had a "did we just become best friends?" moment. Amy and I stayed in touch, and I supported her work in any way I could. I invited her to networking events and introduced her to other interesting women, and she did the same for me. A few years later, as I launched SWAAY and the hype was building, I noticed Amy had gone quiet. Eventually, I realized she had blocked me from her social media channels. Through the grapevine, I surmised that because I had launched a platform in a similar field, Amy now considered me competition. I was disheartened that someone I so admired and supported had shut me out in the name of competition. I felt we could have partnered instead, continuing to elevate and challenge each other. I later heard Amy speak at a women's conference, and when she encouraged the audience to go the extra mile to support each other, I stood up and left.

You might be thinking, *Why didn't you address the situation with her head on?* The truth is, as I grew into my role as a business leader and change agent, distance became my new response to disrespect. Instead of returning such energy, I remove myself from situations outside my control and focus on my own feelings and reactions.

But while not everyone will offer a productive response to jealousy, that doesn't have to stop us from having one. For every instance like the one I just shared, there are hundreds of people who encourage positive relationships with competitors. My fellow media entrepreneur Kellee Khalil is one such example. Although our businesses target different demographics, Kellee and I could be considered competitors because we are both founders building and scaling women's tech platforms. I first read about Kellee's company, Loverly, in 2013 and was eager to feature her story on our home page during SWAAY's launch.

Kellee eventually became a trusted mentor, friend, and investor. My podcast interview with her was one of the most popular episodes because of how raw and genuine our conversations were. Kellee could have seen me as an emerging competitor from day one, but she went out of her way to cultivate our relationship. In 2018, when I was on the verge of giving up on SWAAY, she coached me on my business model and monetization issues to help me approach my business in a way that allowed me to become financially stable. Kellee later confided in me that while helping me rebuild my business, my own progress challenged her to take her company to new heights. And even though we've had our fair share of disagreements and challenges, I credit Kellee with strenghtening my belief in integrating collaboration and healthy competition. Instead of spending our time and energy outshining each other—or worse, ignoring each other out of fear and jealousy—we've fostered a competitive spirit that's helped us both grow into more confident leaders.

"If a friend is good enough to compete with, then she is also someone we can admire, appreciate, and learn from," Diane Barth writes. Letting go of jealousy is simpler if you think of your competitors as being part of the same team and believe that there is enough good fortune for everyone. Ann Friedman and Aminatou Sow, hosts of the *Call Your Girlfriend* podcast, developed the idea of Shine Theory to express this perspective. "Shine Theory is an investment, over the long term, in helping someone be their best self—and relying on their help in return," they explain. "It is a conscious decision to bring your full self to your friendships and to not let insecurity or envy ravage them. Shine Theory is a commitment to asking, 'Would we be better as collaborators than as competitors?' The answer is almost always yes."

Cultivating a spirit of genuine happiness and excitement when your competitors are doing well takes practice.

They further explained that when someone is targeting you as competition, it's often because they themselves lack confidence or support.

To illustrate Shine Theory, imagine you are a nail salon owner with a friend who owns the same kind of business on the other side of town. Technically, yes, you are competitors, but customers tend to frequent the salon closest to their homes, so in reality your clientele is split fairly evenly and permanently. Instead of spending all your cash trying to one-up your friend with promotional activity, why not work with her on designing creative new promotions that can benefit both businesses? Why not take a leadership role in the small business community and divide and conquer the work required? Why not meet for a glass of wine to learn from each other's successes and failures and to brainstorm on issues the two of you are experts on, like hiring aestheticians and ensuring health and safety standards in your salons? By engaging in this way, you preserve your friendship and move toward your own goals. While your collaboration is underway, you can still maintain a healthy competition that keeps both of you on your toes for continuous improvement.

I was fortunate to sit down with fashion icon and successful entrepreneur Rebecca Minkoff for an interview on my podcast and as part of her pop-up women's discussion series in New York City. She told me that the fashion community was like high school. "It was insular and cliquish, and I was never a part of that. I've always just wanted women to support one another." Originally, Rebecca expressed her view by hosting networking dinners for women from different industries. But she realized she could help more women if she scaled her message, so she launched a series of fireside chats, a podcast called *Superwomen*, a nonprofit organization called the Female Founder Collective (FFC), and a women's educational platform called 10th House.

I asked Rebecca how the FFC came about. She shared that when she engaged with investors, they often had no idea which organizations on their rosters were founded by women. "Many women in my network have exited their companies quite successfully and are in a position to galvanize and invest in other women launching startups," she said. "The FFC and the symbol we developed for it make it simple to identify women founders and woman-led businesses you want to help lift up."

The Female Founders Collective is now a national endeavor, with thousands of members (myself included) sharing excitement around new female-founded brands. This degree of support has been instrumental in many founders' trajectories.

Rebecca's FFC is another example of Shine Theory at work. And yet, enthusiastic and unconditional support for other women isn't always a given—and it doesn't need to be. Recall what we covered on likability in chapter 2 and understand that always stepping down from competition because you want to be liked will not serve you. You don't have to be best friends with everyone simply because you share a gender identity, an interest, an industry, or a bloodline. The *Call Your Girlfriend* hosts concur. "Don't mistake this for networking. Shine Theory is not about trying to help everyone you meet along the way in your career, because if you're doing it right, it's simply not possible to invest deeply in that many people. There are only so many hours and so many email replies in any given day."

Generally speaking, I feel that Shine Theory is a good principle to live by. We all have enough obstacles to overcome. Helping someone out does not take away from your own accomplishments or potential—in fact, it sets up opportunities that can result only when two or more talented people join forces. When you do choose to compete rather than collaborate, there's no reason to view the other side as the enemy. As long as everyone plays fair, competitors should respect each other's efforts and abilities.

Voices from the SWAAY Community

Climbing Alongside Other Women

Celeste Durve

Working Girl, 1988. It's a beloved little comedy centering on Tess McGill (Melanie Griffith), new to the cutthroat business world and secretary to Katharine Parker (Sigourney Weaver). When Katherine steals a tip from Tess to further ascend the corporate ladder, Tess "borrows" Katharine's identity to regain what is rightfully hers. The movie closes with Tess winning the showdown while a scorned Katharine fades into irrelevance with her tail between her legs. Oh, and Tess also manages to steal Katharine's boyfriend along the way. It is a heartwarming tale about two women battling for a seat at the boys' table that just so happens to be written by a man.

Pop culture, literature, and real-world anecdotes have been telling us for decades that women are in competition with one another. The mythos surrounding Corporate America says that everything is dog eat dog, which often translates to woman versus woman. This, unfortunately, is not entirely untrue and is likely due to the fact there are so few seats available at the countless tables where women rightfully belong but are conspicuously absent from.

It's a grueling climb to the top, and it seems like every woman for herself along the way. As of this year, women hold 6.6 percent of Fortune 500 CEO roles. That does not occur by happenstance; it is systemic. But we at VIPER want to have a hand in changing this.

VIPER is an all-female nightlife team in Los Angeles. We're no strangers to the occasionally nuanced but more often blatant patriarchal paradigms of working in a world that was built for men. Because of this, we understand and embrace the idea of collective evolution, leaving doors open for women wherever we can. From the beginning, we knew that we wanted our company's principles and culture to be unmistakably female-focused; it has never been a gimmick for us. As co-CEOs and founders of VIPER (born under our parent company KCH Group), not only do we look to leave doors of opportunities open, we also work to empower the individuals who will eventually walk through them.

While we are highly selective of whom we employ, the number-one characteristic we search for in a potential VIPER Girl is enthusiasm. There is so much room for growth, independence, and creativity in our company; we seek out the people who will be inspired by the environment we strive to cultivate. This is why we never want our VIPER Girls to feel they've been simply "hired." We want them to feel brought into the fold.

We know firsthand that it is entirely possible for a woman to carve out a path for herself without the help of women in positions of power. We also know that it is entirely unnecessary. There is no hesitation on our end to lift other women up, nor should there be from any other females in high places. There is a huge danger in fanning the flames of resentment and competition. Every day, our bodies, our livelihoods and even our rights are threatened by middle-aged men in power. Furthermore, our victories are ridiculed and consistently opposed by those exact men who are maintaining a status quo that exists to hold all others back.

We cannot keep putting up with relentless discriminatory restrictions placed on us in retaliation to our brave steps forward. We need to take back the standards and redefine them for ourselves, together. We don't require assistance from men in setting the bar. We set the bar higher than they could ever hope to. We want to prove, through positive influence, that professional growth and economic independence are possible for women, and we want to show that it isn't without sacrifice or mistakes.

Since day one, we've chosen to be transparent about our flaws as leaders. Our VIPER Girls have seen us stand up for ourselves and soar. They've also seen us fumble and deal with the fallout. In order for us to evolve together, we need to show one another that we don't have to be perfect to build a beautiful world. If the world were perfect, it would never be beautiful.

This is what we've always believed in. And maybe that's why we were always able to believe in ourselves. We started our company in our early twenties with only $1,500. In the last three years we have dominated the nightlife industry and gained clientele that is unmatched. We understand, now more than ever, the impact women are capable of if we support and provide agency for each other. If we can thrive in the male-dominated business environment, we can certainly work to fix it. We will expand our reach and bring insurmountable change. Our futures can be reimagined and renegotiated. We can do it, together. We must.

"It's Not a Competition, It's a Climb" was written by Celeste Durve and published on SWAAY.com. Celeste is the cofounder of VIPER by KCH, a high-end, front-of-house operations company running doors at some of the biggest clubs and events in Hollywood.

LEADERSHIP SPOTLIGHT

When you're a leader, it can be difficult to ascertain when you should encourage competition among your team. Post-COVID, we live in a gentler world in which some leaders are afraid that competition will disincentivize their people. While it's true that nonstop or inappropriate means of competition are not called for—for instance, a competition that unfairly rewards some forms of hard work over others or distracts team members from pre-established group goals—some friendly team rivalry can build rapport and camaraderie as well as catapult performances to new levels.

According to Ben Olds, a leadership coach and writer on the Fistful of Talent blog, leaders who want to facilitate productive competition must identify the right scenarios. "First, you need situations that don't require collaboration across competing groups. People are less likely to help one another if helping isn't aligned with their ability to win," he says. "Second, you want to avoid situations where the 'losers' of the competition would be demoralized. That could cut down on risktaking and lead to everyone playing it safe and not stretching. Instead, look for situations where winning can be celebrated while losing isn't devastating." Olds says that

as a leader, you want to introduce elements that bring out the natural human urge to try a bit harder.

"You want situations that have clearly measurable outcomes, Olds says. If you can't measure it objectively, it's tough to ensure integrity in the outcome. You need the competitors to clearly and directly impact the outcome without too much left to chance, and you want a situation in which people are competing for something that matters to them."

Olds suggests these exercises as potentially fruitful team competitions:

- The first team to complete 100 percent of its performance reviews.
- The team with the highest participation in wellness initiatives.
- The team with the best workplace safety record.
- The team with the highest number of aggregate community service hours.

Note that competitions like these will be most effective when they take place over a specified time period, when online communication forums are used to heighten engagement and excitement, and when timely rewards are offered to the winning team.

CUE THE REAL WORLD

Now that we've reviewed some of the nuances around competition, let's put them to work in your life. Write your responses to these questions in your journal.

- Identify a competitor you believe is doing something more effectively than you. What can you learn from this person?

- How might you approach this person for mentorship or a potential partnership?

- Has someone in your space who might be perceived as a competitor ever reached out to you? How did you respond? How might you be more open and generous to such overtures in the future?

COMPETITION LEDGE REVIEW

- If we want to get ahead, we must design positive beliefs around healthy competition with both men and women and embrace it as a **growth strategy**—so long as we play fair!
- Smart competitors know when they have the chops to compete with something they can **differentiate** and when to let others have the niche or the spotlight.
- Acknowledging that you are **jealous** of someone is definitely a hurdle to overcome. Jealousy may manifest as dislike, so if the other person hasn't done anything to offend you, consider whether jealousy might be the culprit and you are being catty in response.
- By developing **positive relationships** with competitors, you preserve friendships and move toward your own goals. While collaboration is underway, you can still maintain a healthy competition that keeps both of you on your toes and focused on continuous improvement.
- **Team competitions** are most effective when they take place over a specified time period, when online communication forums are used to heighten engagement and excitement, and when timely rewards are offered to the winning team.

"Oh, I can't do that, I don't have any experience in it."

"I've been in this field ten years; I know what I'm doing."

"If I just keep hammering away, I'll eventually get it."

"The men here just make it too difficult."

"I don't have the right training to move forward."

"It's too late for me to transition into something new."

"I don't have the experience to comment on that."

"How can she have more expertise? We're at the same level!"

"That's not my area; I can't get involved."

"I started a business; I can't go back now!"

Chapter Nine

EXPERTISE

As I mentioned earlier in the book, I've spent the last couple of years offering free, one-on-one coaching sessions to women who were looking to build their authority and raise their industry profiles. SWAAY's mission is to elevate women's stories and give aspiring and established thought leaders an outlet to increase their visibility as go-to experts. I've noticed, though, that even when offered extensive support, some women are still apprehensive about the value of their expertise.

Over the course of hundreds of meetings, I've heard women say over and over that they lack expertise to speak or write on a subject. And when I follow up with the questions, "What does expertise mean to you, and why do you think you lack it after X years in the field?" they usually don't have an answer. I vowed to get to the bottom of this in *The Glass Ledge*.

You may be familiar with the statistic that men will apply for jobs when they meet 60 percent of the qualifications, while women tend to apply only if they meet 100 percent. In an article for *Harvard Business Review*, Tara Sophia Mohr argues that the issue is not a crisis of confidence but rather a misunderstanding of what expertise really means. Mohr cites a Hewlett Packard survey in which women shared a common refrain: "I didn't think they would hire me since I didn't meet the qualifications, and I didn't want to put myself out there if I was likely to fail." Most women think they have to be perfect right out of the gate, when in fact many others (especially men) are going for jobs in which they have some—but not all—of the right expertise.

Don't fall off the glass ledge by giving up immediately on something you want because you think you don't have the expertise you need.

I am the woman I am today because I've been willing to delve into careers based on my interests rather than bullet-proof expertise. Following my passion for impact, I embarked on global medical missions with a team of accomplished doctors when I hadn't even gone to medical school. I believed in my value as a leader despite a lack of formal training. Later, I confused investors by launching a media company without expertise or experience in journalism or business. I was labeled an "outsider," but little did they know I thought this was a positive attribute. It meant I'd have a fresh and innovative perspective, that I wasn't stuck in the old ways of doing things.

Seeking to be "an expert" was never my goal because I didn't want to stop learning. But "gaining expertise" has been a different story. I've always sought to uncover new ways of navigating my business by drawing lessons from others. In my one-on-one coaching, I've listened to my clients' challenges and come up with ways to evolve our services and platform features in response.

Then there was my podcast venture. When I first started listening to shows by entrepreneurs from my corporate cubicle in our Madison Avenue office building, I was clueless about running a business and had no "million-dollar ideas" of which to speak. While I learned a ton from these entrepreneurs, I wished their stories related more directly to my demographic. I thought that with my own podcast series, I could accomplish a few things at once: I'd have a chance to network with intriguing women role models, and I could share inspiring stories and advice with millennial women who want to do big things but don't know where to turn. It sounds simple, but in reality I had no podcasting experience whatsoever. For some people, that would have been the end of the road, but I hired a podcasting mentor to coach me in buying the right audio equipment, recording the interviews, and doing the editing. As the series grew and my platform evolved, I hired people who were actual experts in areas where I simply understood the basics. In other words, I eventually became "expert enough" to achieve my goal of hosting a podcast.

Before we go further, let's explore the notion of expertise in greater detail, including the facets that are truly important and those that are less relevant.

Expertise might be defined as elite performance in or mastery of something, from craftsmanship to sports. A few years ago, it seemed like everyone had read Malcolm Gladwell's Book *Outliers*, and the most quoted section of the book was about expertise and the ten thousand hours it allegedly takes to become proficient.

In an article for the Association for Talent Development, Patti Shank shares that the ten thousand–hour idea is actually based on a misrepresented area of research by K. Anders Ericsson, a psychologist and professor at Florida State University. Ericsson said that while the world's best violinists might practice an average of ten thousand hours, this number isn't a hard and fast rule for every area of expertise. And more importantly,

expertise isn't really about the number of hours you put in at all. Rather, it's about how you use those hours.

Shank describes Ericsson's notion of "deliberate practice" using a scenario involving two graphic designers who work on the same type of projects in the same department. One of them, Dominic, is driven to gain new skills and improve the skills he already has. He has a mentor outside of work and looks for regular feedback from people with more advanced skills. He reads what experts in the field say, asks questions, and folds what he is learning into new work. His focused effort is paying off in better designs and expanded skill set. The other designer, Jenny, is an adequate designer, but to her, it's simply work. She is satisfied with what she knows how to do. In this way, Dominic is gaining expertise, but Jenny isn't. "We cannot confuse deliberate practice with normal work," writes Shank. "Same ol', same ol' does *not* equal better performance."

Reading Ericsson's work, you might assume that deliberate practice is the secret sauce, and anyone who does it well or long enough can become an expert. Not everyone agrees with this, however. In a groundbreaking study reported in the journal *Psychological Science*, Brooke Macnamara, a psychologist from Princeton University, and her colleagues David Hambrick from Michigan State University and Frederick Oswald from Rice University found that deliberate practice accounted for just 12 percent of the individual differences found in performance. The degree to which this type of practice helped also depended on the domain, improving performance on games by 26 percent, music by 21 percent, sports by 18 percent, and education by only 4 percent. So practice matters, but it's by no means the only factor. Other variables including physical and mental abilities, personality, and environmental support play a role as well.

And here's another thing. I recently came across an article on Medium that caught my attention. Writer Elizabeth Burnam claims that expertise, in the traditional sense, has become obsolete. "In the past, expertise was a valuable trait—a thing to be valued, bragged about, and put on a pedestal," she writes. "But businesses no longer need expertise. Today, everyone with Internet access and well-developed media literacy has a comprehensive and authoritative knowledge or skill at their fingertips. When the whole world has access to the same level of knowledge that you have, expertise is no longer confined to those who've spent years studying and working in a particular position."

According to Burnam, we must extend the definition of an expert to suit the twenty-first century. An expert today is someone who knows enough about a subject to stretch the limits of that subject and advance current knowledge. True expertise lies in one's adaptability, creativity, and willingness to take calculated risks. But, she adds, "When you've spent most of your life building up your credibility as an expert, admitting that you're ignorant about new developments in that subject can be a terrifying experience. It's this fear that causes so-called experts to forge ahead with outdated strategies rather than admit that the old way is no longer the best way. If you want to maintain your status as an expert in the twenty-first century, then you need to confront your blind spots, accept that certain knowledge has an expiration date, and learn to develop creative, future-facing solutions even in the midst of uncertainty."

I love this notion of an expert as someone who evolves with their field of study and is comfortable changing course and pushing boundaries, because that's what my career has certainly proven!

Serial entrepreneur Sara Al Madani is one of my dearest friends and a role model for women who want to push into areas in which they have little to no experience. She has confidently ventured into every field she wanted to, even when others said she had no business in those industries. At a time when she knew only men's tailors in the United Arab Emirates, Sara desired to change women's clothing in her country. "I was told you have to shop to become a fashion designer, but I didn't have the money for that. I didn't give up because I didn't have the knowledge, I just sought the knowledge," she told me. Sara asked the tailors she knew about design and stitching. She interned and modeled for other designers and raised $10,000 to buy a small store of her own. Gradually, her take on mixing traditional and modern sensibilities became the biggest women's clothing brand in the Middle East.

Later, Sara wanted to start a restaurant for people with food allergies, so she consulted a famous English chef. She told me: "The guy was like, 'You can't do that. You don't have the right background. Do you even know how to cook?" But she didn't let that stop her. "I Googled 'how to open a restaurant' and hired people who could teach me everything. No matter what you want to do, you don't have to have expertise at the start."

Sara didn't think twice about switching from fashion to restaurants, but this is something most women tend to struggle with. Once we select a college major and embark on a career, we often believe we're stuck with that path. I've learned through my own twisty career in STEM, philanthropy, pageantry, and the entrepreneurial world that we can hold a variety of roles. And there is no shame in pivoting until you find your ultimate field of expertise.

Also, keep in mind that soft skills are expertise too. Regardless of where your professional journey takes you, you can always work on skills like interpersonal communication, diplomacy, and problem-solving. The best thing about soft skills is that you can always practice them with your partner, children, a friend on a walk through the woods, or in a random conversation with a stranger on an airplane!

In addition to rethinking the concept of expertise, we must develop our ability to pivot and *learn* to learn. In the rest of this chapter, we'll look at strategies, including holding our own in male-dominated fields, building cross-functional and cross-industry expertise, and driving an agile career long-term.

LEDGE PROTECTOR #1: CHALLENGE THE "LEAN-IN" PHILOSOPHY

According to the global nonprofit Catalyst, male-dominated industries are particularly prone to reinforcing masculine stereotypes that make it difficult for women to excel and gain expertise. In 2018, only 7 percent of women worked full time in male-dominated occupations. This trend of women and men remaining concentrated in different fields is known as occupational segregation. It gets even worse: in the US, male-dominated occupations generally pay more than female-dominated occupations. Catalyst reports that 26 out of the 30 highest-paying jobs in the US are male-dominated, while 23 out of the 30 lowest-paying jobs are female-dominated. In Canada, women who participate in apprenticeship programs in male-dominated fields earn 14 percent less than men in median hourly wages, and they are less likely than men to attain a job related to their field after the program.

When you do select a traditionally male occupation, equal pay isn't the only challenge you can expect to face. Others include high levels of anxiety and stress, fewer professional development opportunities, sexual harassment, and negative gender stereotypes pertaining to a woman seen as a weak leader or as the "mother hen."

On Equal Pay Day 2021, I published an article on SWAAY that featured a research study by Girls in Tech, a global nonprofit that works toward erasing gender gaps in technology. The research revealed an alarmingly high rate of burnout among working women with male bosses. According to the data, 63 percent of participants with male supervisors reported feeling burned out compared to the 44 percent of participants with female supervisors. In organizations where top executives are male, even higher rates of burnout were reported by a startling 85 percent of participants.

These obstacles don't mean that you shouldn't pursue a field in which women are in the minority. In fact,

I encourage women who feel passionately about transforming

male-dominated professions to push their way in, showcase their level of expertise, and make changes that will benefit other women.

If there ever was a male-dominated field, boxing is it. So it surprises people when Cary Williams, an incredible woman I interviewed for my podcast, tells people she's an Olympic boxer and coach, as well as an entrepreneur with a franchise of boxing clubs. "I've often been asked why I would want to be a boxer," Cary told me. "People were disappointed that I would mess up my pretty face. They'd test my knowledge of boxing, and as I schooled them through the conversation, they eventually relented and respected my skill set as a woman. I took it upon myself to help them become less ignorant. Instead of getting mad, I educated them. I also suggested they come watch me fight!" When Cary opened her boxing club, visitors constantly assumed her head trainer was the owner, "As if there was no way I could own a gym by myself." Cary would simply correct them and move on. "Women need to stand up and own what we know," she advises. "It starts with us individually and how we allow others to perceive us."

Here are some other suggestions for making the best of the opportunity to be among a rare group of accomplished women.

Don't assume you have to act like a man

You don't necessarily need to lean in. Some who paved the way for women in business did so by adopting masculine norms of behavior. After fighting for a spot on the boys' team, they felt they needed to be harsh, aggressive authoritarians to survive. But as we've talked about throughout this book, these old ways of leading are not the answer. Although Sheryl Sandberg meant well, her "reform from within" strategy did not bring the hoped-for tolerance and diversity in the workplace. So why not try a more assertive approach that's authentic? If you're a woman in a male-dominated field, your advanced interpersonal skills may be a sorely needed asset that can also serve as a powerful differentiator.

Find a senior advocate

Occasionally, a lone-wolf woman might feel threatened. She might hesitate to draw too much attention to herself and may isolate herself from other colleagues, particularly other women. Your game plan should actually be the reverse. According to a study by Nilanjana Dasgupta and Shaki Asgari published in the *Journal of Experimental Social Psychology*, women who hang out with accomplished female role models are more likely to internalize positive beliefs and reject gender-based stereotypes about women leaders. So if there's a woman in your midst whom you admire, ask her to lunch. Share your development goals, ask her advice, and think about ways you can assist her in return. If she's willing, arrange to meet regularly to grow the relationship while also finding ways to provide value in return.

Elevate Your Skills Through Thought Leadership

While it can be uncomfortable to be the only woman in the room, you don't have to allow your solo status to derail your development potential. In the next and final chapter, I'll discuss skills a lot more, as well as impostor syndrome and how you can use this potentially negative phenomenon as a tool for growth. Acquiring expertise is also an avenue for growth and self-development. Rather than being satisfied with what you currently bring to your organization, look for pathways to unlock additional value.

Thought leadership is one such pathway. Increasingly, expertise is judged not on how much experience or knowledge you actually have but on how well you communicate and promote what you know both inside and outside your organization. Thought leadership is the ability to develop and describe innovative ideas with a strong voice that captures an audience's attention while elevating your personal brand and message. Whether it's telling a story on your company blog, writing on community publishing platforms like SWAAY, speaking at company events, or launching your own podcast, thought leadership is an excellent technique for building and positioning your expertise.

LEDGE PROTECTOR #2: GAIN CROSS-FUNCTIONAL AND CROSS-INDUSTRY EXPERTISE

When you operate cross-functionally, you perform different tasks and interact and work with people in groups outside your immediate sphere.

For example, if you are a graphic designer for an agency, learning how your sales team closes deals is working cross-functionally.

Operating cross-industry is similar. If you work in corporate graphic design in the energy industry, attending professional development meetings with corporate graphic designers in the financial industry is working cross-industry.

Working cross-functionally and cross-industry isn't just for business either. If you volunteer in marketing for your house of worship, for instance, you can gain cross-functional expertise by familiarizing yourself with the organization's fundraising. And you can gain cross-industry expertise by investigating how nonprofits outside the religious sector manage their marketing.

Given the speed of today's world, the ability to operate cross-functionally and cross-industry will broaden your expertise and make it easier to pivot into new areas when needed.

But when you're busy with your own work and life, reaching outside may not seem like the highest priority. Here are a few tips for building it into your day.

Talk to one new person a week

We're routinely contacted by people whose activities or knowledge base seem foreign, and we're tempted to ignore them because their information isn't relevant to what we're doing. The next time this happens, consider answering the call. Be curious about the person's journey, skills, and daily tasks and inquire about the biggest challenges and opportunities in their role.

Proactively reach out to other groups

Sure, you might not need to understand the ins and outs of your organization's IT function, but down the road, it might come in handy to know why the group selected the software you use and how to trouble-shoot problems with it. Think about asking your IT rep if you can do an informational interview, or if you can, shadow them in a few meetings. Listen carefully to what you hear and work to connect the dots back to your own area.

Share your enthusiasm for the organization

If you work for or volunteer with a large organization, this is the most obvious place to gain cross-functional expertise. However, the way in which you seek this expertise is important. Everyone has a different agenda, and people might not immediately see why they should spend their time educating you. Show potential partners that you are eager to help the organization achieve its overall mission and help them achieve their goals too.

Bring a diverse group together

You've probably heard that team brainstorming is an effective technique for creative idea generation. But did you know that the more you can vary the perspectives of the brainstormers, the richer your output will be? Inviting individuals with other lenses to help you solve a problem will expand everyone's view and help you build bridges at the same time.

Follow up and follow through

After your initial conversation or gathering, try to keep learning from your cross-functional partners. Shoot them a note or meet up for coffee every so often, keeping your eyes and ears open to news that might be of interest to them too. If they switch jobs or industries, maintaining the relationship can continue to pay additional dividends on your own expertise!

◆ Ledge Work: Taking Stock of Your Personal Methodology

If you've made it to your twenties and certainly beyond, you likely have a fair amount of expertise. Take a few moments to think about how you acquired this knowledge. For example, if you are a skilled writer (even if it's not your full-time job), how did you get there? Did you practice multiple times a week? Did you work with a coach? Did you read books or articles about writing? Did you take courses or learn tools to improve your skills? Since one of the best predictors of future success is past success, write about your methodology in your journal, including how this approach might apply to other areas where you are now seeking expertise.

LEDGE PROTECTOR #3: DRIVE YOUR CAREER LONG TERM

According to Jonathan Black, who heads up career services at Oxford University and writes an advice column for *Financial Times*, one of the marked changes to recent uncertainties in our world is an increase in planning. Prior to the COVID pandemic, Black's students were coping with a job market already impacted by Brexit and adverse climate events. Far from being in denial about the current state of affairs, Oxford graduates are adapting their career ambitions accordingly.

One such student is Anna. An Oxford doctoral student in biophysics, Anna considered drastically changing her trajectory. As she told Black, "On reflection, Brexit will just make staying (in academia) and finding research funding more difficult, but not impossible." She was concerned that her research in medical diagnostic tools would be irrelevant because of the new focus on climate problems. While Anna decided to stick with her doctorate program, she also initiated a new direction in climate activism. This path "has made my life much more interesting, bonding together with a whole new community of people. I feel freed from career expectations and am much more open-minded on where my life will take me," she shared with Black.

In *Inside Higher Ed*, Lauren Easterling explains that external factors can influence how we progress in our career goals and what progress looks like.

"Many of us may not have the option to follow the plans we had or the paths we have mapped out for our lives—at least, not right now," she writes. "But normal life obstacles and a global health and financial crisis do not mean that progress on a career journey must stop. It may just take a different shape than we originally expected it would." Our own definition of success also influences career plans. "Some of us may be driven more by individual goals toward a desired outcome; others find their purpose in their communities or value systems, while others have still different motivations or a combination of them," Easterling says. "We do what we need to do, what we want to do, for the reasons we do it, and we should not try to impose our version of what progress toward a career goal looks like on someone else. I encourage us all to avoid comparing our progress and success to those of others."

And some individuals have curvier paths than others. As you know, both my career and my journey building SWAAY have been far from linear, so I loved this anecdote from Easterling:

> If we imagine standing on the shore at one point along a rela-tively round pond, and we see a place we want to go or a person we want to talk with directly across from us, we have a few choices. Yes, the fastest way to the other side is going across the pond—through the water to the other side. Some will choose that way and have the skills, abilities, privileges and so forth to do well. Others will choose not to go that way, while still others cannot choose that option. Many of us will pick a side of the pond to walk around. Some will walk off into the woods and take a longer route to get there. Others may only be able to use paved paths or go back to our car, drive around the block to the entrance of the pond on the other side, park, and get to our destination that way.

Easterling illustrates how there's more than one way to get to a desired outcome, and we might do it differently than others or even differently than we started out at first. But we don't have to insist on knowing the end of the story at this moment, nor do we have to give up on all planning in a fit of fear and frustration. Driving a career and building a path to long-term expertise in the mid-twenty-first century involves a middle-ground approach, including the following steps.

Determine the twelve-month plan

In chapter 7, we talked about goal setting. The key to successful long-term planning in an uncertain work climate is to focus on the immediate next step. Leverage your knowledge of current circumstances to inform the actions you'll take over the next year. For example, you might want to switch fields, but the post-pandemic job market isn't the best time to do it. So, related to this chapter's topic of expertise, you might set a twelve-month goal to take coursework in specific technical skills so that you're competent and up to date when you're ready to start interviewing in the new field.

Think holistically

One of my least favorite questions during job interviews and pageants was: "Where do you see yourself in X years"? Even in more stable times, it's rare for people to definitively know where they'll be in five or ten years. However, I've noticed that over time, work preferences tend to change more than core belief systems. Remember the ledge protector on planning your life strategically from chapter 7? It applies here as well. Understanding the overall lifestyle you're looking to create (e.g., urban dwelling, child rearing, financial freedom, entrepreneurial, or health focused) will provide clues about your long-term career direction.

Forge ahead without *all* the information

As I briefly mentioned earlier, when I was first approached to write a book, I hesitated. I considered rejecting the offer because I didn't think I had the right expertise to succeed as an author. But one evening, after a long chat with my agent, I recalled how I'd handled other situations in which I didn't feel 100 percent prepared. I had counted on learning the essentials along the way and seeking support and guidance whenever I felt stuck. Don't be afraid to try new things. Don't reject a potentially life-changing opportunity just because you think you need more experience or industry expertise. A bestselling author was once a beginner. A multimillion-dollar empire was once a simple idea. Everyone has to start somewhere.

Ran Ma is a wonderful example of these principles at work. Ran is a biomedical engineer by training and comes from a long family line of medical professionals. She was working on wound care for war veterans before she became an entrepreneur and started her company, Siren

Care—their first product was a smart sock designed to monitor and prevent further nerve damage for diabetic patients.

When I heard about Ran's company, the main thing I wanted to know was how she created a prototype from scratch with no background in this kind of hardware. "Well, it's one thing to have an idea in your mind and quite another to make it physical. I became part of the maker movement, sewing my first prototype by hand with electronics from Amazon," she told me. "Those initial ones were horrendous, with wires coming out everywhere." Ran acknowledges she didn't know everything and made a conscious effort to supplement what she did know. She hired one person who was skilled in electrical engineering and hardware manufacturing and another with connections in technology outsourcing and fashion. She also referenced research on diabetic patients from her prior employment at Northwestern University's wound lab, taking advantage of existing clinical trials to inform how temperature monitoring can prevent diabetic foot.

Ran's willingness to apply her previous expertise in new ways resonated with me. "I had traveled around the world, been exposed to a lot of companies, taken many curved paths," she told me. "Together, all these experiences gave me the knowledge to solve the problem. Sometimes, people questioned me. They said, 'You could be a doctor. Why are you doing this? What makes you think *you* can build it?'" As it turned out, the appropriate question wasn't "Why Ran?" but "Why not Ran?"

Realize it's okay to go "backward"

In the world of career guidance, there's the term *boomeranging*, which refers to people leaving a job or industry, doing something new, and eventually returning to their original path. There is zero shame in this. Instead of looking at your detour as time wasted, consider that every work experience provides color and depth to a career, whether it's the one you started in or not.

Voices from the SWAAY Community

Success in a Male-Dominated Work Environment

Sandi Harari

Over the last year, I've been asked a lot about how it feels to be a female in the predominantly male advertising industry. More often than not I respond with a puzzled look because truth be told, I have never really faced adversity in my career. So I have to wonder, why? Why has my experience been different from so many others? After all, it's true—I'm a female creative director, and when I started climbing the career ladder, I was one of the 3 percent. I have worked for men in almost all of my jobs and sat in many conference rooms where I was the only female, and yet I still didn't feel like this was any kind of "predicament."

I needed to understand *why*.

What I discovered was a commonality among the people I surrounded myself with and worked for. As I moved along my career path and interviewed and accepted positions, I ended up working for men who naturally empower women. These men were expressive, kind mentors who challenged me and wanted to give me the floor when I was ready. No different than the way people have habits in romantic relationships, being drawn to people who may treat them in a certain way (good or bad), I believe I had a natural inclination toward bosses who would give me responsibility, let me shine, mentor me with respect, value my opinion, but most importantly, allow me to challenge them.

Challenging myself and those around me is part of my DNA and something that I am realizing comes from my Jewish upbringing. Growing up, I attended private yeshivahs where it was common to juggle nine Hebrew subjects, many of which were devoted to "probing ancient Jewish texts" to seek deeper meaning and truth.

These were deep commentaries where one could spend hours agonizing about the meanings behind a single word or examining multiple viewpoints.

At the time, I probably complained about staying in school for twelve hours, but now I am thankful I have the rigor to volley with the best strategists, argue the merits of a headline, question the briefs or our goals and objectives. At the heart of this learning style is also the ability to walk around and see things empathetically from various points of view.

As I envision the environments in which women don't succeed—it is where their opinions are not equal or valued or aren't being *heard* or given the credit or credence for their point of view. It's not like I haven't encountered the industry clichés.

I have had to shut down unwelcome advances and have shouted above the fray of male colleagues with a booming voice, but I now realize that I am lucky it wasn't worse. I was fortunate to be spared a lot of what has plagued my industry—women who have been shamed, coerced, and made to feel uncomfortable. Sadly, it is becoming clear that my situation is unique.

So, my advice to women of all ages, ethnicities, levels of seniority, and even industry: Be careful where you spend your time. Don't just size up the work opportunities when deciding on your next move—consider the ecosystem.

Think about the way you felt in an interview, ask to meet the people you will be working with directly—make sure the environment is hospitable toward not only you but women as a whole. Even after you have accepted a position, always continue asking yourself if you feel heard, supported, and equal. If the answer is no, move on and find your tribe—because it's out there. I promise you.

We are living in exciting times—with a seismic shift upon us—#metoo and #timesup are not just moments but movements that are defining our here and now and also creating a *before* and an *after*. They are allowing our shared voices to have power and conversations to be had out loud.

I hope this movement makes it easier for any woman to walk away from a situation that doesn't serve her—and to find support. Women are lifting others up in a way that I didn't see when I was moving through the ranks, and it's thrilling to witness.

I know that as a female leader in my field, the most important role I have is possibly as a shelter, where other women can come to talk or seek advice, but it is also my job to create a safe, welcoming environment for anyone who hasn't had a voice in the past.

"I Am Often the Only Woman in the Room, Yet It Was Never a Predicament" by Sandi Harari was published on SWAAY.com.

Sandi joined BARKER in 2006, making the ad agency one of only 3 percent in the business to boast a female creative director at the time. Sandi has been recognized in industry publications, including *Ad Age*, *Adweek*, and *Forbes*, and is a champion advocate for women in the workplace. She was also named a 2017 Working Mother of the Year by She Runs It.

◇◇

LEADERSHIP SPOTLIGHT

One day when surfing social media, I came across a *Fast Company* article with a line that read: "The hard skills that got you the job won't be the ones that get you promoted." This reminded me of my friend Rish, who built a billion-dollar AI startup with two other founders. When I visited his headquarters in London and asked about the other cofounders, I was surprised to learn that they no longer had the same amount of skin in the game. "Just because you start off as a cofounder doesn't mean you will remain one throughout the course of the company's trajectory," he told me. "Your skills and added value need to grow proportionally to the company's success. Otherwise, you become a pawn in a much bigger game."

Similarly, *Fast Company* writer Ximena Vengoechea went on to say: "At the start of your career, chances are good that you'll be hired primarily for your hard skills—the stuff you know that's relevant for the job. When you're fresh out of college or even a few years into your career, things like what software you've mastered, the knowledge you've picked up during internships and in school, and your other technical credentials really matter.

But what no one quite tells you is that while you might've been initially hired for those hard skills, they gradually matter less.

The further you get in your career, the less you'll be *evaluated* on those same skills—and this is especially important once you reach your mid-career point."

This shift is even more significant once you become a leader. Whether you are in a supervisory role now or planning one in the future, you can develop your expertise and thought leadership in the following areas.

- **Producing:** Can you get high quality work done—on time—both independently and collaboratively?
- **Leading:** Can you motivate and guide others to do their best work, and can you effectively represent your team within and outside the organization?
- **Persuading:** Can you develop strong relationships based on trust, and can you encourage people to follow you based on your reputation as a credible and capable leader?

Knowing exactly what expertise to develop as you take on increasingly senior roles is a critical aspect of navigating the glass ledge. If in doubt, ask your manager, inquire with a mentor or human resources representative, or look online for courses that address soft skills like the ones above.

CUE THE REAL WORLD

This chapter's ledge protectors focus on how to gain the necessary expertise to achieve your goals. With that in mind, use these questions to plot your next steps.

- What personal or professional expertise do you wish you could develop?

- What are three things you can do this month to begin building that expertise?

- Outside your immediate circle, who can you consult about gaining relevant expertise in a new area or function? When and how will you approach them?

EXPERTISE LEDGE REVIEW

- An expert today is someone who knows enough to stretch the limits of a subject and **advance current knowledge**. True expertise lies in your adaptability, creativity, and willingness to take calculated risks.
- Don't assume you have to **act like a man**. If you're a woman in a male-dominated field, your advanced interpersonal skills may be a sorely needed asset that can serve as a powerful differentiator.
- Increasingly, expertise is judged not on how much experience you actually have but on how well you communicate and promote what you know both inside and outside your organization. **Thought leadership** is the ability to develop and describe innovative ideas with a strong voice that captures an audience's attention and elevates your personal brand and message.
- When you operate **cross-functionally**, you perform different tasks and interact and work with people in groups that are outside your immediate sphere.
- The key to successful **long-term planning** in an uncertain work climate is to focus on the immediate next step. Leverage your knowledge of current circumstances to inform the actions you'll take over the next year.

"I'm grateful for the promotion, but I don't think I belong here."

⬦⬦⬦⬦

"I don't want to launch my project until it's perfect."

⬦⬦⬦⬦

"I can't lead my company to success. I've never been a CEO before."

⬦⬦⬦⬦

"Oh, I am not that talented or smart. I was just lucky."

⬦⬦⬦⬦

"Every time I achieve something new, I feel like an impostor."

⬦⬦⬦⬦

"I'm not ready to become a public speaker, but someday . . ."

⬦⬦⬦⬦

"I have no idea what I am doing here."

⬦⬦⬦⬦

Chapter Ten

BELONGING

When I started high school in Colorado, I didn't think or expect I would do well given my language barrier and lack of understanding of how high school worked in America. The education system is very different in Morocco. But as I adapted to my new classes, I aced my tests, nailed my talks in speech class, and received student of the month awards. But instead of seeing myself as worthy of that recognition or intrinsically smart and a fast learner, I attributed my academic success to luck. And deep down, no matter how well I did in school or at extra-curricular activities, I still saw myself as "less than" and felt insecure and awkward when it was time to embrace the recognition.

Outside of school, I was a great athlete. My parents raised us as active kids, and our family bonding time revolved around outdoor activities like tennis. I started playing for fun at a professional club in Morocco when I was ten years old, and I grew to love the sport. As I mentioned in chapter 8, in high school, tennis was my only familiar escape from the depression that took over after moving to a new country. While most kids in my school were going to parties, my only social outlet was tennis. When I heard the news that I'd placed among the top players on the girls' varsity team, I found it hard to believe, even though I had put in the work to achieve such a feat. As competitive as I was, I was still anxious every day that my coach would suddenly realize I wasn't as good as the others.

Recounting these moments now makes me sad, and I wish I could go back and shake the teenage me and tell her to enjoy the fruit of her labor because *she deserved it all!*

I have worked (and continue to work) very hard to be the high achiever I am today, but there are still times I struggle to see myself that way. Two years ago, I discovered that these feelings of self-doubt and anxiety associated with achievements had a name, and I wasn't the only one suffering from it. I confided in one of my advisers, Fran Hauser, about this weird feeling I have when someone praises my work and achievements. She replied: "Iman, I've struggled with that too throughout my career. It's called impostor syndrome."

These feelings can be a burden, but in retrospect, impostor syndrome might be the reason why I learned to fight for what I want. It forced me to overprepare in dealing with a society that is constantly questioning women's capabilities and credibility. When I first set out to launch SWAAY, I used the skills acquired in biotech investor relations and public relations to put together a well-thought-out business plan, presentation, and executive summary about the company. But while working on the initial corporate governance and investor material, I felt all the uncomfortable emotions associated with impostor syndrome.

In fact, I was so uncomfortable that I took every step possible to prepare and land my first investment and set up my first team. I made sure I attended every fundraising panel, showed up to every business networking event I could find, emailed every potential investor, and sought counsel from every mentor or adviser who aligned with my vision. I was obsessed with my own growth and sought relief by proving to myself that I was capable after all.

Politician AOC is a great example of this phenomenon. When she defeated a male incumbent of ten years, at twenty-nine Alexandria Ocasio-Cortez became the youngest congresswoman in history. Born in the Bronx to Puerto Rican parents, AOC never thought she'd be on the cover of *Time*. And though she famously danced to the tune of Edwin Starr's "War" outside her new office in Washington, AOC isn't always confident about her rise. "Like many other women and working people, I occasionally suffer from impostor syndrome," she has Tweeted. "Those small moments, especially on hard days, where you wonder if the haters are right."

Pauline Clance and Suzanne Imes identified the phenomenon in 1978 in a paper titled "The Impostor Phenomenon in High Achieving Women."

Impostor syndrome describes individuals who are marked by an inability to internalize their accomplishments and have a persistent fear of being exposed as a fraud. Despite external evidence to the contrary, people with impostor syndrome are convinced they don't deserve their success. They attribute their accomplishments to luck or others' unfounded opinions, and they diminish their successes and amplify their mistakes.

Clance and Imes originally theorized that impostor syndrome was a gendered phenomenon, but as Clance told Amy Cuddy for Cuddy's book *Presence*, it turns out almost everyone has it. "Researchers have found impostorism in dozens of demographic groups, including but not limited to teachers, accountants, physicians, nurses, engineers, pharmacists, entrepreneurs, high school students, people new to the Internet, African Americans, Koreans, Canadians, disturbed adolescents, 'normal' adolescents, preadolescents, adult children of high achievers, people with eating disorders, people without eating disorders, people who have recently experienced success . . . and so on." The "and so on" includes case studies from virtually every field and background.

Impostor syndrome is often context specific and based on areas of growth where we feel most insecure. SWAAY contributor Megan Dalla-Camina says that "impostor syndrome is in large part a reaction to certain circumstances or situations. While you may feel fully confident speaking to a group of more junior people, addressing your peers could completely undo you. Or you could be fine at work, but having to speak up at the local school meeting? Forget about it. And it limits our courage to go after new opportunities, explore potential areas of interest, and put ourselves out there in a meaningful way."

However this behavior pattern shows up for you, it can often lead to harmful self-sabotage. According to 2019 research by the Society for Industrial and Organizational Psychology, high performers who doubt their abilities are more fatigued, dissatisfied, and unable to maintain healthy work-life integration. In their study of more than 450 employees over 18 years old in the southern US, researchers Lisa Sublett, Lisa Penney, and Holly Hutchins found that people experiencing impostor syndrome have greater conflict with both work and family roles due to emotional exhaustion. Live with it long enough, and you'll not only slip off your career's glass ledge, you'll also jeopardize your mental and physical health.

Graduate school was by far my worst example of how impostor syndrome—and an obsession with growth—can ruin your well-being if not dealt with effectively. I was enrolled in a bioengineering master's program, and I was also participating in beauty pageants. This was not well received by my classmates, who would jokingly accuse me of "playing dress up instead of studying." Most students assumed I was brainless and were shocked I'd even made it into the program. At first, I chose to ignore the background chatter and focus on what I did best—studying! I got a 95 percent on a test many found extremely hard (few scored above 70 percent), and when the word got out, people thought I'd cheated.

Although I'd felt like an impostor before, this hurt, because once again my intelligence was openly in question. I internalized the gossip and stereotypes and turned it into my reality. I told my parents and my school counselor that my classmates were probably right. I convinced myself I truly didn't deserve to have a seat in the program and stopped showing up to class. I withdrew from campus courses and pursued online options instead. To be honest, at the time, I felt relief only because I wanted to stop feeling what I was feeling. Did it ruin my graduate school trajectory? Absolutely. Do I regret it? 100 percent! But it was an important lesson in believing in myself first.

In this era of self-improvement, we women are encouraged to hone the most attractive and compelling aspects of ourselves—and yes, as we saw in the last chapter, developing expertise is important. But also,

paradoxically, the more we strive to be better, the more we feel we must take efforts up another level to be as smart and capable as others.

We struggle to keep up on the hamster wheel, dogged by the feeling that our efforts are still not enough. At some point during this never-ending cycle of "doing more and being more," we start to dislike ourselves and negate the progress we've made.

To prevent a fall off the glass ledge, the first step here is to realize you're falling prey to impostor syndrome or other dark aspects of the growth mindset. Look inward and label what you're feeling about yourself and your role; also identify the actions that accompany these emotions. For example:

- Do you doubt your ability to achieve your performance goals?
- Are you afraid to take on a new responsibility because you're worried someone else will do a better job?
- Have you tried to talk your boss out of recognizing your accomplishments?
- Do you break out in a sweat before a client presentation because you're anxious you'll look incompetent?

In the rest of this chapter, we'll explore three primary strategies for finding steadier ground: realistically evaluating your skills, collecting objective evidence, and acknowledging your insecurities and "acting the opposite."

LEDGE PROTECTOR #1: EVALUATE YOUR SKILLS REALISTICALLY

Adam Grant is a social scientist and the international bestselling author of *Originals* and *Give and Take*. In a 2018 article in *The Atlantic*, he shared that people are not always the best judge of their own character and skills. He explained that people know themselves best on the traits that are tough to observe and easy to admit—for instance, emotional stability. "Emotional stability is an internal state, although people might not want to call themselves unstable, the socially acceptable range is fairly wide," Grant writes.

"With more observable traits, you don't have unique knowledge. If you're a raging extrovert or a radical introvert, we don't need to ask you—we can pick it up quickly. And with the most evaluative traits, you just can't be trusted. People consistently overestimate their intelligence and generosity, perhaps because they want to convince *themselves*."

I feel this phenomenon often results from a lack of rigorous evaluation. Considering what makes you most effective and writing it down might serve as a useful reference to help others bring out the best in you and to assure yourself that perhaps you don't need to prove yourself as much as you think. In order to provide the most accurate picture possible, I recommend some steps for evaluating your skills realistically.

Examine a single day

Ask yourself: *What did I accomplish? What skills did I use? What were my results?* Give yourself a grade, as if you were collecting data for a direct report's performance review. If a project or task didn't go well, don't look for someone else or an external circumstance to blame. Reflect on your own role. A skills gap could be responsible for the outcome.

Revisit your job description

Honestly assess how you're doing relative to the "ideal candidate." If you were your boss, would you be happy you made the hire? Even if you don't have a job description, you can still do a variation of this exercise. Write down each of your responsibilities and assess the ones you've achieved extremely well, the ones you've handled competently, and the ones with definite problems. You might simultaneously evaluate each responsibility next to that of a peer in the same role. How do you perform in comparison? Are the standards you set for yourself realistic, or are you judging yourself more stringently than you should?

If you're facing a challenge, consider whether it's a challenge for only you or for *everyone*?

For example, you may know the challenge of managing a team during a global pandemic! You don't need to show these insights to anyone, but they can go a long way toward proving you aren't as deficient in as many areas as you may think.

It's ironic that actual frauds rarely seem to experience impostor syndrome. English philosopher Bertrand Russell put it more poetically: "The trouble with the world is that the stupid are cocksure and the intelligent are full of doubt." So while some of my less qualified peers rarely seem to do this, I research and prepare talking points before any major meeting. This way, I have a clear idea of what I bring to the table and what I want to communicate. And before I make any final decision, I stop and reflect on whether my decision is based on facts or my own feelings. Don't get me wrong: evaluating situations realistically and removing feelings and doubts from my decisions hasn't been easy to implement, but it's an effective weapon when fighting against impostor syndrome.

◆ Ledge Work: Label Unattainable Standards and Perfectionism

Perfectionism is often defined as the setting of and striving to meet demanding standards that are self-imposed and relentlessly pursued despite complications. It involves basing your self-worth on how well these standards are pursued and achieved. Answer these questions in your journal to see if you need to give yourself a break!

- Have other people told you that perfection is the enemy of good or that you're a perfectionist?

- Do you have a pattern of rejecting opportunities or delaying projects because you don't feel ready?

- When you meet a standard, do you immediately set another that's more difficult to achieve?

- Does the pursuit of your high standards prevent you from spending time on other important things in your life?

- Do you ruminate or criticize yourself for failing to meet standards, even when no one else seems to care?

If you answered yes to any of these questions, write down any areas in which you've noticed you have high and possibly unattainable standards—for example, appearance, career trajectory, work performance. Examples of thoughts associated with these areas might be:

Appearance: "I must look flawless and fashionable at all times."

Career Trajectory: "I must make $150K/year right out of college."

Work Performance: "I must always have the best sales record on the team."

◆

LEDGE PROTECTOR #2: COLLECT OBJECTIVE EVIDENCE

As I was waiting to be introduced at the Harvard's Women in Business conference, I felt totally out of place. I had to follow Huda Kattan on stage, the founder of the billion-dollar Huda beauty empire and an Instagram star with millions of followers. I turned to my boyfriend and said, "Why am I here? I feel like an impostor." And then a conference organizer walked up. She thanked me for accepting the invitation to speak at the event and shared how inspired she is by my story and the work I am doing and that I was their first choice when planning their speaker lineup. It restored my confidence and was my first instance of collecting objective evidence about my own value and why I was deserving of being on a Harvard stage. We are in fact our own worst critics.

Studies from the American Psychological Association show that coworkers are more accurate than we are at assessing how our personalities will impact our on-the-job performances. In his *Atlantic* piece, Adam Grant describes research by Simine Vazire, a professor of psychology at the University of California, Davis. Vazire asked people to rate themselves and four friends on a bunch of traits ranging from emotional stability and intelligence to creativity and assertiveness. Then, to see if they had predicted their own personalities better than their friends had, they took a bunch of tests that measured these traits. Vazire reported that when her research subjects tried to predict their performance on an IQ test and a creativity test, they were less accurate than their friends.

Given these results, it may make sense to ask at least two trusted friends and/or coworkers to appraise you on a multitude of work-related traits and skills, including communication, teamwork, work ethic, business savvy, agility, persistence, technical proficiency, problem-solving, and willingness to learn. It's critical to give your peers a purpose and a context for this type of discussion, so share that the feedback is for your eyes only and meant to help you grow as a leader or an employee. Emphasize that you are looking for an honest assessment and that sanitized commentary will not help you evaluate how you're doing.

We've talked about mentors throughout this book; they can also prove useful in this regard. Look for someone on a similar career path, ideally who is a few years ahead of you and may have themselves experienced impostor syndrome or a growth obsession. Once you get to know them, ask for guidance on playing to your strengths and addressing your areas for improvement. And take any encouragement or compliments they offer to heart!

A few years ago, Eric M. Ruiz wrote for *Fast Company* about his own impostor syndrome and the important role mentors played in his recovery. For instance, he once doubted whether he was qualified to take on a new position, but he'd been strongly recommended by his mentor, Stephen. "I was recommended by someone whose counsel I seek and whose opinion I respect. Doubting his confidence in my abilities would imply that *I* was more capable of making such judgments than he was. If that were true, what would be the point of Stephen mentoring me in the first place?" Ruiz explained. "This little mental exercise—reminding myself that I can trust people like Stephen despite my own misgivings—has proved surprisingly powerful." Ruiz added: "Much more than guidance, mentors push us to believe in ourselves—even against our own internal objections. Make your mental bias toward information that comes from people you know and trust work in your favor."

If all this feels gratuitous or self-indulgent, consider O. C. Tanner's *2020 Global Culture Report*, which found that peer-to-peer recognition increases the probability of a constructive team culture by 2.5 times. So, your friends, coworkers, and mentors aren't just helping you, they're also helping the organization.

Peer and mentor informal feedback should give your self-assessment a big boost, but don't forget about existing documentation.

People with impostor syndrome and/ or a growth obsession often overlook evidence of their achievements and emphasize negative feedback instead.

When I was initially fundraising for SWAAY, I engaged in some self-destructive behavior. I printed all the negative feedback I received from investors and looked at it every day. At the time, I thought it would serve as a motivator, but I subconsciously absorbed those statements daily as negative "affirmations," which ultimately led me to develop an unhealthy perspective of my own worth. Don't fall into this same behavior; instead, document and frequently review your accomplishments. You might put together a file with your official performance reviews and items such as

- winning proposals
- improvements you initiated at work that made a difference in the organization
- thank-you or kudos emails from managers, clients, or customers
- LinkedIn recommendations
- awards
- media mentions
- new skill certifications
- anything else that illustrates you're operating at a high level

Today, I keep a list of all my achievements on top of my desk to remind myself how deserving I am and that none of my success is due to luck or being in the right place at the right time. I also keep a folder with screenshots of praise and positive feedback on the work we do from our SWAAY community. I routinely remind myself of the sacrifices, the hard work, the preparation, and the time I have put into becoming the leader I am today. By encouraging myself to look at the evidence of my accomplishments, I have gradually stopped believing that I always need to be more, more, and more.

If you have access to a technology platform that allows for real-time, 360-degree feedback from managers, peers, and direct reports, encourage those people to submit comments regularly. If you don't have a platform available, you can ask for this feedback manually. Don't just read it once; put every item in your file for later reference. On days when you're feeling vulnerable and less than, take out the file and peruse its contents. You'll see that you are where you are for a reason!

Finally, learning from other successful individuals via indirect means such as books, articles, and podcasts can also help with collecting evidence. In 2019, my friend Cheslie Kryst, a North Carolina lawyer, was representing prison inmates for free when she won the Miss USA title. "I've coped with my own impostor syndrome by learning about the failures and humble beginnings of powerful people I admire and respect," Cheslie told me. "There's this belief that everyone else knows what's going on, has all the answers, and is more deserving. Reading about Sara Blakely selling Spanx store to store when she first started is a reminder that everyone is a beginner at some point in time, everyone experiences failure from time to time, and those who are most successful shift the focus from blowing their own shortcomings out of proportion to overcoming real challenges."

LEDGE PROTECTOR #3: ACKNOWLEDGE YOUR INSECURITIES AND "ACT THE OPPOSITE"

One of my dearest friends and mentor, Heather Monahan, is a bestselling author, keynote speaker, entrepreneur, and founder of the company Boss In Heels. After successfully climbing the corporate ladder for twenty years, Heather earned her place in the C-suite. As a chief revenue officer in the media industry, she was a Glass Ceiling Award Winner and one of the Influential Women in Radio. You would never know how insecure she has felt over the course of her career.

"I was at a dinner with a lawyer friend of mine I really respect. I was sharing how nervous I was to become the CRO because I thought I might not be ready for the promotion. She laughed and told me she felt the same every day she walked into her office. She was always questioning if she was smart enough to be a partner," Heather told me. "After taking the CRO role, I considered that reaching the C-suite actually meant I had more support to do good work. I'd been believing this lie that the C-suite was so intense and special that I'd never be ready for it." Heather traded her insecurity and the belief that things were more difficult, which she had when first starting out, for a new belief. She is the same person she'd been back then but with more resources at her disposal, and she sees advancement as an opportunity to succeed as part of a team.

Insecurity, or the fear that we are not good enough, is a common bedfellow of impostor syndrome and growth obsession. "Feelings of insecurity leave us overdependent on external factors—admiration, praise, promotions. But even then, the feeling of achievement is generally temporary. Soon after, we turn inward, digging inside ourselves for a vein of confidence that remains elusive," say Svenja Weber and Gianpiero Petriglieri, psychology professors at INSEAD. In a 2018 article for *Harvard Business Review*, Weber and Petriglieri write, "Insecurity makes it difficult for us to make our voices heard, leaves us unable to dissent, and makes us tentative in our work relationships. It leaves us dissatisfied, undermines collaboration, and renders our teams less creative and efficient. If there is one enemy of authenticity and innovation, insecurity is it."

According to the piece, the academic research on women and minorities in professional settings reveals that insecurity is more a social issue than a psychological one.

While women are constitutionally as confident as men, a cocktail of conflicting messages and personal feedback tinged with bias puts us in circumstances that would make anyone second-guess themselves.

As we've already talked about at length, because we women tend to be people pleasers, we constantly chase the right answer for how we should behave, but the only consistent thread in our feedback is its inconsistency. And when we can't trust what we hear, we start to think the problem is us, that we need to be better. Identifying that you feel insecure is the first step in breaking free and staying on the glass ledge.

And there's no shame in feeling insecure!

After all, insecurity is hardwired in us, and sometimes it helps us recognize when we can legitimately improve. You might try writing down what you're feeling insecure about, and even better, you might talk to a trusted friend, relative, or mentor about it. Remember that outside of the person you confide in, no one knows how insecure you feel. People are too worried about their own insecurities to even notice yours. You aren't going to be "found out."

Sometimes, specific people or situations trigger insecurity. Identifying these so you can protect yourself is important too. For example, there might be a work friend who is always putting you down or boasting about her own accomplishments. If she asks you to go to happy hour, you could decline with a polite excuse. Unless you have no choice, there's no reason to subject yourself to scenarios that make you feel especially vulnerable.

Once you've processed how your insecurity shows up, you can try a technique called "acting the opposite." Remember when I mentioned that many men "fake it till they make it?" They may not be 100 percent qualified or competent in an area, but they are so convincing that everyone else believes in them. Realize that you have a great deal of control over how you are perceived, and every time you show up and act "as if," you influence perception in the desired direction. Do you have to make remarks in a large meeting but you're insecure about your public speaking ability? Prepare carefully, practice beforehand, and then when you're at the podium, act the opposite of how you are feeling in the moment. Tell yourself you're up there because you deserve to be. Forget your sweaty palms, and nail it!

Voices from the SWAAY Community

Winning Against Imposter Syndrome

Dr. Amy Athay

Have you ever played the game Among Us? It's an online, multiplayer social-deduction game. You can play with four to ten people you know or with Internet strangers. The goal of the game? Rout out the player who's playing the impostor before they can kill the rest of you.

Among Us is a great case study in how we, as humans, can also be played—by impostor syndrome. Impostor syndrome isn't related to an accurate view of our skills or abilities. In fact, 70 percent of people will experience impostor syndrome at some point, meaning they will:

- feel like a fraud or a fake

- be unable to realistically assess their skills

- sabotage their own success or attribute it to external factors

- experience self-doubt

- feel fear that they won't live up to expectations

So, how do we rout out impostors in real life?

In Among Us, one way for the impostor player to get busted is to go through the vents and be caught by the other players. Players can also enter a security room and watch others on the cameras and catch the impostor that way.

Sometimes, like in the game, we're really aware of our impostor. They'll make moves or create an internal dialogue that's so ridiculous we can easily call them out. For example, say you go into a nonthreatening room to give a talk you've given fifteen times before to an audience that's eager to hear what you have to say. If the impostor creeps into that situation and whispers that you're going to bomb, it's easy to spot them and say, "I don't believe you." We can easily move on, kick the impostor out, and keep going.

But at other times in our lives, the impostor is pretty sneaky and quick—and they can get into our heads without our even realizing it.

Right now, we're in a systemically stressful time—we're going through personal loss, there are community stressors from the pandemic, resources are being shut down or modified, and people are feeling more physically disconnected and socially isolated. Those conditions mean that it's easier for the impostor to sneak up because the stakes are so high.

When the impostor is being sneaky, here are some takeaways to banish them—and win the game:

- First, we need to recognize what kind of game we're in—and that means increasing our situational awareness. More stress increases the likelihood that an impostor can get in and question our readiness and experience. Being aware of our situations, like knowing we're tired because we were up with a baby or we have an intense work deadline coming up that's causing us stress, helps us blow up some of the impostor's cover.

- Next, we need to recognize which tools have worked for us in the past and dip back into that toolbox. This is probably not the first time in your life that you've experienced feelings of self-doubt or questioned your readiness and experience. What has helped you in the past? Taking a deep breath and recentering on the task at hand? Imagining yourself kicking ass at a task before doing it? Reminding yourself of advice from a mentor that helped you reframe a past experience? All such tools are available for you to use again.

You can also add new tools, given that these are unprecedented times:

- You can train yourself to be your own ideal coach by asking what you need to hear in a specific situation. What would you want your ideal coach to say or do? What would be the timing of the statement? Would it be instructional? Would it be challenging? Would it be supportive?

You know best how you need to be spoken to right now. Your running dialogue can be your friend in helping you make it through a particularly challenging or frightening day.

- You can also regulate your emotions with breathing exercises, like box breathing. In stressful situations, breathe in for a count of four, pause for a count of four, breathe out to a count of four, and pause for a count of four. Continue this breathing pattern for two to five minutes, depending on your comfort and skill level.

- You can build a "confidence resume" to draw on in more challenging times. List one thing you've done of late that you're proud of. Personal, social, work, whatever comes to mind. Then make a list beginning with "I am the type of person who" and list your strengths from above. For example, "I am the type of person who cares about helping a customer." Finally, rewrite your strengths so that they're global rather than unique to that experience. For example, "I am someone who cares about helping others, so I know I will make a difference."

- Apps like Confidently train the mindset tools of a high performer. If you're looking for more support, these can be a great tool to try.

Life isn't a game (especially these days!), but we can still use the framework of Among Us to put together some powerful tools to rout out and expose our impostors—before they can get to us.

"How to Win Against Impostor Syndrome" by Dr. Amy Athey was published on SWAAY.com. Dr. Athey is a national leader in performance psychology and the training of mental fitness, with over twenty years working with elite performers, coaches, teams, medical professionals, and organizational leadership. She is currently the chief wellness officer at the University of Arizona.

LEADERSHIP SPOTLIGHT

As a leader, it's critical to be on the lookout for growth obsession in your high-performing employees. Why? Because you want to retain them, and people who feel inferior are more likely to quit.

If an employee seems to overprepare for everything, is single-mindedly focused on the job, rides herself down for small mistakes, or dismisses your positive feedback with comments like "I can't take all the credit," consider starting a conversation. Take the woman in question to lunch and begin with an empathic statement like "You know, every time I moved to a new senior role, I felt undeserving because I wasn't sure I was ready for the opportunity. I wonder if you ever feel that way?" More generally, educate your team about impostor syndrome so they are more likely to recognize it in themselves. The earlier in their careers people receive information and guidance on the subject, the better.

Focusing on others can indirectly help you too. For example, in the last few years when I failed to raise sufficient venture capital funds for SWAAY, I pushed through the negative feelings by focusing on the women we bring value to. Not investors, not shareholders—but the women who use our platform daily and appreciate having a safe space to discuss their perspectives on life's most important issues. Speaking with SWAAY members helps me see that it's not always about me or my growth ambitions. It's bigger than me, and whether I want to acknowledge my own achievements or not, I owe it to our community and my team to show up as the leader they need.

CUE THE REAL WORLD

This chapter's ledge-protector strategies target ways to increase your comfort with desirable growth and the belief that you belong. Respond to these prompts in your journal whenever you feel the stirrings of impostor syndrome:

- Are you currently holding a role you feel unqualified for or feel you don't belong or deserve to be where you are?

- Take the perspective of the person who placed you in this role and consider why you were selected. What traits make you the best person for the job?

- What are some steps you can take to feel less insecure?

BELONGING LEDGE REVIEW

- In 1978 Pauline Clance and Suzanne Imes identified **impostor syndrome,** which describes individuals who are marked by an inability to internalize their accomplishments and a persistent fear of being exposed as a fraud.
- According to 2019 research by the Society for Industrial and Organizational Psychology, high performers who doubt their abilities are more fatigued, dissatisfied, and unable to maintain **healthy work-life integration.**
- **Evaluate your skills** realistically by examining a single day. Ask yourself: *What did I accomplish? What skills did I use? What were my results?* If a project or task didn't go well, don't look for someone else or an external circumstance to blame. Reflect on your own role and how a skills gap might be responsible.
- **Gain objective evidence** of your accomplishments by tapping in to trusted friends and/or coworkers to appraise you on a multitude of work-related traits and skills. It's critical to give your peers a purpose and a context for this discussion, so let them know that the feedback is for your eyes only and meant to help you grow as a leader or an employee.
- Overcome insecurity with a technique called **acting the opposite.** Realize that you have a great deal of control over how you are perceived, and every time you show up and act "as if," you influence perception in the desired direction.

CLOSING

This has been a book about acquiring self-awareness and self-knowledge to avoid self-sabotage, specifically the ways we tumble off the glass ledge when we internalize false beliefs about ourselves and what we are capable of achieving. And my hope is that after reading it and journaling your thoughts, you've begun developing a healthier relationship with your self-perception and how you show up in every aspect of your life.

I was just twenty-two years old when I got a close look at the aftermath of the civil war in South Sudan. I was in my first year of graduate school. Although my career as a cancer research scientist was taking off, I felt stuck and wanted a more hands-on learning approach. When I met Dr. Glenn Geelhoed, a professor of surgery at George Washington Medical Center and the founder of Mission to Heal, I asked if I could join an upcoming medical mission. After completing the necessary training and certification, I embarked on a life-changing trip to some of the most remote villages on the African continent.

During that month, I witnessed miracles happen. We slept in tents in the middle of fields with no electricity or clean water; worked in bat-infested, burned-down hospitals with ancient or missing equipment; and interacted with children holding AK-47 guns. I was constantly terrified and uncomfortable. I had gone from my comfort zone to a war zone and stared down the glass ledge. But I made it. And that mission was so personally rewarding that I went on several more, including one that I led in my home country of Morocco.

Although it feels real, the comfort zone is a self-inflicted barrier. It's a boundary you've created that stands between you and your path to self-actualization. It's a way of holding yourself back because you're afraid of failure, of looking foolish, and of judgment, uncertainty, or discomfort. Anna Lundberg describes it perfectly in her essay for Thrive Global: "As kids, we are endlessly curious. But as we go through school, we're taught to look for the right answers, to stay within the lines, and to follow an expected path. So you do as you are told. You get the good grades. You go to a good university, and maybe another good university, and then you get a good job. But without really realizing it, you're gradually settling into a comfort zone. And you experience stagnation, frustration, and a feeling of being stuck as that comfort zone inevitably shrinks around you."

Maybe you started off here, and maybe you're still here today. But you do not have to stay here. Now that you've read this book and are aware of the ways in which we women can objectively evaluate our circumstances and take back control of our own desired paths, I hope that you are ready to take responsibility for where you are today and that you feel the inner power to change any situation for the better.

Break free from that comfort zone. The way to keep from falling off the glass ledge is to commit to your ongoing growth, expand your self-awareness, and act on that awareness in the ways we've looked at here. Tell yourself you will not be pushed off the ledge by your self-deprecating inner dialogue—because you know better. Be patient with your transformation and always remember that you have me and so many other women supporting you and balancing alongside you every step of the way.

Acknowledgments

A lot of hard work went into this book, but it wouldn't have been possible without the support of my family, friends, and team. It truly does take a village to create a masterpiece!

First, I would like to express my immense gratitude to my beloved parents, Souad Benradi and Abderrahim Oubou. Thank you for all your sacrifices and for the courage that it took to move to a new country in pursuit of the American Dream. I am proud to be your daughter and to have you both as my role models. Your unconditional love and support are what keep me going.

To my one and only brother, Adil, you have been my voice of reason throughout my biggest breakdowns and my biggest cheerleader throughout my breakthroughs. Thank you for consistently pushing me to believe in myself and to get out of my own head. The lessons I shared in this book wouldn't have been possible without your co-leadership in life and in SWAAY.

To my aunt Rachida and her loving family for showing us the ropes and welcoming us into your home when we first moved to the US and had nowhere to go. You gave us hope and taught us the most important lessons to ensure a smooth cultural transition, and for that I am forever thankful.

To my extended family and the Kingdom of Morocco, thank you for elevating my work and my story, even from thousands of miles away.

To my life partner, Marko Ciklic, for sticking by my side and believing in my vision even in the darkest of times. Thank you for fostering a safe space for my creativity to thrive. I am grateful for your love and to have you on this completely unpredictable roller coaster of a journey with me.

Thank you to my agent, Heather Jackson, and the whole team at Sounds True, including my rock-star editor, Haven Iverson, and production editor, Jade Lascelles, for valuing my story and seeing my potential as an emerging author even when no one else did. You all have been a source of motivation as I stepped into this new path, and I will forever be grateful for your guidance, kindness, and support.

Finally, to my circle of friends and my SWAAY community, I wouldn't have written this book without your constant encouragement and your support along the way. Thank you for trusting me with your stories; they have constituted the inspiration for this book.

Cheers to writing your own stories and swaying your narratives!

References

PROLOGUE

Michelle Riddell, "Talk Her Off the Ledge," ManifestStation.net, August 3, 2016, themanifeststation.net/2016/08/03/talk-off-ledge/.

INTRODUCTION

Alison Rogish et al., "Women in the C-Suite," Deloitte.com, March 4, 2020, deloitte.com/us/en/insights/industry/financial-services/women-in-the-c-suite.html.

"America's Women and the Wage Gap," NationalPartnership.org, March 2021, nationalpartnership.org/our-work/resources/economic-justice/fair-pay/americas-women-and-the-wage-gap.pdf.

Kate Clark, "US VC Investment in Female Founders Hits All-Time High," TechCrunch.com, December 9, 2019, techcrunch.com/2019/12/09/us-vc-investment-in-female-founders-hits-all-time-high/.

Roxy Szal, "The Media's Gender Gap Isn't Improving," MsMagazine.com, March 4, 2019, msmagazine.com/2019/03/04/medias-gender-gap-isnt-improving/.

CHAPTER ONE: POWER

Rachel Vogelstein and Jennifer Klein, "Let's Make Women's Power Culturally Acceptable," ForeignPolicy.com, September 3, 2020, foreignpolicy.com/2020/09/03/lets-make-womens-power-culturally-acceptable/.

Hillary Clinton, "Power Shortage," TheAtlantic.com, October 2020, theatlantic.com/magazine/archive/2020/10/hillary-clinton-womens-rights/615463/.

Mary Beard, *Women & Power: A Manifesto* (New York: Liveright, 2017).

Gloria Feldt, *No Excuses: Nine Ways Women Can Change How We Think About Power* (New York: Seal Press, 2012).

John French and Bertram Raven, "The Bases of Social Power," ResearchGate.net, originally published January 1959, researchgate.net/publication/215915730_The_bases_of_social_power.

Heifer International, "What Does Women's Empowerment Even Mean?" Heifer.org, May 9, 2018, heifer.org/blog/what-does-womens -empowerment-even-mean.html.

Deirdre Maloney, "The True Definition of Power," MakeMomentum.com, January 4, 2011, makemomentum.com/the-true-definition-of-power/.

J. B. Rotter, "Generalized Expectancies for Internal Versus External Control of Reinforcement," *Psychological Monographs: General and Applied* 80, no. 1 (1966): 1–28, doi.org/10.1037/h0092976.

Michael F. Steger et al., "Genetic and Environmental Influences on the Positive Traits of the Values in Action Classification, and Biometric Covariance with Normal Personality," *Journal of Research in Personality* 41, no. 3 (June 2007): 524–39, sciencedirect.com/science/article/abs/pii /S0092656606000791.

Sara B. Algoe and Baldwin M. Way, "Evidence for a Role of the Oxytocin System, Indexed by Genetic Variation in CD38, in the Social Bonding Effects of Expressed Gratitude," *Social Cognitive and Affective Neuroscience* 9, no. 12 (December 2014): 1855–61, researchgate.net/publication /259608367_Evidence_for_a_Role_of_the_Oxytocin_System_Indexed _by_Genetic_Variation_in_CD38_in_the_Social_Bonding_Effects_of _Expressed_Gratitude.

Jinting Liu et al., "The Association Between Well-Being and the COMT Gene: Dispositional Gratitude and Forgiveness as Mediators," *Journal of Affective Disorders* 214 (May 2017): 115–21, pubmed.ncbi.nlm.nih.gov /28288405/.

Summer Allen, "The Science of Gratitude," Greater Good Science Center, May 2018, ggsc.berkeley.edu/images/uploads/GGSC-JTF_White_Paper -Gratitude-FINAL.pdf.

Soul Pancake, "An Experiment in Gratitude: The Science of Happiness," YouTube.com, July 11, 2013, youtu.be/oHv6vTKD6lg.

The Editors of The Cut, "Powerful Women Talk about Power," TheCut.com, October 18, 2018, thecut.com/2018/10/women-and-power-introduction.html.

Hillary Clinton, "Remarks for the United Nations' Fourth World Conference on Women," UN.org, September 5, 1995, un.org/esa/gopherdata/conf /fwcw/conf/gov/950905175653.txt.

CHAPTER TWO: LIKABILITY

Robert Graves, *I, Claudius* (New York: Vintage, 1989).

Matthew Jacobs, "On Hating Madonna," HuffPost.com, July 1, 2019, huffpost.com/entry/madonna-madame-x-career-retrospective_n_5d08fb17e4b0e560b7097d3b.

Ilene Rosenzweig, *The I Hate Madonna Handbook* (New York: St. Martin's Press, 1994).

Abigail Johnson, "Why Do Women Hate Angelina Jolie?" Villainesse.com, November 26, 2018, villainesse.com/think/why-do-women-hate-angelina-jolie.

Steven Goldstein, *The Turn-On: How the Powerful Make Us Like Them—From Washington to Wall Street to Hollywood* (New York: Harper Business, 2019).

Molly Schwartz and Sam Van Pykeren, "A Likability Expert Explains Why If You Want to Be Liked, You Need to Have These 8 Traits," MotherJones.com, January 29, 2020. motherjones.com/politics/2020/01/likability-expert-warren-clinton-klobuchar-traits/.

Barbara Lee Family Foundation, "Politics Is Personal: Keys to Likeability and Electability for Women (2017)," BarbaraLeeFoundation.org, barbaraleefoundation.org/research/likability/.

Leonie Gerhards and Michael Kosfeld, "I (Don't) Like You! But Who Cares? Gender Differences in Same-Sex and Mixed-Sex Teams," *The Economic Journal* 130, no. 627 (April 2020): 716–39, doi.org/10.1093/ej/uez067.

Ilene Strauss Cohen, "How I Learned to Stop Being a People-Pleaser," PsychologyToday.com, March 16, 2018, psychologytoday.com/us/blog/your-emotional-meter/201803/how-i-learned-stop-being-people-pleaser.

Joan Williams, "How Women Can Escape the Likability Trap," NYTimes.com, August 16, 2019, nytimes.com/2019/08/16/opinion/sunday/gender-bias-work.html.

Anna Rova, "True Feminine Power and Why Modern Female Empowerment Has Got It All Wrong," AnnaRova.medium.com, September 21, 2018, annarova.medium.com/true-feminine-power-why-modern-female-empowerment-has-got-it-all-wrong-6a7578d40c3e.

CHAPTER THREE: PRESENTATION

Amy DeKlerk, "Tarana Burke on How We Need to Shift the Narrative Around #MeToo," HarpersBazaar.com, October 25, 2018, harpersbazaar .com/uk/culture/culture-news/a24205132/tarana-burke-metoo-reflecting/.

Jessica Bennett, "The Beauty Advantage: How Looks Affect Your Work, Your Career, Your Life," Newsweek.com, July 19, 2010, newsweek.com/beauty -advantage-how-looks-affect-your-work-your-career-your-life-74313.

Shamontiel Vaughn, "My Hypocritical Views on Chivalry," Medium.com, October 27, 2019, medium.com/we-need-to-talk/my-hypocritical-views-on -chivalry-6001d85c40b5.

New York University, "Chivalry Is Not Dead When It Comes to Morality," NYU.edu, June 8, 2016, nyu.edu/about/news-publications/news/2016 /june/chivalry-is-not-dead-when-it-comes-to-morality.html.

Janine Willis and Alexander Todorov, "First Impressions: Making Up Your Mind After a 100-Ms Exposure to a Face," *Psychological Science* 17, no. 7 (July 1, 2006): 592–98, doi.org/10.1111/j.1467-9280.2006.01750.x.

American Psychological Association, "Young Children Judge Others Based on Facial Features as Much as Adults Do," APA.org, April 18, 2019, apa.org /news/press/releases/2019/04/judge-facial-features.html.

Mindy Isser, "The Grooming Gap: What Looking the Part Costs Women," InTheseTimes.com, January 2, 2020, inthesetimes.com/article/grooming -gap-women-economics-wage-gender-sexism-make-up-styling-dress-code.

Kellie Scott, "How a Woman's 'Glam' Appearance Affects Her Career," ABC .net.au, June 8, 2020, abc.net.au/everyday/how-a-womans-glam-appearance -affects-her-career/11671912.

Chioma Nnadi, "Meet Bozoma Saint John, the Most Fashionable Woman in Silicon Valley," Vogue.com, May 29, 2018, abc.net.au/everyday/how-a -womans-glam-appearance-affects-her-career/11671912.

Alison Doyle, "What to Wear When There's No Dress Code," TheBalanceCareers.com, November 25, 2019, thebalancecareers.com/what -to-wear-when-theres-no-dress-code-2061189.

Mallory Stark, "Creating a Positive Professional Image," HBSwk.hbs.edu, June 20, 2005, hbswk.hbs.edu/item/creating-a-positive-professional-image.

Amy Gallo, "How to Give an Employee Feedback about Their Appearance," HBR.org, May 26, 2017, hbr.org/2017/05/how-to-give-an-employee -feedback-about-their-appearance.

CHAPTER FOUR: AUTHENTICITY

Tchiki Davis, "Develop Authenticity: 20 Ways to Be a More Authentic Person," PsychologyToday.com, April 15, 2019, psychologytoday.com/us /blog/click-here-happiness/201904/develop-authenticity-20-ways-be-more -authentic-person.

Herminia Ibarra, "The Authenticity Paradox," HBR.org, January–February 2015, hbr.org/2015/01/the-authenticity-paradox.

The Gottman Institute, "Marriage and Couples," Gottman.com, gottman .com/about/research/couples/.

Toni Parker, "Six Steps to Mindfully Deal with Difficult Emotions," Gottman.com, September 28, 2016, gottman.com/blog /6stepstomindfullydealwithdifficultemotions.

Claire Eagleson et al., "The Power of Positive Thinking: Pathological Worry Is Reduced by Thought Replacement in Generalized Anxiety Disorder," *Behaviour Research and Therapy* 78 (March 2016):13–18, doi.org/10.1016/j .brat.2015.12.017.

Sonja Lyubomirsky et al., "The Benefits of Frequent Positive Affect: Does Happiness Lead to Success?" *A Psychological Bulletin* 131, no. 6 (2005): 803–55, apa.org/pubs/journals/releases/bul-1316803.pdf.

Ron Carucci, "Ways to Manage an Emotionally Needy Employee," HBR.org, September 27, 2019, hbr.org/2019/09/4-ways-to-manage-an-emotionally -needy-employee.

CHAPTER FIVE: CONFLICT

Josie Glausiusz, "Would the World Be More Peaceful If There Were More Women Leaders?" Qz.com, October 30, 2017, qz.com/1115269/would-the -world-be-more-peaceful-if-there-were-more-women-leaders/.

CPP, "Workplace Conflict and How Businesses Can Harness It to Thrive," July 2008, shop.themyersbriggs.com/Pdfs/CPP_Global_Human_Capital _Report_Workplace_Conflict.pdf.

Dean Tjosvold and David Johnson, "Deutsch's Theory of Cooperation and Competition," *Work Teams: Past, Present and Future* 6, 131–55, doi.org/10 .1007/978-94-015-9492-9_8.

Natalie Semczuk, "The 10 Most Effective Workplace Conflict Resolution Strategies," TheDigitalProjectManager.com, January 15, 2021, thedigitalprojectmanager.com/10-effective-conflict-resolution-strategies/.

Alina Morkin and Pini Yakuel, in "13 Ways to Get Better at
   Delivering Bad News," Forbes.com, April 3, 2019, forbes.com/sites
   /forbescommunicationscouncil/2019/04/03/13-ways-to-get-better-at
   -delivering-bad-news/?sh=6cc81bc065f0.

Abbey Slattery, "How to Fight Verbal Abuse at Work," InHerSight.com,
   August 24, 2019, inhersight.com/blog/guide/verbal-abuse-at-work.

Sarah DiGiulio, "9 Tips for Talking to People You Disagree With,"
   NBCNews.com, September 28, 2019, nbcnews.com/better/lifestyle/9-tips
   -talking-people-you-disagree-ncna1059326.

Kat Boogaard, "How to Disagree with Your Co-Worker's (Bad) Idea Without
   Ruining Your Friendship," TheMuse.com, themuse.com/advice/how-to
   -disagree-with-your-coworkers-bad-idea-without-ruining-your-friendship.

Jeanne Brett and Stephen Goldberg, "How to Handle a Disagreement on
   Your Team," HBR.org, July 10, 2017, hbr.org/2017/07/how-to-handle-a
   -disagreement-on-your-team.

CHAPTER SIX: CONFIDENCE

Aisiri Amin, "Nanette: Powerful End to Self-Deprecating Humour," The
   -Inkline.com, July 8, 2018, the-inkline.com/2018/07/08/nanette-powerful
   -end-to-self-deprecating-humour/.

Brad Bitterly and Alison Wood Brooks, "Sarcasm, Self-Deprecation, and
   Inside Jokes: A User's Guide to Humor at Work," HBR.org, July–August
   2020, hbr.org/2020/07/sarcasm-self-deprecation-and-inside-jokes-a-users
   -guide-to-humor-at-work.

Maria Daniela Pipas and Mohammad Jaradat, "Assertive Communication
   Skills," *Annales Universitatis Apulensis Series Oeconomica* 12, no. 2
   (December 2010): 649–56, researchgate.net/publication/227367804
   _Assertive_Communication_Skills.

Lolly Daskal, "The Best Way to Offer an Opinion on Anything,"
   LollyDaskal.com, lollydaskal.com/leadership/the-best-way-to-offer-an
   -opinion-on-anything/.

Leon Ho, "Why You Have the Fear of Failure (and How to Overcome It),"
   Lifehack.org, March 2, 2021, lifehack.org/articles/lifehack/how-fear-of
   -failure-destroys-success.html.

Gartner Press Release, "Gartner Survey Shows Only Half of Business Leaders Feel Confident Leading Their Teams Today," Gartner.com, July 23, 2019, gartner.com/en/newsroom/press-releases/2019-07-22-gartner-survey-shows -only-half-of-business-leaders-fe.

CHAPTER SEVEN: BALANCE

Arghavan Salles, "I Spent My Fertile Years Training to Be a Surgeon. Now, It Might Be Too Late for Me to Have a Baby," Time.com, January 3, 2019, time.com/5484506/fertility-egg-freezing/.

Jory MacKay, "The State of Work Life Balance in 2019," RescueTime.com, January 24, 2019, blog.rescuetime.com/work-life-balance-study-2019/.

Elisette Carlson, "Work-Life Balance Is a Load of Bullshit. Here's Why," SWAAY.com, November 17, 2019, swaay.com/the-myth-of-work-life -balance-why-its-a-load-of-bs-and-how-to-better-redefine-your-life.

Amitava Chattopadhyay, "The Little-Known Quirk in the Way Our Brain Evaluates Goals," INSEAD.edu, November 28, 2018, knowledge.insead.edu /marketing/the-little-known-quirk-in-the-way-our-brain-evaluates-goals-10526.

Michael Singer, *The Surrender Experiment* (New York: Harmony Books, 2015).

Alvin Powell, "When Science Meets Mindfulness," Harvard.edu, April 9, 2018, news.harvard.edu/gazette/story/2018/04/harvard-researchers-study -how-mindfulness-may-change-the-brain-in-depressed-patients/.

Katie Hoare, "Average Worker Significantly Overworked Due to Pandemic," Happiful.com, January 12, 2021, happiful.com/pandemic-causes-culture -overwork/.

The Conference Board News Release, "Survey: Companies 3 Times More Willing to Hire Remote Workers Anywhere in US or World," Conference -Board.org, November 2, 2020, conference-board.org/pdf_free/press/Press %20Release-Survey%20of%20HR%20Executives.pdf.

OECD Better Life Index, "What's the Better Life Index?" OECDBetterLifeIndex .org, oecdbetterlifeindex.org/about/better-life-initiative/.

Sarah Coury et al., "Women in the Workplace 2020," McKinsey.com, September 30, 2020, mckinsey.com/featured-insights/diversity-and -inclusion/women-in-the-workplace#.

Claire Ewing-Nelson, "Nearly 2.2 Million Women Have Left the Labor Force Since February," NWLC.org, November 2020, nwlc.org/wp-content /uploads/2020/11/October-Jobs-Day.pdf.

Sherrie Bourg Carter, "The Tell Tale Signs of Burnout . . . Do You Have Them?" PsychologyToday.com, November 26, 2013, psychologytoday.com /us/blog/high-octane-women/201311/the-tell-tale-signs-burnout-do-you -have-them.

Allison Pohle, "How to Improve Your Work-Life Balance," WSJ.com, March 31, 2021, wsj.com/articles/how-to-improve-your-work-life-balance -11608244271.

CHAPTER EIGHT: COMPETITION

Diane Barth, "Women Shouldn't Have to Feel Bad about Competing with Each Other," Qz.com, March 22, 2018, qz.com/work/1235541/women -shouldnt-have-to-feel-bad-about-competing-with-each-other/.

Melissa Batchelor Warnke, "Jessica Knoll: It's Time to Stop Pitting Women Against Each Other," Girlboss.com, May 16, 2018, girlboss.com/read /jessica-knoll-on-women-and-competition/.

Melissa Matthews, "Women and Competition: Females Not Driven to Compete with Other Females, Only Themselves, Study Suggests," MedicalDaily.com, January 31, 2017, medicaldaily.com/women-and-competition-females-not -driven-compete-other-females-only-themselves-409759.

Colin Robertson, "How to Use Your Natural Competitive Fire to Increase Your Willpower," Willpowered.com, March 9, 2015, willpowered.com /learn/competition-increases-willpower.

Aminatou Sow and Ann Friedman, "What Is Shine Theory?" shinetheory.com.

Ben Olds, "Embracing Competition in the Workplace," FistfulofTalent.com, April 10, 2015, fistfuloftalent.com/2015/04/embracing-competition-in-the -workplace.html/.

CHAPTER NINE: EXPERTISE

Tara Sophia Mohr, "Why Women Don't Apply for Jobs Unless They're 100% Qualified," HBR.org, August 25, 2014, hbr.org/2014/08/why-women-dont -apply-for-jobs-unless-theyre-100-qualified.

Patti Shank, "Science of Learning 101: What Kind of Practice Makes Expert?" TD.org, May 26, 2016, td.org/insights/science-of-learning-101-what-kind -of-practice-makes-expert.

Princeton University Office of Communications, "Becoming an Expert Takes More Than Practice," Princeton.edu, July 3, 2014, princeton.edu/news /2014/07/03/becoming-expert-takes-more-practice.

Elizabeth Burnam, "Your Idea of 'Expertise' Needs to Change," Medium .com, August 13, 2019, medium.com/swlh/your-idea-of-expertise-needs-to -change-21a5bdcc1421.

Catalyst, "Quick Take: Women in Male-Dominated Industries and Occupations," Catalyst.org, February 5, 2020, catalyst.org/research/women -in-male-dominated-industries-and-occupations/.

Iman Oubou, "How Gender Parity in the Boardroom May Relieve Burnout for Women in Tech," SWAAY.com, March 30, 2021, swaay.com/how -gender-parity-in-the-boardroom-may-relieve-burnout-for-women-in-tech.

Nilanjana Dasgupta and Shaki Asgari, "Seeing Is Believing: Exposure to Counterstereotypic Women Leaders and Its Effect on the Malleability of Automatic Gender Stereotyping," *Journal of Experimental Social Psychology* 40, no. 5 (September 2004): 642–58, doi.org/10.1016/j.jesp.2004.02.003.

Jonathan Black, "Take Control of Your Career in an Uncertain World," FT .com, February 2, 2020, ft.com/content/dbf6d632-2e55-11ea-84be -a548267b914b.

Lauren Easterling, "Your Career May Take a Different Path Than You Expected," InsideHigherEd.com, July 27, 2020, insidehighered.com/advice /2020/07/27/your-career-may-take-different-path-you-expected-opinion.

Ximena Vengoechea, "How to Know Which Skills to Develop at Each Stage of Your Career," FastCompany.com, April 29, 2016, fastcompany.com /3059358/how-to-know-which-skills-to-develop-at-each-stage-of-your -career.

CHAPTER TEN: BELONGING

Nikki Schwab, "Ocasio-Cortez Says She No Longer Suffers from 'Impostor Syndrome,'" NYPost.com, March 26, 2019, nypost.com/2019/03/26 /ocasio-cortez-wonders-if-haters-are-right-until-she-hears-mike-lees-speech/.

P. R. Clance and S. A. Imes, "The Imposter Phenomenon in High Achieving Women: Dynamics and Therapeutic Intervention," *Psychotherapy: Theory, Research & Practice* 15, no. 3 (1978): 241–47, doi.org/10.1037/h0086006.

Amy Cuddy, *Presence* (New York: Little, Brown and Company, 2016).

Megan Dalla-Camina, "The Reality of Imposter Syndrome," PsychologyToday
.com, September 3, 2018, psychologytoday.com/us/blog/real-women
/201809/the-reality-imposter-syndrome.

Society for Industrial and Organizational Psychology News Release, "The
High Cost of Perfectionism," EurekaAlert.org, July 12, 2019, eurekalert.org
/news-releases/753737.

Holly M. Hutchins et al., "What Imposters Risk at Work: Exploring Imposter
Phenomenon, Stress Coping, and Job Outcomes," *Human Resource
Development Quarterly* 29, no. 1 (November 2017): 31–48, doi.org/10
.1002/hrdq.21304.

Adam Grant, "People Don't Actually Know Themselves Very Well,"
TheAtlantic.com, March 1, 2018, theatlantic.com/health/archive/2018/03
/you-dont-know-yourself-as-well-as-you-think-you-do/554612/.

Bertrand Russell, "The Triumph of Stupidity." In *Mortals and Others:
American Essays, 1931–1935, Volume II*, edited by Harry Ruja (London and
New York: Routledge, 1998), 27–28.

Simine Vazire, "Who Knows What about a Person? The Self-Other
Knowledge Asymmetry (SOKA) Model," *Journal of Personality and Social
Psychology* 98, no. 2 (2010): 281–300, doi.org/10.1037/a0017908.

Eric M. Ruiz, "Other People Can Help You Beat Imposter Syndrome (and
Never Know It)," FastCompany.com, November 28, 2017, fastcompany
.com/40499114/other-people-can-help-you-beat-imposter-syndrome-and
-never-know-it.

O. C. Tanner Institute, "2021 Global Culture Report," octanner.com/content
/dam/oc-tanner/images/v2/culture-report/2021/GCR-2021-sm.pdf.

Svenja Weber and Gianpiero Petriglieri, "To Overcome Your Insecurity,
Recognize Where It Really Comes From," HBR.org, June 27, 2018, hbr.org
/2018/06/to-overcome-your-insecurity-recognize-where-it-really-comes-from.

About the Author

Iman Oubou is a Moroccan American entrepreneur, published scientist, and a national beauty pageant winner on a mission to change the women's media landscape. She won the title of Miss New York United States and was second runner-up at the 2015 Miss United States Pageant. Iman was awarded the "Women's Advocate of the Year" Award for 2019 in Dubai and has been featured in *Harper's BAZAAR, Cosmopolitan, Forbes, Inc., Fortune, Vogue Arabia*, and the *Huffington Post*.

She is the founder and president of SWAAY Media, a leading publishing platform aimed at championing female thought leadership. By providing access to editorial and writing support, as well as a supportive community of like-minded women, SWAAY has helped thousands of women tell their stories, share their expertise, and elevate their voices. Partnering with companies like Unilever and *The Wall Street Journal*, Iman has led national events that feature conversations about female empowerment and thought leadership in the workforce. Her podcast, *Women Who SWAAY*, has reached millions of listeners, was number two on iTunes in 2015, and was ranked in the top five best podcasts for women entrepreneurs by *Inc.* magazine.

Before founding SWAAY, Iman earned a degree in biochemistry/molecular biology and a masters in bioengineering, which led to her work in cancer research. She accompanied the Mission to Heal organization to South Sudan, Kenya, and Ecuador and organized a medical mission to her own native country, Morocco, in 2013 before moving to New York to work on the corporate side of biotech. She traded her lab coat for a science communication specialist position working with Big Pharma and start-up biotech companies.

Named as the number-one "female entrepreneur to watch" in 2018 by *CIO* magazine that same year, Iman was a keynote speaker at both the Harvard Women in Business and MIT STEM Conferences. She was the first-ever "Face of Morocco" Ambassador, a new initiative uplifting female voices in Morocco and the Middle East. She was also part of the first all-female judge panel at Miss Universe 2018 and judged Miss Teen USA, Miss Earth USA, and other state pageants.

About Sounds True

S ounds True is a multimedia publisher whose mission is to inspire and support personal transformation and spiritual awakening. Founded in 1985 and located in Boulder, Colorado, we work with many of the leading spiritual teachers, thinkers, healers, and visionary artists of our time. We strive with every title to preserve the essential "living wisdom" of the author or artist. It is our goal to create products that not only provide information to a reader or listener but also embody the quality of a wisdom transmission.

For those seeking genuine transformation, Sounds True is your trusted partner. At SoundsTrue.com you will find a wealth of free resources to support your journey, including exclusive weekly audio interviews, free downloads, interactive learning tools, and other special savings on all our titles.

To learn more, please visit SoundsTrue.com/freegifts or call us toll-free at 800.333.9185.